AMERICAN
ECONOMIC POLICY
TOWARD THE
PHILIPPINES

THE INSTITUTE OF PACIFIC RELATIONS

The Institute of Pacific Relations is an unofficial and nonpartisan organization, founded in 1925 to facilitate the scientific study of the peoples of the Pacific area. It is composed of autonomous National Councils in the principal countries having important interests in the Pacific area, together with an International Secretariat. It is privately financed by contributions from National Councils, corporations, and foundations. It is governed by a Pacific Council composed of members appointed by each of the National Councils.

The Institute as such and the National Councils of which it is composed do not advocate policies or express opinions on national or international affairs. Responsibility for statements of fact or opinion in Institute publications rests solely with the authors.

AMERICAN
ECONOMIC POLICY
TOWARD THE
PHILIPPINES

BY SHIRLEY JENKINS

With an Introduction by Claude A. Buss

Published Under the Auspices of the
American Institute of Pacific Relations

Stanford University Press, Stanford, California

STANFORD UNIVERSITY PRESS, STANFORD, CALIFORNIA

PUBLISHED IN GREAT BRITAIN, INDIA, AND PAKISTAN
BY GEOFFREY CUMBERLEGE, OXFORD UNIVERSITY PRESS,
LONDON, BOMBAY, AND KARACHI

THE BAKER AND TAYLOR COMPANY, HILLSIDE, NEW JERSEY

HENRY M. SNYDER & COMPANY, INC., 440 FOURTH AVENUE, NEW YORK 16

W. S. HALL & COMPANY, 457 MADISON AVENUE, NEW YORK 22

PRINTED AND BOUND IN THE UNITED STATES OF AMERICA BY STANFORD UNIVERSITY PRESS

Library of Congress Catalog Card Number: 53-9962

FOREWORD

Economic and commercial factors have always exerted a major influence on the course of American relations with the Philippines, but their dominant role has been particularly evident since the Philippines became politically independent. For one thing, it soon became clear that despite its political autonomy the new Republic was still tied by many commercial and financial apron strings to the United States, whether on the government level (as in the case of war damage payments and ECA and MSA aid programs) or on the level of private business (as in the case of investments by American firms and the regulations controlling imports and foreign exchange in the Philippines in recent years). But there is no doubt that the legal fact of political independence, together with the political fact of an increasingly self-conscious Filipino nationalism, has made the problem of Philippine-American economic relations more complex and a greater potential source of misunderstanding than in former years.

For that reason the present study, appearing soon after an important election in the Philippines, is particularly timely and useful. It should help to provide some much-needed perspective on immediate economic issues and also to enable American and other readers outside the Philippines to have a more sympathetic understanding of the deep-rooted and painful economic weaknesses which still beset the Philippines as well as of the signs of economic advancement which have here and there been manifest.

Mrs. Jenkins' book is an outgrowth of a study begun in 1946 for the international research program of the Institute of Pacific Relations and is intended as a contribution to the series of studies on the relations of the United States with various Asian countries since World War II. Other volumes already published are *America and Japan*, by Edwin O. Reischauer and others, and *The United States and the Far East, 1945-1951*, by Harold M. Vinacke. A forthcoming study by Miriam S. Farley will deal with American relations with Southeast Asia in recent years.

Mrs. Jenkins was formerly Associate Editor of the *Far Eastern Survey*, and later served as a member of the Secretariat of the United Nations. She is the author of an American IPR booklet, *Trading with Asia*, and has been a student of Philippine problems for a number of years. In the preparation and revision of her study she has had the valuable assistance of Miss Miriam S. Farley.

v

Others who have given useful advice and criticism on the manuscript include Professor Rupert Emerson, Professor Claude Buss (who has been kind enough to write the Introduction), and Mr. Laurence E. Salisbury. It should be noted that though the study appears under the auspices of the Institute of Pacific Relations the author alone is responsible for statements of fact or opinion expressed in the book.

WILLIAM L. HOLLAND
Secretary General
Institute of Pacific Relations

NEW YORK
November 1953

CONTENTS

TABLES

(Pages 171–77)

THE SETTING OF AMERICAN ECONOMIC POLICY TOWARD THE PHILIPPINES

By Claude A. Buss

AMERICAN economic policy toward the Philippines has developed against the background of changing conditions in the Islands themselves. A consideration of this historical setting may enrich the interpretation of past controversies and enigmas and may shed some light on the way ahead. An analysis of the role of economic policy in recent over-all international relations between the two countries—as seen from the Philippines and as seen from the United States —should contribute to the definition of perspective and the formulation of a balanced judgment.

I

The Filipinos—some 20 million of them—are remarkably homogeneous. With the exception of some scattered tribes throughout the Islands, the mountain people in Luzon, and the Moros in Mindanao and the Sulu Archipelago, the Filipinos have a common outlook on national and international affairs. Before the coming of the Spaniards, "all the natives lived in their villages, applying themselves to the sowing of their crops and the care of their vineyards, and the pressing of wine; others planting cotton, or raising poultry and swine so that all were at work; moreover the chiefs were obeyed and respected, and the entire country well provided for."[1] The Philippine earth is good, and the climate is kindly. Then as now, food came easily and population pressure was unknown. Economics played a minor role in the business of living.

After the excitement of discovery and the disappointments of the spice trade, the Spanish founded and administered their colony in the Philippines in the interests of religion rather than of commerce or industry. The political grandees profited from the land grants or the storied galleon trade, but the Indios themselves continued their ancient economic way of life. They were attached more servilely to the land, and subjected to the political domination of the cacique, and they were absorbed completely in the fold of the Catholic church.

During three centuries in the Spanish imperial system, some Filipino leaders

[1] E. H. Blair and J. A. Robertson (eds.), *The Philippine Islands 1493–1898*, VIII, 87.

sporadically sought the same freedom and independence which marked the political evolution of the West. Internal revolt reached its climax in 1898, when Admiral Dewey assisted the return of Aguinaldo. Americans replaced the Spanish as alien masters, but even the most well-meaning paternalistic "imperial" regime could not postpone indefinitely the demand for independence. Americans felt an instinctive sympathy for Filipino aspirations, and therefore tended to rationalize or apologize for those practical or unavoidable attitudes which their self-interest seemed to dictate. On a nation-wide scale, Americans had no stomach for overseas responsibilities. They remained ignorant about or indifferent to relations with the Philippines. The American masses accepted the economic preachments of those few to whom the Philippines became a source of prosperity or wealth. Americans experienced an understandable pride of participation in a noble experiment in education, democratization, and missionary endeavor in the far Pacific.

To many it seemed wise, to others vital, that the Philippines should be tied into the American economic system. American trade and investment in the Philippines needed a free market in the United States. This closed-door relationship contradicted our favorite theory of the Open Door. It suited our immediate economic requirements even if it ran counter to our long-run desires. Some of us realized that eventually our economic primacy in the Philippines would have to disappear as a casualty of political independence. But we did not prepare for the consequences of ultimate separation. Individuals or corporations which profited from their legitimate operations naturally exerted every effort for the continuation of the status quo. The executive branch of the government did not or could not exert the same energy to promote the kind of adjustment which the general interest demanded. Timid statements pointed out the necessity for providing a sound economic foundation for a new independent Philippines, but efforts at implementation were never more than half-hearted. Ordinary procrastination, indifference, preoccupation with other issues, inability to see clearly what should be done, and honest differences of political opinion were greater enemies of constructive action than any malevolence on the part of those interests which had built up substantial stakes in the Philippines. We continued to ride the easy economic highway with scant regard for the hardships at the end of the road.

These economic shortcomings are only a part of the American record. Filipinos were given the guaranties of our Bill of Rights and the highest degree of participation in government for which their education and increasing experience would fit them. The system of government from the beginning was designed, according to the instructions of President McKinley to the Philippines Commission,

not for our satisfaction, or for the expression of our theoretical views, but for the happiness, peace and prosperity of the people of the Philippine Islands, and the measures adopted should be made to conform to their customs, their habits, and even to their prejudices, to the fullest extent consistent with the accomplishment of the indispensable requisites of just and effective government.

In the short span of a half-century Americans brought better health, wider education, and a common English language. They not only gave a superficial physical stamp of Americanism to city and country but also invigorated a whole people with a yearning for and devotion to "the American way of life." No amount of economic maladjustment or social inequity could erase the fundamental spiritual tie of the Philippines to the United States.

During the bitter years of the occupation the Japanese were not able by cajolery, bribery, or force to accomplish the "moral rehabilitation" of the Philippine people. The Filipinos' love of music, hatred of military discipline, and aversion to heroics and sustained effort were the despair of the Japanese military administration. The Japanese were not given ample time to effect fundamental changes in the international economic orientation of the Philippines, although they tried desperately to diversify the crops, replace cigar tobacco by Japanese-style cigarette tobacco leaf, and coax from the land a surplus of food to provide for invading troops. War pressures thwarted their schemes. The Japanese occupation meant an economic program of robbery, fantastic inflation, poverty, discontent, and disaster. It meant a million casualties, and wholesale destruction of productive assets. The occupation left the Philippines a house divided, guerrillas versus collaborators. The economic shambles of the war, coupled with spiritual exhaustion, constituted a most unpromising foundation for the inauguration of political independence. The war left its ugliest psychological and physical scars in the Philippines. In his inaugural address, President Roxas said:

. . . there is hunger among us. . . . Plagues of rats and locusts gnaw at our food supplies. Public health and sanitation have been set back a quarter of a century. Housing . . . is shocking in its inadequacy and squalor. Our communications are destroyed, stolen or disrupted. . . . Schools have been burned and teachers have been killed.

This was the setting in which our postwar economic policies were launched. Among their citizens who escaped torture and pain, cynicism uprooted faith, chicanery replaced open dealing, stealth and intrigue destroyed the sentimental appeals of honest effort. Still, the Filipinos found a new life in the midst of the feverish activities of the American Army. The sentiment of anti-imperialism, which caused so much damage elsewhere in southeast Asia, created scarcely a ripple in the Philippines. Filipinos were eager to assume political responsibilities which we were eager to cast aside. Even had we wanted to, we could not escape our own responsibility in contributing to the shambles of the Philippines. Our defenses had been inadequate, our liberation policy cost their blood and devastated their property. The least we could do was to offer compensation, to help rebuild.

There was never any intention to go back on our promise of independence. Nothing has contributed more to the prestige of the United States in southeast Asia than the fact that we made a promise and we kept it. Some Filipinos were tempted with the easy way out of their difficulties, perhaps a commonwealth relationship with the United States, but the tempting idea never evolved into a practical program. In spite of the war, and in spite of the enormity of the economic handicaps, independence was declared exactly as scheduled.

II

As seen from the Philippines, American postwar economic policies had to be judged and executed primarily against the background of their own internal conditions. At the end of the war it was difficult to restore law and order and to preserve and foster democratic processes. Manuel Quezon was missed. His strong will and unflinching courage would have been bulwarks in time of crisis. The primordial struggle for existence gave a degree of lawlessness and criminality to practically every province and section of the country. Robberies, kidnappings, and daylight assaults on buses, trucks, and trains were almost daily occurrences. The traditional respect for individual freedom and human rights was insufficient to counteract the petty criminals, the bandits, and the Communist-led groups who debauched the cities and disturbed the countryside. President Osmeña and his government were circumscribed in their powers and limited in their operations. The national welfare and the national security were large problems which were neglected because of the immediate tasks of getting individuals straightened out. Individuals needed food, shelter, clothing, jobs, and protection.

When American relief money came trickling in, then pouring in, it brought life and hope and a measure of joy to millions of individuals. It can be argued that the funds were frittered away on luxury goods, or consumer items, rather than intelligently invested in capital goods. But the money was distributed widely to persons who wanted to do what they pleased with the compensation they received for their suffering. Nylons, lipsticks, and new shirts looked better and felt better than lathes or spinning machines, and these human foibles were the economists' despair. But that spiritual uplift was far from unimportant in reviving the enthusiasm and supplying the momentum for the troubles ahead. True, it brought opportunities for sharpers, gamblers, and big-time operators, political or otherwise, but the picture was not one of unrelieved waste and corruption. Nor should those in the Philippines who blame the United States now for not having been more severe in its restrictions forget the splurge they enjoyed on the come-easy American dollars. They needed relief, they got it, and they spent it, and then they demanded that their government look after the larger aspects of their social or community welfare.

Prices were high, profits were pleasing, and jobs were good—temporarily. The national cash position was strong, the banks were in an excellent position, abacá and copra made up for the losses in sugar, and the trends in building construction and gross sales seemed constantly upward. The rehabilitation program beautified the face of Manila and contributed to the basic improvement of the economy of the entire Philippines. But, as Mrs. Jenkins shows so ably, the pendulum had to swing in the opposite direction. The imbalance of international payments, the crisis in the national budget, the fundamental maladjustments in agriculture, and the lag in industrialization forced the Philippines to turn her eyes inward. Filipinos could justifiably complain about their inequitable historical economic heritage, but they could not erase it. They could look to others for assistance, but they could not escape their own responsibilities. They were obliged to make decisions, in some cases harmonious with American interests, in some cases (like the re-examination of the Bell Trade Act) counter to expressed American policies. We in the United States may sometimes object to those decisions, but we must respect the right and the reason of those who made them.

In an agricultural country such as the Philippines, land problems are paramount. In the thickly populated areas of Luzon, illiterate tenant farmers long insisted upon overdue reforms in matters of excessive rents, usury, and absentee landlordism. Without knowing anything of the subtleties of Marx or Lenin, or anything about the power or promises of the U.S.S.R., they indulged in peasant uprisings in the decade before World War II. They received scant satisfaction in the program of "Social Justice" under the Commonwealth and they took matters into their own hands during the Japanese occupation. Tenants had always been suspicious and oppressed, landlords unsympathetic and resentful. When the landlords turned to the Japanese for protection, they became in the eyes of the tenants not only the exploiters of the masses but also traitors to their country.

Leaders of the peasantry, like Pedro Abad Santos, Juan Feleo, and Luis Taruc, joined forces with labor leaders like Mariano Balgos, Guillermo Capadocia, and Mateo del Castilla (the latter two Moscow-trained) to organize the Hukbalahap, or People's Anti-Japanese Army, as the fighting guerrilla arm of a "United Front of the Socialist and Communist Parties, the Civil Liberties Union, labor unions, peasant groups, some intellectuals and middle class elements, religious organizations, groups representing the large Chinese colony and others."[2]

Communism had obtained a foothold in the Philippines after the visit of the Indonesian Communist Tan Malaka in the late 'twenties. On November 7, 1930, Crisanto Evangelista established a Communist party of the Philippines, and the next year he and nineteen others were convicted of sedition and illegal

[2] Bernard Seeman and Laurence E. Salisbury, *Cross Currents in the Philippines* (New York, 1946), p. 33.

association. In 1932 the Communist party was outlawed, and at once Pedro Abad Santos, the peasant leader of Pampanga, organized the Socialists. In 1934 Evangelista was pardoned and left immediately for Moscow. In the wake of the world-wide United Front policies, in 1938, the Communist party in the Philippines emerged from the underground and joined forces with the Socialists. A local Popular Front was formed, which nominated its own political candidates for public office, published its own official organ, operated its own book center, and carried on its own propaganda in Pampanga, Tarlac, and Bataan, where the Huks became most active.

During the war communism or lack of it among the Huk leadership was of less consequence than the struggle for survival. Most testimony is that the Huks fought bitterly against the Japanese, capturing guns and supplies and keeping the rice of central Luzon out of the hands of the enemy. In the areas of their operations, they took over the functions of local government. They seized the estates of the landlords, organized a system of political administration, and put a *de facto* end to the abuses of the cacique. After the war they resisted the return of the landlords—often killed outright any who tried to reclaim their properties—and continued their wartime regime. They were strengthened by an estimated half-million rifles, with ammunition, which came into their hands during the liberation. They were in no mood to subordinate themselves to the rival guerrilla groups which had won the support of the United States military officials, and they showed no disposition to disband themselves on the orders of the central government. The Huks protested against the fraternization between Americans and *hacenderos*, and called the Philippines' administration a mere puppet of the American "imperialists."

A cleavage between the hard core of Huk leadership and the rank and file of the peasant membership began to appear in 1946. The rank and file wanted to become eligible for the back pay which the United States government was allotting to other guerrillas. There is every evidence that they would have preferred to return to their farms and to look to the government for the improvement of their well-being. The role of loyal opposition looked much more attractive than that of outlaws and bandits. The hard core leadership was more skeptical and decreed open hostilities against Manuel Roxas, the Liberal candidate for the presidency. These leaders looked upon Roxas as a cacique, related by marriage to one of the most powerful and reactionary families of central Luzon. In their opinion he had a dubious war record and was a thoroughgoing tool of the capitalists. The Huk leaders adopted a program which went far beyond the requirements of agrarian reform. They came out against the Bell Trade Act and against the "mock independence" which had been obtained from the United States. As an agricultural program, they advocated a 70-30 division of the crop between tenant and landlord, redistribution of large estates, crop loans for small farmers, tax relief, government-financed tractor and experimental stations, extension of co-operatives, aid for construction of homes, and a beginning of collectivization. They supported the losing Nacionalista ticket, and ran their own candidates for Congress.

Seven of their candidates, including the leader, Luis Taruc, were elected to Congress but were refused their seats by the Committee on Elections. (If they had been seated, it is doubtful whether the Bell Trade Act could have mustered the necessary majority in the Philippine Congress.) Violence ensued. President Roxas ordered the Constabulary to give neither rest nor quarter to the hooligans and bandits who were seeking power through force. He said their methods were to create social disorder, confusion, and chaos, to foster widespread discontent, and to drive the people to desperation. He insisted that they did not seek agrarian reform, otherwise they would co-operate with the government in enforcing its own reform program. As long as they continued to defy the government, they must be dealt with as public enemies. He proceeded from the premise that they were Communists, and as Communists deserved no place in the scheme of government. Roxas declared himself to be for

free but guided enterprise. Defend it against the deceptive allures of communism, militarism and fascism. We will not give comfort to or countenance those anti-democratic creeds. Proponents of those views will be protected in their right to hold and openly advocate them. They will not be protected in subversive schemes to destroy the structure of this nation or its free institutions.

In 1947, while Manila wrestled with problems of American economic policies, the Huk situation in the countryside went from bad to worse. The rice-bowl provinces were kept in a state of constant uneasiness and isolated villages were deserted. The Constabulary intensified its crack-down policies, and the tenants were often caught between its exactions and the depredations of the Huks. In March 1948 the Huks were outlawed and their forays for food became increasingly brutal and vicious. The ordinary procedure was to attack Constabulary headquarters in a town, set up roadblocks, cut telephone and telegraph wires, burn and sack municipal and provincial buildings, stores, and select private homes, raid banks and hospitals (for medicines), and on retreat distribute handbills against "crooks" and "warmongers."

In April 1948, when Quirino succeeded to the presidency, he tried new tactics: truce negotiations, and amnesty. He permitted the Huk representatives to take their seats in Congress, Luis Taruc came to Manila and promised to have his men surrender their arms. During the fifty days accorded for turning in arms, only one hundred Huks registered and less than fifty actually gave up their guns.

Quirino promised a six-point amelioration program which provided for government purchase of haciendas for conversion into model agricultural communities; opening up of new agricultural lands; construction of roads and bridges in rural areas; opening of schools in "Huklandia"; extension of crop loans to small farmers; and the granting of immediate relief in the form of food, clothing, and medicine. But here the nonagrarian character of the Huk leadership began to assert itself. As the world situation worsened in the mid-summer of 1948, the Huk leadership displayed its sensitivity to Moscow's global policies. The Huks could not have reasonably asked President Quirino for more concessions in the interest of their basic agricultural grievances in Luzon. So they switched their demands to a larger arena and called for the abrogation of the trade agreement with the United States, the expropriation of all haciendas over fifty hectares, and the amelioration of the plight of the populace struggling, as it were, in the clutches of the American imperialists. Taruc also insisted that he had never agreed to surrender his arms; he only agreed to register them. Each man, Taruc and Quirino, accused the other of failing to live up to his promises.

Disorders multiplied, and the adamant attitude of the Huks brought neither rice and reforms to the peasants nor peace and prosperity to the nation. The Huks launched vitriolic attacks on President Quirino and his government, accusing them of graft and corruption and of utter subservience to the fascistic imperialism of the United States. Taruc attacked the United States as the source of all ills of the Philippines, and singled out our economic policies as the most pernicious of all. On August 15, 1948, he asserted at Nueva Ecija that the Communist party of the Philippines, "of which I am a member," stood for the eventual achievement of socialism, land for the peasants, and full and complete independence from all forms of foreign domination.[3] He refused to "submit to a fascist peace."

When the spread of terror was climaxed by the cold-blooded murder of Mrs. Quezon and members of her party on April 28, 1949, the righteous anger of decent citizens was aroused. The Huks, it was felt, had sacrificed their claim to championship of agrarian reform and adopted an unmitigated Communist program. Labor leaders who were thoroughly indoctrinated took over the active direction of the movement and rechristened their army the HMB, initials for the Tagalog words meaning People's Liberation Army. Their propaganda became the familiar jargon for the "New Democracy." They insisted that the people's basic problems of food, land, freedom, and peace could no longer be solved except through the armed overthrow of the rule of the imperialists, the feudal landlords, and their puppets. Power must be taken from the Liberal party and its backers, the feudal landlords and the business compradors, and given to the Filipino peasantry, the proletariat, the intelligentsia, and the national bourgeoisie. The international aspects of their propaganda called for boycott of trade with Japan, recall of U.S. military

[3] Quoted in Henry Wells, "Communism in the Philippines," *American Perspective*, Winter, 1950.

forces from the Philippine Islands, and the linking up of their program with that of their counterparts in Malaya, Korea, Viet Nam, and China.

The Communist leadership in the Huks found its sources of support primarily among the peasants, labor, and the Chinese minority. The Catholic laity was bitterly opposed to the communism of the Huks, and the intelligentsia preferred to progress with democracy rather than to revolt with the Communists. The Communists garnered little but hatred with their violence and unfulfilled promises. But whenever or wherever the government showed signs of appeasement or weakness, the Huks increased their depredations. They continued their state within a state on Luzon and spread to the Visayan Islands and even to Mindanao.

In his inaugural address in January 1950 President Quirino indulged in a bit of optimism. He said, "There is no organized movement of any consequence that can be considered a threat to the stability of our government." At this time the villages were undergoing their worst sufferings at the hands of the Huks (and the Army and Constabulary) and their hopes for the improvement of local conditions were at a low point. For an entire year President Quirino tried a policy of force. He failed, and blamed his failure on the insufficiency of the force at his disposal. The Constabulary, the civil guards, the temporary police, and the Army itself had neither the equipment nor the audacity to suppress the Huks. Too often the Constabulary went out to chase Huks, simply fired their machine guns over empty fields, and returned to base with a report of "mission accomplished." They refused to leave their jeeps and pursue the Huks to their mountain hide-outs. While landlords were left to arrange their peace with the Huks and Constabulary, President Quirino called for an organization of barangays (local political units) and ordered the suspension of the writ of habeas corpus for those accused of complicity with the Huks. When the Bell Economic Survey Mission from the United States was in the Philippines in 1950, the Huk situation seemed at its very worst.

In September 1950 Ramón Magsaysay took over as Minister of Defense. Scrupulously honest himself, rough and tough, he inaugurated spectacular new attitudes in the government's drive against the Huks. He gave his own soldiers leadership and appreciation; he faced the Huks with effective force, plus an alternative offer of help. Magsaysay said:

They are fighting the government because they want a house and land of their own. All right, they can stop fighting, because I will give it to them. And if they are not satisfied with that, by golly, I have another big deal for them. I am going to make the Huk a capitalist. I am going to set up a carpentry shop and let the Huks run it.[4]

Magsaysay shook up the top command of the Army and Constabulary and enforced strict discipline. As his intelligence reports improved he was

[4] *Time*, November 26, 1951, p. 25.

able to raid liaison offices of the Huks in Manila and other cities, to detain hundreds of Red leaders including influential Chinese Communists, and to capture valuable documents. In a series of campaigns throughout 1951 he seized the initiative from the Huks. He cut off their food supplies and gave comfort and protection to the terrorized villagers in the country. The guerrillas were forced to scatter and thousands of them surrendered. The military threat of the Huks was on the wane when in February 1953 Magsaysay resigned his office, "not as a millionaire, but as a poor man."

Antonio Quirino, the President's brother, charged that the resignation was a good thing because the Army had bungled the campaign against the Huk rebels; he suggested again that all the Huks should be granted amnesty. In reply, Magsaysay said, "It's a fight to the finish, either the Huks surrender or the government must." Magsaysay had disagreed with the President's negotiations for the surrender of Luis Taruc and Jesús Lava, Huk leaders hidden in the swamps of Pampanga. Quirino authorized Dr. Emilio Cortez, a member of the Pampanga provincial board, to conduct the negotiations, and authorized the chief of staff of the Philippine Army, Major General Calixto Duque—over Magsaysay's protest—to order a cease fire for the duration of the negotiations. Magsaysay opposed the entire procedure, primarily because he feared trickery on the part of the Huk leaders and a repetition of the abortive amnesty negotiations of 1948. He charged that the Huk tactics smacked of the peace offensive along the party line of Moscow. In resigning, he told the President:

. . . it would be useless for me to continue as Secretary of National Defense with the specific duty of killing Huks as long as the administration continues to foster and to tolerate conditions which offer a fertile soil for Communism. Merely killing dissidents will not solve the Communist problem. Its solution lies in the correction of social evils and injustice, and in giving the people a decent government free from dishonesty and graft.

Magsaysay's parting blast was, "the government says one thing and then does another. The government is full of crooks and grafters who suck the blood and money of taxpayers to enrich themselves."

When Magsaysay gave up the portfolio of National Defense, he stepped into the larger arena of presidential politics. In the Philippines, politics is more enticing than economics, and few people bother about the economic policies of the United States when election news is in the headlines.

The democratic heritage of the United States in the Philippines contained many serious imperfections. Abuses with which we are familiar—stuffed ballot boxes, padded election lists, five percentism, and peddling of influence, for example—were aggravated in the Philippines by the overcentralization of power in the hands of the nation-wide party machine, which in turn was dominated by a single individual or cabal. Before the war there was only one issue, independence, and only one party, the Nacionalistas. Manuel Quezon tended to be a personal *jefe*, and he juggled positions and appointments to suit his immediate whims. Nomination meant election. The provincial politicians were merely dedicated followers or seekers after the favors of Manila. Decisions in matters of policy, either economic or political, were usually made in the presidential palace, Malacañan, and approved by rather obedient legislatures.

Traditional patterns were subjected to serious strains after 1945. President Osmeña lacked the determination of Manuel Quezon, and President Quirino was overshadowed by his brilliant predecessor, President Roxas. Quirino's administration was marred by scandals, "inefficiency and even corruption," as the Bell Report expressed it. The regular and respected government services were honeycombed with graft. As the press mercilessly exposed the most flagrant abuses of the public trust, the executive continued to place politics above economics. The public charged the government with failure to implement a vigorous agrarian policy; blamed it for being too subservient to the caciques and economic tycoons; and accused it of inefficiency, extravagance, and seeking for wealth and power for its own benefit. No one (except the Communists, of course) called for a change in the form of government, but many wanted a change of attitude, a change of methods, and a change of personalities. Choices between two parties, and two candidates, were offered to the voters, but too often the differences between parties and platforms were more apparent than real, and depended more upon individual loyalties and hope of personal gain than upon moral issues or political principles. Party ranks were torn by factionalism, and the party in power had tactical advantages which consistently thwarted the attacks of the opposition.

The elections of April 23, 1946, depended largely, but not completely, on Roxas' interpretation of American policies. Roxas convinced the electorate that he was the favored son of the United States, but the convincing process demanded an excessive amount of dubious practices. Roxas created the Liberal party, the Liberal wing of the Nacionalistas, as he chose to call it, and defeated the incumbent, discouraged President Osmeña. The Popular Front elected seven members to the Congress, who were refused their seats. Perhaps the brutalities, the bitter denunciations, and the flamboyant promises were to be expected in the atmosphere of 1946, which was so charged with the flames and the casualties of the war.

In the election of 1949, also, there was far too much coercion, violence, and disorder. The Liberals won the presidency, sixty-eight out of one hundred seats in the House, and eight seats in the Senate. José Laurel, who had been President of the Philippines under the Japanese, as the nominee of the Nacionalistas gave Quirino a close race, and might well have won had there been less fraud and intimidation at the polls. While the real issues before the people should have been rehabilitation, recovery, and economic development, the political battles raged about the personalities of Quirino and his supporters, Cuenco and Pérez, or of Quirino's foes within the Liberal party, Senator Avelino, or of José Laurel. The Liberal administration, which had been in office for nearly four years, took credit for all the joint United States–Philippine rehabilitation achievements, obscured or underplayed its approaching domestic economic crisis, and adroitly brushed aside the criticisms of corruption which were leveled at it.

By 1951 the pendulum began to swing. The economic crisis had reached the surface, the Huks had carried their excesses to the point where violent revolution seemed a grim possibility, and internal politics had degenerated to depths where an outspoken press and public-spirited citizens demanded action and reform. The Bell Mission had made its report public, so the people of the Philippines were in a position to know exactly what they were up against. There was no presidential election in 1951, but there were congressional and local elections. The outcome would determine the control of the election machinery which would be in power in 1953.

Liberals and Nacionalistas opposed one another with the customary shadowboxing on their points of difference. On economic issues the Nacionalistas talked about less emphasis on government planning, the abolition or reduction of government controls, the disposal of government corporations, and the reduction of expenditures and taxes. The Liberals warned of continued controls, more planning, and higher taxes. The parties differed only on matters of timing and administrative methods with regard to industrialization, attracting Filipino capital into long-term investment, relief of credit stringency, cutting into foreign (chiefly Chinese) commercial domination, and adjustment of the unfavorable international income account.

On foreign policy (which is discussed in more detail below) both stood for fundamental friendship and good relations with the United States, and more U.S. aid, but the Nacionalistas advocated renegotiation of trade relations. The Liberals advised the ratification of the peace treaty with Japan while the Nacionalistas wanted a prior agreement on reparations. Politically, the Nacionalistas threw all the mud they could: the surplus property scandals, the sale of political influence in obtaining privileges under import quotas and controls, failure to collect more than 25 percent of the taxes due, the use of temporary police and civil guards by local landlords and politicos, and the half-hearted and costly execution of an inadequate program of land reform. Their attacks were vicious, but their constructive alternatives were conspicuously lacking.

President Quirino maintained his position in control of the Liberal party. He switched his favor from the regular party bosses, Cuenco and Pérez, and restored it to Senator Avelino. Since the Liberal candidates were often picked by the party bosses rather than by the President himself, he had little to lose if the regular party nominees were defeated. They were Cuenco men, or

Pérez men, and they did not represent the President. He permitted some candidates running as Liberals to make a deal with a Nacionalista candidate in order to defeat the official candidate of his own party, and he rather astutely proclaimed himself to be a partisan of clean elections. Let the best man win, said Quirino, and he ordered Magsaysay and the Army to guarantee fair play at the polls. He had assented to the enforcement of the revised election code, which called for the abolition of block voting and the permissible presence of representatives of third parties (in this instance, he anticipated that third parties would be "Independent" representatives of his new friend, Senator Avelino) on the election boards. He bowed to, and seemed to be in the vanguard of, the National Movement for Free Elections, which under the sponsorship of leading civic organizations set up 150 offices throughout the Philippines.

The fact is that the elections were fairly free and orderly.[5] The Nacionalistas won all nine Senate seats contested and captured twenty-three out of forty-five provincial governorships. They made sufficient gains in the local elections to guarantee for themselves protection of their interests when the votes would be counted in the presidential elections of November 1953.

The election of 1951 produced a temporary feeling of optimism about politics, in that it seemed to herald better days ahead. Still a certain amount of caution was called for in observing trends in 1953. The presidential race got off to an early start by Quirino's announcement that he would run again. This caused intraparty disappointment to those who thought the Liberals would lose with Quirino, but would win with almost anyone else. Since Quirino had the position and the power, his renomination loomed as a foregone conclusion. However, failing an amendment to the Constitution, he would be limited to eight years as President. This would mean that after two years in office he would ordinarily be succeeded by his Vice-President. Thus the number two spot became particularly desirable, and it was given to the Negros sugar baron, José Yulo.

President Quirino made it crystal-clear that he intended to take and to keep the initiative in maintaining himself and his friends in office. Through his retention of emergency powers, which the Congress was unable to take from him, he increased the pork-barrel expenditures in the political twilight zones. It was alleged that part of the rake-off on import licenses went into party coffers and that official advertising went to those outlets which were "Liberal" in outlook. One Lacson, the mayor of Manila, was ousted and another Lacson, the governor of Negros Occidental, was kept in office over protest in the interest of party control. It was openly charged that the pardon of Kamlon, the Sulu outlaw, was a sop to the Moro vote and that the negotiations with the Huks were initiated primarily from considerations of political advantage.

[5] See James J. Dalton, "Ins and Outs in the Philippines," *Far Eastern Survey*, July 30, 1952.

The so-called purge of Magsaysay in one sense removed a threat to President Quirino's political designs. Magsaysay was getting too popular. After his resignation, the President removed from important posts high-ranking officers who had worked closely with Magsaysay, and shifted certain military offices and branches, including psychological warfare (which was very effective against the Huks but allegedly was too active in glamorizing Magsaysay) from the office of the Secretary of Defense to the office of Chief of Staff. This made possible more of the playing of both ends against the middle. President Quirino insisted that he wanted the Army to keep the elections of 1953 free and clean, but there were those who asserted that while the cleanup of 1951 might have suited Quirino's purposes, he might desire a little more leeway for maneuvering in 1953.

It was only in one sense that Quirino gained from Magsaysay's resignation. In another, he lost. The Nacionalistas needed a platform and a candidate. José Laurel was not eager to run again, and the other leading candidates, including Claro Recto and Camilo Osias, lacked Magsaysay's color and popular appeal. On March 9, 1953, Magsaysay joined the Nacionalistas because, he said, "the Liberals were unable or unwilling to honor the standards of public service which its members and the citizens of the nation have a right to expect." Within two months he was nominated for the presidency. Senator Laurel offered Magsaysay as "the man of the masses, the spirit of Juan de la Cruz . . . the embodiment of Bonifacio and Del Pilar." The blue bloods in the Philippines might be inclined to look down upon this former truck mechanic, and his opponents might tend to characterize him as a "dumb but honest" front man for the behind-the-scenes manipulators like Recto, Laurel, and Rodríguez, but he emerged as the man to beat for Malacañan. His running mate was Senator Carlos García, a former governor of Bohol.

While the Nacionalistas were fulminating against the Liberals, and the Liberals were returning the barbs in kind, Carlos Romulo returned to the Philippines. He objected to the "dead hand of entrenched power" which President Quirino held over the Liberals, and he lacked confidence that Magsaysay would measure up to the responsibilities of national or even party leadership with the Nacionalistas. General Romulo took the lead in organizing a third party which called itself the Democratic party, and he teamed up with President Quirino's own Vice-President, Fernando López, to offer the people a third choice at the polls. In 1953 for the presidency and vice-presidency, respectively, it was Quirino and Yulo for the Liberals, Magsaysay and García for the Nacionalistas, and Romulo and López for the "Democrats." In late summer, however, the Democratic nominees withdrew from the race unconditionally because it had become "increasingly evident that the Democratic Party cannot hope to compete with the heavily-financed, strongly-entrenched power of the Administration party machinery." Accordingly, the

Democratic party, retaining its identity, formed a coalition with its former rivals, the Nacionalistas, as the only possible hope of getting a change.

III

American postwar economic policy toward the Philippines asserted itself in a period when the fundamental relationship between the two countries was being altered, and when the Philippines was groping toward independence in fact as well as in name. In the contempoary era of interdependence, nationalism is little more than a will-o'-the-wisp, but it is sought after and cherished with an almost pathological devotion.

Before the war the Philippines concerned itself but slightly with foreign affairs, security, and the national defense. By the Tydings-McDuffie Act these functions were reserved to the United States as its responsibility. President Quezon had an army which guaranteed internal security, and he had in General MacArthur a marshal who at one time assured Quezon that the Philippines had nothing to fear by way of foreign invasion. The political atmosphere in Manila was one of sublime indifference to the implications of the geographic nearness of Asia. The Philippines was in the Far East, but not of it. The Chinese in the Philippines were considered as a blessing or a nuisance as the case might be, but little thought was given to their relationship to China politics on the mainland. Southeast Asians—from Indonesia, Malaya, or Thailand—were given occasional kudos in the press as brothers, but scant heed was given to common attitudes on colonial problems or mutual interest in the social changes which were brewing in the Orient. The Japanese residents, primarily in Mindanao, were looked upon as good citizens and underestimated as potential fifth columns for an enemy invasion. Until the very doomsday in 1941 there was a blind confidence in Uncle Sam, and a mixed confidence and hope that it could not happen there.

The war changed all that. Invasion and liberation gave them a new appreciation of their own nationalism. In the future it would not be enough to be anti-Spanish, or anti-American, or anti-Japanese. They would have to be pro-Philippine. They could not afford to be exclusively a passenger on an American ship, they would have to sail their own craft, and they would have to cope with the tides and currents of the Asia in which they lived. They would have to prepare against the revival of a powerful Japan, they would have to take cognizance of the Red tide surging over, and they would have to seek new friends and allies among all the nations of the Western world.

The Japanese problem was most immediate. The Philippines wanted to make sure that, through supervision and advice, the democratically minded nations would guarantee the continued development of Japan as a peace-loving state. It was straining human credulity, so they said, to believe that the occupation had achieved for Japan an enduring or permanent transformation from an aggressive, feudal, militarist police state into a practicing and thoroughgoing democracy. Aside from the psychological tensions involved, the Philippines already had enough budget problems without the added costs of rearmament against a new menace from Japan.

The Philippines demanded more reparations; its original demand was for $8 billion. Japan offered services like building of ships and rolling stock; processing of trucks, tractors, farm implements, mining machinery, communications equipment, machine tools, and power-generating equipment; and the salvaging of ships which were lying on the bottom of Manila Bay. Japan also offered co-operation in industrial development, like salt and abacá production, but the sums involved were modest and the terms were far from outright reparations payments. Trade between the two countries revived—iron ore, logs, abacá, copra being exchanged for textiles, iron and steel, and manufactured products—to the point where in 1951 Japan took 7 percent of all trade with the Philippines. These were storm signals perhaps for Western commercial nations.

The Philippines realized that Japan had great contributions to make to the peace and stability of the Far East, particularly to President Quirino's proposed Pacific Union if that defense organization were to become a bulwark against Communist aggression. Yet it was difficult to forgive and forget. Ambassador Romulo looked directly at Prime Minister Yoshida at the San Francisco peace conference and said:

You have done us a grievous injury, and words can never repair it, nor all the gold or worldly goods you have. But fate has decreed that we must live together as neighbors, and as neighbors we should live in peace. . . . We are eager that the fangs of hatred shall be buried forever between us, but before that is done, before we extend the hand of forgiveness and brotherhood, we shall await some clear sign from you of spiritual contrition and renewal.

The Philippines signed the treaty with the greatest possible reluctance because "we had to act in a painfully limited area of choice." Ratification was delayed, pending a bilateral understanding on reparations. This was also a method of expressing resentment against the alleged betrayal of Philippine claims in the interest of "America's new darling, Japan." A front-page editorial in the *Manila Chronicle* showed the depth and intensity of the Philippines' bitterness:

Fifty years from now when the Japanese once more ride over Asia and the Far East as lords and masters they should set aside one day to pay tribute to the great American heroes of 1951, chief among whom is John Foster Dulles who was responsible for Japan's resurgence as economic and military power. By that time, thanks to the United States the Philippines will have become a nation of slaves worshipping at the temple of the Japanese goddess Amaterasu Omikami and paying obeisance to the Emperor of Japan.

Throughout the Philippines one senses the attitude, "We did so much for you during the war, how can you do this to us now?" As internal problems multiplied, there grew the perfectly understandable tendency to look abroad, in this case to the United States, as the source of help, perhaps, but also as the source of trouble. Memories emphasized the unpleasant features of the days when the GI's were there, rather than the benefits of the GI's associations and his dollars. The essential contribution of the Tydings Rehabilitation Act was forgotten in the rising protest against the Bell Trade Act. The Philippines had accepted the unpleasant medicine of the Trade Act at a time when a very harassed doctor had too many patients to take care of and needed a moment to look after his own health. After years of taking the medicine, the Philippines was unsure of the effectiveness of the remedy, and was developing an allergy to it.

The commercial dependence upon the United States continued. Imports overbalanced exports, capital shied away from the Philippines, and industrialization lagged. The satellite economic relationship took new forms, but it was as strong and as humiliating as it had been before the war. The National Policy Association, the National Economic Council, the Central Bank, the Department of Commerce, the Philippine Chamber of Commerce preceded the Bell Economic Survey Mission in condemning certain features of the Bell Trade Act. They demanded genuine economic sovereignty and a new treaty of friendship, commerce, and navigation based on the time-honored relationships of equality and reciprocity.

The American aid program, no matter how well conceived and how generous in American eyes, gave rise to arguments and misunderstandings. Money or credit was extended to the Philippines through the sale of surplus property, payments of the War Damage Commission set up under the Tydings Act, a Reconstruction Finance Corporation budgetary loan, veterans' pensions, military expenditures, back pay to guerrillas, and assistance through the Mutual Security program. It is impossible to cite exact figures for "aid" (some say $150 million and some say $2 billion), because the Philippine government insisted that payments for services rendered (for example, wages paid to laborers on military bases) could not be counted as aid. Furthermore, it was held, when the U.S. government made payments directly to individuals in the Philippines, the Philippine government was not responsible for how the money was spent. Nor, Filipinos believed, should the United States claim credit for expenditures which it had made in the Philippines in the interests of its own security.

After the Bell Economic Survey Mission made its recommendations, looking to an aid program of $250 million over a five-year period, the Philippines and the United States entered into an agreement under which special and technical missions from the United States should begin operations in the Philippines. Quirino's political opponents criticized this agreement by saying, "We might have driven a better bargain if we had had an administration which could have offered the United States more reliable collateral than proven incompetence, ill repute, and prodigality." No matter what sums were extended, good reasons were adduced for more. A "Marshall Plan for Asia" found active support in the Philippines. The aid pattern envisaged a progression from grant aid to government loans and then to the investment of private capital. Grant aid was intended to help to assure the internal security and basic economic and social preconditions for the development of the Philippines.[6]

American reports frequently drew fire from the Quirino administration. The Rivera-McMillan report on "feudalistic" conditions in the villages stated that nearly half the village residents in the Philippines were worse off today than ten years ago. The Hardie report on land reform (September 1952) intimated that the United States might have to intervene unless something drastic was done about land redistribution. The report asserted that the pernicious problem of land tenure threatened the very existence of the Republic and the stand of the United States against communism in the Pacific. Unless conditions were corrected, the report found, the United States could conceivably be forced to take direct, expensive, and arbitrary steps to insure against the loss of the Philippines to the Communist bloc.

The Philippine Congress was up in arms over the Hardie report and wanted Quirino to lodge a formal protest against it. Quirino refused but the election year overtones were obvious. Rumors were bruited about that the United States assistance programs themselves were infiltrated by Communists subversive to the Philippine government. Speaker Pérez suggested that the Philippine government should be allowed to screen American personnel and, in apparent pique, he asked, "Do our officious American friends expect us to do in 7 years what they failed to do in 47 years? The MSA is in position to help us yet its assistance is lagging." Aside from imperfections in its own organization and program, the mission had to cope with problems of delay and with political advice and interference. There was a world of implications in the affirmation that "There is no sense in putting an irrigation pump anywhere else but where it is needed most to increase the rice yield."

Military assistance was deemed as vital as economic aid from the American point of view. While the Americans looked upon the agreements for military assistance in the training of the Philippine Army and for the joint use of bases

[6] Mutual Security Administration, *Third Report to the Congress for the Six Months Ended December 31, 1952*, p. 10.

in the Philippines as measures for *mutual* security, the Filipinos thought they were getting the short end of the deal. In 1950 Senator Osias said, "Our show window of democracy in the Far East is fragile and easily smashed," and charged that the United States had not developed its bases or furnished adequate military assistance. In his words, "The United States has turned over to us arms deteriorated, battle worn, insufficient and inadequate even to cope successfully with internal order." Until our action in Korea there was a real fear that we would leave the Philippines as exposed as it was in 1941, and that we would be tempted to abandon our position in time of crisis "unless our national security and interests were directly and vitally threatened or if our national honor and prestige were formally committed." Filipinos were not blind to our mercurial oscillations in China and Korea and they wanted a formal binding guaranty that we would come to their assistance if they were the victims of aggression. Until they got this guaranty in the Defense Treaty of August 16, 1951, they considered it sheer madness to rely on the promises of policy makers who were not even authorized by the United States Constitution to declare war in the name of their people. This category included President Truman, who had assured the Filipinos that any attack on them would be considered dangerous to American peace and safety.

The "great debate" in the evolution of Philippine foreign policy after the war centered about this precise point of relations with the United States. President Quirino, and his able representative, Ambassador Romulo, sought to make the Philippines a respected member of the international community, loyal to the principles of the United Nations, dedicated to the maintenance of international peace and security, with the fullest support of the peoples of Asia and elsewhere in their struggle for freedom and independence. They endeavored to foster a regional consciousness in southeast Asia, as shown in their attendance at the New Delhi conferences on Asian relations and on Indonesia, the convocation of the Baguio conference on cultural relations, and active participation in the sessions of the Economic Committee for Asia and the Far East and other United Nations agencies in southeast Asia. Above all, they worked to prevent the impact of independence from resulting in chauvinistic nationalism and the severance of close ties with the United States. They insisted that they were not subservient to the United States, that they were not mendicant beggars with hat in hand inviting foreign intervention to do what their government could not do for itself, and that full and free participation in the struggles of the free world was a preferable alternative to the myth of neutralism.

Thus, while President Quirino was involving himself constantly in quarrels with the United States (we do not like your Japan policy, we do not like your trade monopoly, we do not like your interference in our internal affairs, we do not need you to teach us democracy), he was at the same time a target for the Nacionalistas and their most eloquent spokesman—Claro M. Recto—who reminded Quirino constantly that the foreign policy of the Philippines must be dedicated to the permanent peace and safety of the Philippines, not the United States. Recto was not by any means anti-American, for he openly expressed his hope for a *pax Americana* in eastern Asia. However, he proclaimed his patriotic devotion to the welfare and security of his own country first. If war should come, he asked, "Into what burrow could the Philippines crawl to hug the illusion of security in an atomic world?" His plea for equality and for independence in judgment and action was framed in these graphic words:

If America really believes that war is inevitable, then let her give Asia a resolute leadership we can trust; let her give us the same unconditional pledges and guarantees and the same actual evidence of a spiritual equality and common fate that she has given to her kinsmen and allies in the Atlantic community; and we shall have justification for the risk of war and incentive to make common cause.

Otherwise we must restrain our enthusiasms, dissemble our sympathies, moderate our words and actions, and in fulfillment of the primitive duty of self-preservation, make no enemies where we can make no friends, and hold our peace. . . .

Let not Macaulay's traveller from New Zealand, exploring the spectral ruins of Manila in the course of his post–atomic war peregrinations, and cautiously testing the radioactive waters of the Pasig, from the broken arches of Quezon Bridge, have cause to ponder that in those shattered tenements and poisoned fields and rivers once lived a nation unique to the annals of mankind; free men who put their liberties on the auction block, a sacrificial race with a mysterious urge to suicide, who, being weak and weaponless, took upon themselves the quarrels of the strong, and having been warned of their abandonment still persisted in their lonely course, and whose brutalized and deformed survivors, scrambling with stunted limbs in the infected debris of their liberated cities, had forgotten even the echo of the memory of the strange illusion for which their race had fought and perished.[7]

IV

American economic policy toward the Philippines gave rise to the foregoing considerations when interpreted in the context of its impact on the Philippines. It should also be examined and judged as a single segment of the tremendous complex of internal and international factors which determined the major directions of all United States foreign policies after the war.

From the days of the Atlantic Charter, American leadership devoted a great deal of study to the world's fundamental economic problems which contributed to misunderstandings, rivalry, and war. A deep appreciation of the dilemmas of the underdeveloped or underprivileged areas, particularly in the Far East, prompted rather far-reaching plans for immediate aid and long-term rehabilitation. During the fiercest days of the fighting in the Philippines, there was conscientious planning in the Department of the Interior, the War De-

[7] Commencement address at University of the Philippines, *Manila Times*, April 18, 1951.

partment, and the office of the Philippine government in exile for postwar reconstruction. Conflicting ideas, as between Americans and Filipinos and as between different Americans, prevented the translation of plans into action. With the sudden ending of the war the Filipinos subordinated economics to politics, while the Americans, who held all the economic potential, found themselves overwhelmed by their responsibilities in Europe and elsewhere in Asia. When one considers the demands of our Allies, France and the United Kingdom, our problems with the U.S.S.R., the preservation of the remnant life and spirit in Germany and devastated Europe, the occupation of Japan, the restoration to national power in China of Chiang Kai-shek and the Kuomin-tang, and the world-wide responsibilities flowing from our role in UNRRA and the young United Nations, it is little wonder that the Philippines seemed neglected in the evolution of our postwar policies.

The personal interest of men like General MacArthur, Secretary Ickes, High Commissioner McNutt, Senator Tydings, and Judge Bell guaranteed that the Philippines would not be buried in the government maelstrom, but it could not attract more than cursory and inadequate attention. When the Tydings Commission went to the Philippines to estimate the extent of dam-age, it stayed only a matter of days. This speed typified the general attitude of "let's do something, but do it quick" with which most Americans viewed admitted responsibilities in the Philippines. While the government agencies argued, the prewar firms with established interests and reputations in the Philippines went back to the job, primarily on their own resources but with hopes of compensation for their wartime losses. New firms flocked to the Philippines, and hundreds of GI's came up with flyers in trade which they had dreamed about and prepared for while they were in service during the libera-tion. These conditions were often hectic and exasperating, but perhaps normal and healthy in our free and competitive system. No apologies can erase the irregularities and the delays of red tape in government activities, and no ex-planations can wipe out the schemes of the illegal and unscrupulous who took advantage of the longing and despair of the terrorized Filipinos. The flood of GI dollars took care of immediate economic needs in the Philippines, but the Congress seemed to take an unconscionably long time in getting around to measures for rehabilitation and trade. Meanwhile, the returned Philippine government was helpless, the American High Commissioner's office (the arm of the executive branch of our government) was circumscribed in its powers and responsibilities, and the American Army in the Philippines was deter-mined to escape any long-term commitments for long-run economic restora-tion. These inactivities meant little to American welfare, but everything to Philippine welfare. The Philippines was always in the unenviable position of meaning infinitely less to the United States than the United States meant to the Philippines.

Egged on by the pressures of approaching independence for the Philippines, the American government evolved an embryo program. This program was a single entity. It included President Truman's instructions regarding Philippine affairs to the High Commissioner, the Alien Property Custodian, the Attorney General, the Secretary of War, the Secretary of the Treasury, the administrator of Veterans' Affairs, the president of the Export-Import Bank, the administrator of the War Shipping Administration, and the chairman of the Reconstruction Finance Corporation. It also included the Tydings Rehabilitation Act, the Bell Trade Act, the Military Assistance Act, the Military Bases Agreement, the surplus property disposal, and the General Relations Treaty which recognized the independence of the new nation. Any estimate of American activities, intentions, and motivations must be weighed in the light of the entire program, not any single part of it.

A psychological indifference or neglect seemed to characterize American relations with the Philippines between the declaration of Philippine independence and the outbreak of the Korean war. There was a general disposition to criticize local conditions in the Philippines, perhaps to preach a bit, but very little inclination to admit our own historical shortcomings. Some few publicists accepted the challenge of presenting Philippine facts to the American people, and some few government agencies, authors, and scholars endeavored to maintain a balanced perspective and to seek future remedies for present ills.

The intensification of the cold war metamorphosed American attitudes. We were still overwhelmingly preoccupied elsewhere, psychologically and politically. The United Kingdom, France, and Spain; Germany and Japan; the Middle East and China—all weighed heavily on our collective conscience and presented themselves as phases of a global necessity to contain the totalitarian communism of the Soviet Union. But after the attack in Korea awakened us to the deadly perils which we faced, it seemed fundamental common sense to look to our relations with the Philippines, accept their friendship where we would find it, and address ourselves to the twin challenge of expanding the bases of that friendship and doing away with the causes which would mar or destroy it. This meant carrying on a process which had emerged during World War II: not blinding ourselves to realities and not seeking to perpetuate a satellite relationship, under any guise whatever, but airing our grievances and endeavoring to build a relationship upon mutual understanding, mutual respect, and mutual devotion to a common cause. Political policies, military policies, and economic policies must stand or fall as they contribute to or detract from that fundamental premise.

V

Neither wholesale condemnation of our policies nor blanket approval serves any useful purpose. The goal is clear, the standards are unmistakable, but the tactics demand continuous reappraisal and readjustment. Our political and military policies require constant scrutiny, and the experts need to provide the public with sufficient information to inspire confidence and support. The psychological results of international activities—whether government instrumentalities like the United States Information Service, the International Exchange of Persons program, or the Voice of America, or private contracts between businessmen, tourists, teachers, or students—must be kept in tune with the temper of the times. A hair's breadth divides sympathy from resentment. An ill-timed venture, a careless word, or a brash deed often complicates the job of preserving harmony between the best of friends.

It is characteristic of human nature for each party to a relationship to tend to exaggerate his own contribution to that relationship and to underestimate the importance or misinterpret the motive of the other party. Americans are inclined to think that they have done everything possible for the Philippines, politically, economically, and militarily. Filipinos are inclined to think that we could have done more, that we have been primarily concerned with our own welfare, and that we have taken care of the Philippines' problems only as suited our own convenience and our own security.

There is no black and white to any of these attitudes. Both countries are entitled to a great deal of credit, both deserve a certain amount of criticism. Neither can be blamed for primary preoccupation with its own national interests, whether it be the American Congress in the matter of the Trade Act, or the Philippine Congress in the ratification of the Japan peace treaty. It cannot be said with justification that we in our search for our enlightened self-interest have sought naked power or ruthless exploitation; nor can it be substantiated that the Filipinos in their quest for what they feel to be their rightful position in the world have been unmindful of the benefits, as well as the weaknesses, which they have inherited from the American regime. It seems rather that on occasions both nations have given vent to their temporary exasperations and have lost sight of their common ties and their opportunities. Those were the times which called for soul-searching and wise statesmanship on both sides of the Pacific.

In spite of the shortcomings of American economic policy in the Philippines, and the often dismal picture of conditions in the Islands, the long-range picture is by no means discouraging. Faith in our own future can well be matched by confidence in the Filipinos. Their human qualities are excellent; lesser spirits might have withered in the catastrophes of the last decade. Their basic political and economic institutions are sound and their resources are ample. Their fundamental economic problem is the creation of new wealth by agricultural improvement or industrialization. Any American aid program, whether technical assistance or modest investment of capital, has every prospect of success. We must insist upon intelligent and efficient use of our aid under conditions of peace, order, and more efficient administration, but we must not underestimate the past sufferings, the culture, the traditions, the ambitions, and the pride of our Filipino friends. If we can assist the better elements in the Philippines in planning a constructive development program, we shall be doing something positive to counteract both sovietism and administrative ills. To fail is unthinkable; that would augment unrest and provide a field day for Communist agitators. To succeed is to record a significant step toward more stability, enhanced welfare, and the achievement of the kind of world to which both our nations are irrevocably dedicated.[8]

STANFORD UNIVERSITY
October 1953

Note.—November 15, 1953. The election five days ago was one of the most truly democratic elections ever held in Asia. In a campaign which scorched the grass roots, the people elected Ramón Magsaysay as their president and returned Nacionalista majorities to both houses of the Congress. The voters believed the humble, sincere young candidate who promised, "I will get rid of the crooks; I will make the officials get out and work in the barrios; and when I am president, the masses will be the first to benefit." The traditional blue-blooded oligarchy was called upon to turn over its political power to a new government dedicated to the welfare of the ordinary citizens.

President Magsaysay is a friend of the United States and an enemy of communism. He intends to prove that his way of life can cope with the problems of economic and social distress which are the earmarks of underdevelopment. The election is a tribute to the political maturity of the Philippines and an unimpeachable demonstration of the power of the democratic ballot, even in Asia.

—C. A. B.

[8] See address by Michael J. Deutsch, formerly industrial adviser to the Bell Mission, before the Society for the Advancement of Management, December 7, 1950.

Chapter One

THE PHILIPPINE PATTERN

Bound to the United States by military and economic commitments, as well as by the ties resulting from almost half a century of former colonial status, the Philippine Republic today is a key outpost of American arms and American policy in Asia. Strategically, the Islands are considered a vital link in the United States' chain of Pacific defenses. This was apparent on June 27, 1950, when, at the same time that American troops were ordered to South Korea and the Seventh Fleet to the Formosa Strait, President Harry S. Truman directed that American forces in the Philippines be strengthened and that military assistance to that country be accelerated. On August 30, 1951, the military relationship between the two countries was restated in a mutual defense agreement signed in Washington.

Strategic considerations appeared to be uppermost in the minds of American policy makers at that time, but long-standing economic, social, and political problems also had to be met if the Philippine Republic was to achieve a degree of stability. Many of the conditions which had caused upheavals elsewhere in Asia were also present in the new state. Aware that a bankrupt country would be a poor ally in the Pacific, the President of the United States dispatched an American Economic Survey Mission to the Islands in the summer of 1950. After careful study, this group, known as the Bell Mission, concluded that inefficient production and low incomes were the main Philippine economic problems, and made recommendations for their solutions. In January 1952 President Elpidio Quirino of the Philippines, in his address at the convening of the Philippine Congress, called for a review and readjustment of the provisions of the Philippine Trade Act of 1946, which defined United States-Philippine economic relations, in order to meet changing conditions and achieve a more stable and balanced economy.

These problems are of direct concern to Americans today not only because of the historical responsibility associated with sovereignty over the Islands, but also because of the continuing American financial and military interests in the Republic. Present-day decisions, however, are an outgrowth of past policy, which must be understood in order to evaluate the position today.

In contrast with such older imperial powers as Britain, France, and the Netherlands, the United States acquired the Philippines at a comparatively recent date. Political techniques suitable to twentieth-century conditions had to be worked out by a country which lacked experience in colonial administra-

25

tion. Moreover, the American economy was larger and more complex than those of the European countries, and conflicting interests, as between urban and rural areas, led to frequent disagreement on United States economic policy toward the Philippines.

At the turn of the century the conquest of the Islands received, from various quarters, both strong support and vigorous opposition. Once political sovereignty had been established, the argument continued on economic issues. In congressional discussions of every United States legislative act on the Philippines, protectionism was weighed against free trade, and commercial and financial groups clashed with domestic agricultural interests. During the Commonwealth period in the Islands, progress was made toward self-government and "Filipinization" of the administration. But the basic assumption of United States commercial policy, that there were special American ties, responsibilities, and rights in the Philippines, was not altered.

The Pacific war in many ways retarded Philippine economic development; but here as in other colonial countries the anti-Japanese resistance movements released forces of potential social change. The end of the war saw the fulfillment of the American promise for the establishment of the Philippine Republic. Political sovereignty, however, provided no simple formula for Philippine-American relations in the postwar period. Issues that were undecided when the Philippine Independence Act was passed in 1934 were not resolved when the Republic was established in 1946, and still hang in the balance. The recent period, therefore, has been only a new chapter in an old story.

Although the Philippine Republic is an Asian state and its future is inseparable from Far Eastern developments, the Filipinos, who numbered 19,234,000 in the census of October 1948, reflect both European and American influences, ideas, and interests. Aside from certain minorities, the people themselves are a homogeneous group of Malay origin, with a wide diffusion of Chinese and Spanish blood. Over three centuries of Spanish rule produced in the Islands many of the social and political problems that have plagued the Latin-American countries. Among these were the system of large plantation landholdings, semifeudal institutions, and the presence of a powerful minority of European origin controlling many phases of government, trade, and religion. More than nine tenths of the people are Christian, including about 78 percent who are Catholics and 10 percent who are affiliated with the Aglipayan Church, an independent denomination. In addition, there is a small minority Moslem group, called Moros, and some pagan peoples.

The foreign communities are of some significance, particularly the old Spanish group, the important Chinese population, who play a key role in trade and commerce, and the resident Americans. The principal United States influences in the Philippines have been in the spheres of economic development, administrative and governmental procedures, and general alignments in world politics.

Although the archipelago lies in the western Pacific, it has lacked close ties with China, Japan, or Indonesia. Insularity and the Spanish conquest have differentiated the Philippines from the rest of southeast Asia, of which it is considered a part. The land area of the Philippines consists of over 7,000 islands with a total of 115,600 square miles, but approximately 94 percent of the people live in eleven main islands which are in excess of 1,000 square miles each. The two largest of these are Luzon in the north (40,420 square miles) and Mindanao in the south (36,537 square miles). Other important islands are Samar, Negros, Palawan, Panay, Mindoro, Leyte, Cebu, Bohol, and Masbate. The principal cities include Manila, with a population of over one million, Cebu, Zamboanga, Davao, and Iloilo.

The physical isolation of the Philippines from the rest of Asia was intensified as a result of Western political domination, since trade and economic development were inevitably oriented toward the colonial power. It has not been simple, therefore, to characterize the position of the Philippines in comparison with other underdeveloped areas in the Far East. The standard of living and the educational level of the Filipinos, although low, were relatively higher than elsewhere in southeast Asia. From the beginning of United States rule there was slow but steady progress toward self-government. Although this was encouraged by the American promise of political sovereignty, it was rooted in the historic Filipino nationalist struggle, which was never abandoned throughout the colonial period or the Japanese occupation.

High hopes for the future of the Philippines were reflected in discussions at the end of World War II of Asian regional blocs. Filipino spokesmen even put forward proposals for Philippine leadership in any new Far Eastern constellation. Similar optimism was reflected in the economic field, as some Filipinos, interested in industrialization of their country, hoped that the defeat of Japan would clear the way for the development of Philippine resources. Events in Asia, however, and shifts in United States policy soon put a damper on wishful Filipino thinking. Ideological factors came to outweigh geographical facts.

Since V-J Day the magnitude of the changes in the political map of the Far East has surpassed expectations. The new Indonesian state has been established, after serious setbacks. In Viet Nam stubborn resistance has been maintained to the return of the French administration; Burma and Malaya have had their own internal upheavals and conflicts. The partition of the Indian subcontinent into a new India and Pakistan brought on an initial period of migrations and disorders and left a residue of unsettled problems, such as the Kashmir dispute. China moved in new directions, in the most revolutionary change in recent Far Eastern history. When Korea was split in two, both sides struggled for power, and international involvements threatened a new world war. Japan, weakened but still potentially strong, has claimed its place in international society. The strength to lead the hundreds of millions of Asian peoples clearly does not rest with the Philippine Republic, whether the criterion be ideology or population and resources. The Filipinos must find their niche in the new Asia.

In a similar way hopes that the Philippines could have a larger share of Far Eastern business, because of the downfall of Japan, have not been realized. American policy toward the former enemy has shifted drastically from the "deindustrialization" to the "workshop of Asia" philosophy, to the consternation of the Filipino people. Both military and economic considerations had their place in this reversal. Strong economic arguments were advanced for revitalizing Japanese industry to provide capital goods for southeast Asia. United States emphasis on Japan, however, has not meant the abandonment of the Philippines as a possible military base. On the contrary, the advent of the Communist regime in China and the fighting in Korea have spurred efforts to equip the Philippines as a friendly outpost in the Pacific. But the shift in focus has had inevitable economic consequences. For example, few reparations materials moved from Japan to the Philippines, and although the peace treaty left the way open for bilateral negotiations on the subject, the full Philippine claims seemed unlikely to be satisfied. Under the terms of postwar trade agreements, the Philippines sent strategic raw materials such as iron ore to Japan and received consumer goods such as textiles in return.

The internal economy of the Philippines presented a further dilemma. Trade totals in money terms were high after independence, but imports were almost twice as large as exports. Large United States disbursements, including war damage payments and military expenditures in the Republic, made it possible for the Philippines to make large outpayments in foreign exchange, and put off the day of reckoning with an eventual dollar deficit. Highly inflated prices for copra distorted the value of Philippine export crops. Not until the alarming flight of capital at the end of 1949 necessitated exchange controls, followed by rigid import controls in May 1950, was there any serious move to achieve a reasonable balance-of-payments position.

Failing to find substantial private capital willing to take a chance on Philippine investment, the government developed elaborate schemes for publicly financed business enterprise covering the whole range of industry, agriculture, and transportation. These were not put forward as a program of socialism, or even of nationalization of basic industries. They involved state enterprise, with the government taking the initiative and assuming risks and responsibilities in fields where private firms were unwilling to venture. Lack of finances, poor administration, and political considerations, however, resulted in the abandonment of plans for most of the proposed enterprises. Hence industrialization in the Philippines has proceeded very slowly.

Finally, internal political and social problems, demands for agrarian reform, and outright civil warfare have prevented real stability. In open conflict with the government were the forces of the Hukbalahap, renamed Philippine People's Liberation Army, the former anti-Japanese resistance movement which developed into a Communist-led peasant opposition seeking to overthrow the administration. Reports on Huk strength varied from time to time, but in spite of government all-out suppression campaigns it seemed unlikely that efforts to cope with the Huk problem could be finally successful in the provinces unless accompanied by deep-seated reforms in the condition of the peasants, the basic source of discontent.

On both the domestic and the international fronts, the Philippines faced in 1953 an uncertain future. The uncertainty stemmed from many factors. In part, it was the almost inevitable result of over four decades of American rule in the Islands, for while the United States pioneered in fostering political self-rule for its colonial people, it did not plan or encourage the kind of economic development which would have been the basis for real independence. In part, it was the consequence of the failure of Filipino leaders to take advantage of three postwar years, when large dollar resources could, if properly used, have gone far in furthering economic development. In part, it was the difficulty of being a small country in Asia today, where social revolution appeared to be the rule, rather than the exception.

Events in the Philippines have tended to be overshadowed by developments in China and India, the problems of postwar Japan, and the upheavals in the rest of southeast Asia. But a small country may quite suddenly secure the spotlight, as witness Korea, because of the nature of big-power involvements as well as the importance of internal occurrences. The situation in the Philippines is more likely to change than to be static, and what happens there will have a special significance for all Americans. In estimating the future role of the United States in world affairs, there is much to be learned about American foreign economic policy in action from the history of our relations with the Philippine Republic.

CHAPTER TWO

COMMERCIAL OPPORTUNITY:
PREWAR U.S. POLICIES

IN his instructions to delegates to the Paris Peace Conference in 1898, President McKinley, commenting upon the Philippine conquest, said the United States had taken up arms against Spain in "the fulfillment of high public and moral obligations." He went on, however, to remark that "incidental to our tenure in the Philippines is the commercial opportunity to which American statesmanship can not be indifferent."[1] Subsequent American policy toward the Philippines, while conscious of obligations to the Filipino people, was not, in fact, indifferent to the commercial factor. When, in fulfillment of solemn promises, political independence was granted to the Philippines on July 4, 1946, close economic ties with America remained, embodied in the Philippine Trade Act of 1946, the accompanying Rehabilitation Act, and various commercial agreements.

In part, this situation came about because of desperate Philippine needs, the result of an overspecialized agricultural economy and of wartime devastation. A clean break would have wrecked the Philippine economy; some transitional arrangement was unavoidable, but its strength and duration exceeded expectations. By 1951, six years after independence, the economy of the country was as heavily dependent on the United States as in the prewar years. The Filipinos themselves had recognized continuing American interests to the extent of amending their Constitution to allow special rights for United States nationals. Economic ties, parity rights, and military agreements, though accepted by both countries, inevitably imposed some practical limitations on the exercise of Philippine political sovereignty.

The urgency of the postwar period in the United States did not allow time for sober historical evaluation. In the public statements applauding the granting of independence to the Philippines in 1946, it was seldom recalled how divided American public opinion was over the original annexation of the Islands. The history of the period, however, records that American policy on the Philippines was a major controversial issue in the United States Congress and in the press of this country in the last years of the nineteenth century. On the one hand, there was a strong antiexpansionist feeling. On the other hand, there was frank discussion of the economic benefits that would accrue to

[1] "Correspondence with the United States Commissioners at Paris, Instructions to the Peace Commissioners, September 16, 1898," *Foreign Relations of the United States, 1898*, p. 907.

American business by extension of United States sovereignty over the archipelago.

Proponents of American expansion at the turn of the century emphasized that the Philippines would be a base from which to extend United States influence and trade in the Orient, and especially in China. This was illustrated by a statement of John Barrett, former United States Minister to Siam (1894–98), who told the Shanghai General Chamber of Commerce on January 12, 1899, that "it is high time that diplomatically, politically, commercially, the nations interested in the protection and expansion of their commerce and trade in China executed a movement not unlike that of Dewey in Manila Bay."[2] This point of view was also held by Senator Albert J. Beveridge of Indiana, who introduced a joint congressional resolution (S.R. 53) on January 4, 1900, to establish permanent United States sovereignty over the Philippines. Speaking in the Senate on January 9 on the vast markets of the Orient, he commented:

The Philippines are ours forever. . . . And just beyond the Philippines are China's illimitable markets. We will not retreat from either. We will not repudiate our duty in the archipelago. We will not abandon our opportunity in the Orient. . . .

Our largest trade henceforth must be with Asia. The Pacific is our ocean. More and more Europe will manufacture the most it needs, secure from its colonies the most it consumes. Where shall we turn for consumers of our surplus? Geography answers the question. China is our natural customer. . . . The Philippines give us a base at the door of all the East.[3]

In answer, Senator Alexander S. Clay of Georgia, on March 1, 1900, deplored existing greed and commercialism, and called the argument of Senator Beveridge "fanciful and illusory." He said:

There is quite a difference between commercial and territorial expansion. One does not necessarily follow the other. . . . The proposition that we must own vast tracts of land populated by a race of people that can never assimilate with our people, adjacent to Asia, across the Pacific, to induce the teeming millions of China to become our customers is absurd and is not supported by the laws of trade and commerce. . . .

Wars, entangling alliances, domestic insurrection are not the proper means to induce foreign consumers to buy our goods and wares and to become our customers. The laws of business, commerce and trade, friendly alliances, cheapness and quality in comparison with other countries contending for the same trade and business, are elements that must shape and regulate the volume of our business with other coun-

2 John Barrett, "The Philippine Islands and America's Interests in the Far East," an address before the Shanghai General Chamber of Commerce, January 12, 1899, p. 15.
3 Senator Albert J. Beveridge, in *Congressional Record*, 56th Cong., 1st sess., January 9, 1900, p. 704.

tries. . . . If we desire the trade of China, we must make it to the interest of her people to trade with us. . . .[4]

The expansionist group prevailed, and the Philippines came under the sovereignty of the United States. This policy was not, however, unopposed by many leaders in American public life. Philippine policy became an important political issue in the United States. Planks calling for some form of Philippine independence appeared in successive Democratic party platforms through 1912, and American policy toward the Islands was the subject of perennial criticism.

Although the Philippine Islands fell to the United States as a result of the Spanish-American War, the actual terms of the agreement indicated that sovereignty was transferred almost as the result of bargain rather than of conquest.[5] Article III of the Treaty of Paris, December 10, 1898, provided that Spain cede the Islands to the United States and that the United States pay $20 million to Spain. Thus the territory was not actually bought but some "consideration" was given to the former Spanish rulers. Furthermore, Article IV of the treaty provided that for a ten-year period Spanish ships and goods would be admitted to Philippine ports on the same terms as ships and goods of the United States, an unusual concession to a defeated enemy.

This last provision delayed for a decade the establishment of any real preferential arrangement between United States goods and Philippine products, as it would have been necessary to extend any such system to Spanish commodities as well. In addition to the treaty restriction, the United States was faced, at the turn of the century, with somewhat the same dilemma as at present. The establishment of preferential rates with the Philippines at that time would have been embarrassing to the major American objectives of securing equal rights in the China market.[6] There was, therefore, little objection to retaining the status quo in trade relations with our newly acquired possession, for a decade at least.[7]

Events in 1909 completely reversed the picture. The United States Tariff Act of August 5 of that year and the parallel Philippine Tariff Act of the same date instituted virtual reciprocal free trade between the two countries. There

---

[4] Senator Alexander S. Clay, in *Congressional Record*, 56th Cong., 1st sess., Appendix, March 1, 1900, p. 111.

[5] "Treaty of Peace Between the United States of America and the Kingdom of Spain, Signed at Paris, December 10, 1898," *Foreign Relations of the United States, 1898*, pp. 831–40.

[6] Grayson L. Kirk, *Philippine Independence* (New York, 1936), p. 57.

[7] The United States Revenue Act of March 8, 1902, however, provided a reduction of 25 percent from United States rates on dutiable goods entering this country from the Philippines. In addition, the $7.50 tax rebate for American importers of hemp, provided in Section 2 of the act, resulted in special benefits for American cordage manufacturers and some loss of revenue to the Philippines. This arose from a stipulation in Section 4 of the act, which provided that all revenue collected on Philippine articles was to be held in a separate fund, and paid to the Treasury of the Philippine Islands. See Pedro E. Abelarde, *American Tariff Policy Towards the Philippines, 1898–1946* (New York, 1947), pp. 52–53.

were several minor limitations. The quantities of Philippine sugar and to-bacco products which could enter the United States duty-free were restricted, although generous annual quotas were allowed. The maximum content of non-Philippine or non-United States materials in Philippine-manufactured goods admissible duty-free was set at 20 percent of the total value. Rice was exempted from duty-free treatment. Even these restrictions, however, were soon eliminated. The United States Tariff Act of October 3, 1913, removed the quantity limitations on duty-free sugar and tobacco products, and allowed rice to move free of duty. The act of 1909 abolished Philippine export duties on shipments to the United States; the act of 1913 abolished all duties on Philippine exports, irrespective of destination.

The Jones Act, approved by President Wilson on August 29, 1916, was an important milestone of Philippine legislation. It gave the Philippines the right to enact its own tariffs, and contained the first American legislative step, even though tentative, toward future Philippine independence. This was expressed in the preamble of the act, which stated:

Whereas, It was ever the intention of the people of the United States to withdraw their sovereignty over the Philippine Islands and to recognize their independence as soon as a stable government can be established therein; and

Whereas, For the speedy accomplishment of such purpose it is desirable to place in the hands of the people of the Philippines as large a control of their domestic affairs as can be given them without in the meantime impairing the exercise of the rights of sovereignty by the people of the United States, in order that, by the use and exercise of popular franchise and governmental powers, they may be the better prepared to fully assume the responsibilities and enjoy all the privileges of complete independence. . . .

Full Philippine control of domestic affairs, however, was not possible within the framework of American sovereignty. This was seen in the history of the free-trade program, a major phase of United States policy which was in fact imposed on the Islands over the strong opposition of the elected Filipino representatives. The National Assembly of the Philippines, in 1909, protested the establishment of free trade with the United States on the ground that such a relationship "in the long run would be highly prejudicial to the economic interests of the Philippine people and would create a situation which might delay the obtaining of its independence."[8] In taking this position, they showed a farsighted awareness of their national interests. The circumstances at the time were described by the late Manuel Quezon, former President of the Philippines, in his autobiography, *The Good Fight*. He said:

My first clash with the American Government while serving in the National Assembly was about a bill pending in the United States Congress to provide for the trade relations between the United States and the Philippines. The bill con-

[8] Philippine Islands Assembly Resolution No. 36, March 27, 1909.

templated the establishment of free trade relations between the said two countries. Certain private interests in the United States were opposed to the bill for selfish reasons and Secretary of War Taft, under whose department the Philippines then were, instructed the Philippine Commission to indorse the proposed bill and to secure the concurrence of the Philippine Assembly to its action. I fought the measure upon the ground that free trade relations between our countries would result in making the Philippines absolutely dependent upon the markets of the United States. This, I contended, would create a most serious situation in Philippine economic life, especially when the time came for the granting of our independence. The Assembly, by overwhelming vote, supported me, only the opponents of immediate independence taking the other side. My contention was proved sound when finally the question of Philippine independence was taken up by the Congress of the United States.[9]

By the time the United States was ready to act on the question of political independence for the Philippines, twenty-five years of free trade had tailored the economy of the Islands to fit the American market. The fears of the early Filipino legislators had proved to be well founded.

In the United States the move to grant independence to the Philippines was supported by interest groups with varying motives. Philippine independence had been a plank of successive Democratic party platforms, although the formulation became more vague as the years went on. American labor took an anti-imperialist position in general. Specific concern was voiced by the American Federation of Labor over the supposed threat of competition from cheap labor in Asia and from Oriental immigration to the United States. There was a determined Filipino group in this country which repeatedly urged an independent status for its homeland. But while all these were important, the major pressure for action on the independence issue came from the American farm lobby, whose members saw in continued Philippine preferences a threat to domestic agricultural production.

In a revealing study of the farm groups supporting Philippine independence,[10] Dr. Grayson Kirk analyzed the experience of American agricultural producers in the nineteen-twenties, when, coincidentally, imports from the Philippines rose substantially and American agricultural prices fell year after year. American agriculture did not share in the industrial expansion which followed World War I. Preferring to seek an external explanation, rather than to look at the inner workings of the domestic economy, these farm groups put the blame on Philippine competition. It should be recalled that, over these years, American tariff walls rose steadily and Philippine products were placed in an increasingly favorable position. For the decade 1920–30 Philippine sugar exports to the United States rose by 450 percent, coconut oil exports (including copra) by 223 percent, and cordage by over 500 percent. But, as Dr. Kirk

[9] Manuel Luis Quezon, *The Good Fight* (New York, 1946), pp. 107–8.
[10] Kirk, *op. cit.*, pp. 73–101.

pointed out, no causal relationship between these increases and the lowering of domestic prices has been shown.

The anti-Philippine group flourished, however, supported by the dairy organizations, general farm groups, domestic sugar producers, and cordage manufacturers, with the moral backing, at least, of the Cuban sugar lobby. The Tariff Defense Committee of American Producers of Oils and Fats was formed. Representative Harold Knutson of Minnesota included as part of his remarks in Congress, on December 14, 1929, a letter he had written to the editor of the St. Paul *Pioneer Press*, which stated, "It is generally agreed that the Philippine Islands today constitute the greatest single menace to our dairy industry because of their huge exports to our country."[11] Failing to secure what they considered adequate protection in the form of quotas and duties from the Smoot-Hawley Tariff of 1929, these groups gave their whole-hearted support to the move to cut the Philippines loose from the American free-trade bloc.

From 1930 to 1932 various Philippine independence bills were discussed in Congress, and finally the Hare-Hawes-Cutting Bill was approved. Agreement was reached on provisions for a ten-year transitional period of free trade, for imposition of quotas on Philippine products, for immigration restrictions allowing fifty Filipinos a year entry to the United States, and for special American rights in the Islands. The bill received a decisive veto in January 1933 by President Herbert Hoover, who stated that the readjustment period was too short, and insufficient security was provided for the Islands. It was, however, promptly repassed by Congress over the President's veto. Congressional support for the bill arose in response to the desperate domestic agricultural situation. The drop in farm incomes in the depression years sent legislators grasping at any tariff or quota straws to protect American products from overseas competition. When the American election of 1930 resulted in a shift of power to a slim Democratic majority in the House, some action on Philippine affairs was bound to occur.

The Hare-Hawes-Cutting Act created a storm of dispute in the Philippines, and resulted in a factional fight within the leading political party. President Quezon opposed the act, while both Sergio Osmeña and Manuel Roxas were in favor of accepting it. President Quezon was finally able to secure the passage of a resolution against the measure in the Philippine legislature on October 17, 1933. Four main objections were listed: the trade provisions, the immigration restrictions, the allocation of indefinite powers to the High Commissioner, and the military and naval restrictions, which were considered to be "inconsistent with true independence."[12]

President Franklin D. Roosevelt, who took office in March 1933, recommended to Congress that the measure be modified by eliminating provisions

[11] *Congressional Record*, 71st Cong., 2d sess., December 14, 1929, p. 690.
[12] Kirk, *op. cit.*, p. 125.

for permanent military bases, except naval stations. The Tydings-McDuffie Act was speedily enacted, and became effective on March 24, 1934. It was accepted by the Filipinos, primarily because it was considered to be the best that could be secured at the time, and also because there was implied a promise of later review. This was apparent in the resolution of the Philippine legislature which, in accepting the act, quoted from President Roosevelt's message to Congress, which declared, "Where imperfections or inequalities exist, I am confident that they can be corrected after proper hearing and in fairness to both peoples." This statement, according to the Filipino legislators, "gives to the Filipino people reasonable assurance of further hearing and due consideration of their views."

The Tydings-McDuffie Act included both political and economic provisions. On the political side, it defined the steps toward independence. The Philippine legislature was authorized to arrange for a constitutional convention to result in a document "republican in form" and including a bill of rights. Also stipulated for inclusion in the framework of the interim government were a number of provisions defining American sovereignty in the Islands for the ten-year transitional period. Thus no foreign Philippine loans could be made without the approval of the President of the United States; the United States retained control of Philippine foreign affairs; all decisions of Philippine courts could be reviewed by the United States Supreme Court; and American citizens were to have equal rights with Filipino citizens in the Islands. Filipino immigration to the United States was limited to the minimum quota of fifty a year. Most of these restrictions applied only in the transitional Commonwealth period. On July 4 of the independence year the President of the United States was to surrender all sovereignty and recognize the independence of the Philippines.

Major portions of the Tydings-McDuffie Act were devoted to defining economic relationships between the two countries. Free trade was to be continued from 1935 to 1940, but the quantities of products entering the United States duty-free were restricted to 850,000 long tons of sugar, 200,000 tons of coconut oil, and 3 million pounds of cordage each year. Imports in excess of these quotas were to pay full duty. There were no restrictions on United States products entering the Philippines. In the period 1941–46 products receiving preferential treatment were to be subject to a Philippine export tax of an initial 5 percent, increasing annually by 5 percent to 25 percent in 1946. Full United States tariffs were to be paid after July 4, 1946, the independence date. Tariff revenues before independence were to be applied to liquidate the bonded indebtedness of the Commonwealth.[13]

Domestic American producers were not satisfied with the new law and promptly sought more protection. Under the Jones-Costigan Amendment to

[13] The Philippine Commonwealth and Independence Law (Public Law No. 127, 73d Cong., 2d sess.), also known as the Tydings-McDuffie Act, March 24, 1934.

the Agricultural Adjustment Act of 1934, an absolute quota was substituted for the duty-free quota on sugar, and the Philippine allocation was set at a relatively low figure. Domestic producers of fats and oils also became vocal, and the Revenue Act of 1934 provided for a processing tax of 3 cents a pound on coconut oil coming to the United States or extracted therein from Philippine copra. The proceeds of the tax were to go to the Philippine Treasury. This tax still gave some preference to the Islands, however, as compared with a 5-cent tax on oil extracted from non-Philippine copra. The following year the Cordage Act of 1935 substituted an absolute quota of 6 million pounds for the duty-free quota of 3 million pounds provided in the Independence Act. Commenting on the events of 1934, Dr. Kirk said:

With this coconut oil tax the Seventy-third Congress closed its Philippine account. It had offered independence to the Islands and that independence had been accepted. But whatever nobility there may possibly have been in the gesture was completely overshadowed by an appalling indifference to Philippine welfare. Statesmanship had surrendered openly and callously to the dictates of lobbyists.[14]

While the American producers had succeeded in obtaining increasing protection from Philippine products, the Filipinos were far from satisfied. The Tydings-McDuffie Act had been supported because it promised political independence, but with that assured the Filipinos sought to make a better economic bargain.

The abrupt termination of trade preferences, once independence was achieved, was a particularly hard blow, as time was needed to develop alternate sources of income, to diversify production, and to seek new markets. On April 14, 1937, the Joint Preparatory Committee on Philippine Affairs, including both Filipinos and Americans, was created to study trade relations. After careful analysis it proposed extensive revisions in the existing legislation, including the substitution of a series of annually declining duty-free quotas instead of increasing Philippine export taxes, and it suggested that the transitional period of preferential treatment be extended after independence by increasing the tariff by 5 percent annually.[15] A major purpose of the proposed changes was to strengthen the infant industries of the Philippines. Representatives of American domestic industries, however, were still reluctant to give competitive advantages in the American market to Philippine products.

Sections of the recommendations dealing with quotas and special treatment for certain commodities were accepted by Congress, but others, particularly those relating to extension of preferences, were rejected. In the 1939 amendments to the Independence Act few important changes were made. Annually declining duty-free quotas were instituted in place of increasing Philippine export taxes for coconut oil, cigars, pearl buttons, and certain

[14] Kirk, *op. cit.*, p. 134.
[15] *Report of the Joint Preparatory Committee on Philippine Affairs*, May 20, 1938 (Washington, 1938), Vol. I, *passim*.

tobacco products. In 1941 the provisions of the Independence Act with regard to the export tax and to quotas were suspended for 1942, to begin instead in 1943.[16]

While such minor details of trade relations were being debated, major issues of Far Eastern and world politics had reached a critical stage. Japanese expansionists, who had promoted military conquest in China and economic penetration in southeast Asia, now sought to extend their control over all of the Far East. The Philippines was a first step on the road to such conquest. For United States legislators events in Asia diverted discussion from quotas and preferences to defense and counterattack. After Pearl Harbor there was only one item on the agenda for the Philippines and that was the war with Japan.

To say merely that the prewar Philippine economy was tied to that of the United States would be an understatement, overlooking the economic potentialities of the Islands. For one thing, Philippine overseas trade was conducted primarily, and for some commodities exclusively, with the American market. This was true for both imports and exports. Total trade in the period since American control had grown from $34 million in 1899 to over $251 million in 1940. Trade with the United States, however, had grown from 16 to 75 percent of total trade.[17] Under the Spanish regime, Philippine commerce was divided among various countries, including India, the United Kingdom, the United States, Spain, and China. This was soon to change under the free-trade policy, which brought increasing concentration on the American market.

The nature and extent of prewar Philippine foreign trade illustrate, with some variations, the pattern of colonial development familiar throughout southeast Asia. To the United States came agricultural raw materials and products needed for manufacture in this country, and from this nation went industrial goods and commodities vital to an underdeveloped economy. American exports also included foodstuffs such as wheat and flour, for owing to excessive specialization on export products the Philippines, though an agricultural nation, was unable to feed itself.

American investments in the Philippines in the years just before World War II were on a small scale compared with the investments of European powers in their Asian colonial spheres. They amounted to only about $258 million, or approximately 60 percent of total foreign investment in the Islands. This represented 30 percent of American investment in the Far East, but only one percent of all American foreign investment. A large part of American investment in the Philippines was the result of savings by United States nationals residing there, and the plowing back of profits by American-owned

16 Shirley Jenkins, "Our Ties with the Philippines," *Far Eastern Survey*, May 23, 1945, pp. 121–28.

17 *American-Philippine Trade Relations*, "Report of the Technical Committee to the President of the Philippines" (Washington, 1944), p. 32.

corporations. United States investments were concentrated in mining, public utilities, and industries producing for export to the American market.

Of major importance in the prewar Philippine economy was the sugar industry, on which about 2 million people, or 12 percent of the population, depended for their livelihood. The sugar centrals in operation had an annual capacity of about 1.5 million tons. Investment in centrals was estimated at $93 million, while about $181 million was invested in land and improvements and $25 million in crop loans. Of the total capital invested in sugar, approximately 50 percent was Filipino, over 30 percent American, and 15 percent Spanish.[18]

Estimates of investments in the coconut industry were unreliable because of the large number of small enterprises. According to Philippine figures, before the war the total investment in the industry was $221,215,000, of which $209,320,000 was in land and improvements. Of this latter figure, about $194,-665,000 was Philippine capital and $8,375,000 American. Investment in mills and refineries totaled $11,895,000, of which only $905,000 was Philippine, $5,545,000 American, and $3,495,000 British. The American Trade Commissioner in Manila reported on July 9, 1936, that six American companies held investments amounting to $1,112,500 in land and buildings, and $1,200,000 in machinery and equipment.[19]

The undeveloped character of the Philippine economy was evident from the small amount of money invested in industry, and also from the large role of foreign capital. In 1938 manufacturing assets in the Philippines amounted to $178.2 million, of which 35 percent was Philippine, 19 percent American, 14 percent Spanish, and 7 percent Chinese. The total investment in electric light and power companies was $28.2 million, of which 73 percent was American and only 20 percent Philippine. In the mining industry, invested capital amounted to $100.6 million, of which 48 percent was Philippine, 37 percent American, and 6 percent British. The Philippines had extensive lumber resources, but total funds invested in forestry were only $18.5 million, of which 39 percent was Philippine, 36 percent American, 10 percent Chinese, and 7 percent Japanese. Assets of commercial establishments in the Philippines amounted to $293.8 million, of which 35 percent was Philippine, 21 percent American, and 25 percent Chinese.[20]

These figures on investment illustrate the low level of industrialization in the Philippines. Was this a result of inherent deficiencies in the country, or merely of inadequate development?

Repeated surveys of Philippine resources have shown that the land is rich, and that there are many possibilities for expanding production, raising living

[18] Data on industry from *American-Philippine Trade Relations, op. cit.,* and *Report of the Joint Preparatory Committee, op. cit., passim.*

[19] *Report of the Joint Preparatory Committee, op. cit.,* p. 51.

[20] *Yearbook of Philippine Statistics, 1946* (Manila, 1947).

standards, and increasing self-sufficiency. In his authoritative work, *The Philippines: A Study in National Development,* the late Dr. Joseph Ralston Hayden (former vice-governor) said of the Philippines: "Their population has more than doubled in the past 35 years, and even with the means of production which are at present known to mankind their territory is capable of supporting probably three times as many people as it now contains."[21]

Declaring that sugar was overproduced and should be drastically curtailed, Dr. Hayden stated that both Manila hemp and copra could be sold at a profit on the world market without tariff protection, and possibly also sisal, tobacco, and other minor products. For home consumption, and perhaps also for export, the country could produce more rice, rubber, quinine, kapok, cotton, coffee, and tropical fruits. Cattle could be raised, and more timber exploited. Dr. Hayden pointed out that of 18.6 million hectares of potential agricultural land only 4.3 million were under cultivation in 1937; that fisheries could be more productive; that exports of chrome ore, copper, iron, and manganese ore could be increased; that there existed iron, lead, and molybdenum deposits, as well as asbestos, zinc, platinum, and sulphur; and that streams represented potential hydroelectric power. The material requisites for a light industry manufacturing goods for home consumption and export have been present in the Philippines. Their development, however, has been slow.

An undeveloped economy and unbalanced production have been at the root of the poverty-stricken condition of the vast majority of Filipinos. The Philippine economy has been primarily agricultural, with 80 percent of the population dependent on the production of a few crops, all—except rice—for export. Of this number 6 million were engaged in the production of rice, 4 million in coconuts, 2.5 million in abacá, 2 million in sugar, and 500,000 in tobacco.[22]

Although levels of living undoubtedly improved as a result of American control in the Islands, real incomes were still very low, and general conditions have been far below minimum standards of health and efficiency. The per capita income of Filipinos was estimated by Manuel Roxas, when he was Secretary of Finance in 1939, at $40 annually.[23] With the economy tied to high-cost United States imports, real income continued low even though money incomes rose over the years. According to E. D. Hester, former Economic Adviser to the United States High Commissioner, "Much of our high wage level is artificial because also we have high food and clothing costs for the plain people, so that real wages—purchasing power—are not as high as the wage rates expressed in pesos would indicate."[24]

What were these wage rates? In 1939 a Department of Labor study esti-

[21] Joseph Ralston Hayden, *The Philippines, A Study in National Development* (New York, 1942), p. 4.
[22] *American-Philippine Trade Relations, op. cit.,* p. 1.
[23] Kenneth K. Kurihara, *Labor in the Philippine Economy* (Stanford, 1945), p. 37.
[24] *Ibid.,* p. 41.

mated that the average daily wage of Filipino workers was 45 cents. As for agricultural workers, a 1940 survey by the *Manila Bulletin* revealed that the average farm worker was paid 25 cents a day.[25] Furthermore, income was distributed very unequally. It was reported that, in 1938, about half of the Filipino families received annual incomes, largely in kind, of about $62.50 per family. On the other hand, it was estimated that, although only one percent of the people received over $500 a year, their earned and unearned income together amounted to about one-third of the total national income.[26]

The free-trade relationship, which encouraged producers to concentrate on a few specialized export crops, meant the continuation of a dependent and predominantly agricultural economy in the Philippines. This does not mean that there was any deliberate American policy of discouraging industrialization, but rather that trade preferences for a few products such as sugar, copra, and hemp channeled both Philippine and American investment into these fields, which required unskilled labor and low wage rates. Dependence on plantation products and overspecialized, unmechanized agriculture have produced the same evils the world over: low wages, poor living conditions, and lack of impetus for rationalization of production and modernization of techniques. Displaced agricultural workers have not been able to turn to an expanding industrial system for employment, but have remained a burden on an already exhausted land economy. Similarly, promotion of home industries, such as needlework and embroidery, has not meant raising of levels, but rather has taken advantage of existing low wages.

Low standards have in turn meant poor education, a low level of political development, and frequent inefficiency and maladministration in government. As in many other parts of Asia, there was neither the money nor the determination to push through a program of industrialization, agrarian reform, and diversification of production. These were the needs of the Filipinos before Pearl Harbor, and although they were recognized in many quarters, only a small beginning had been made toward reshaping the economy in preparation for independence. The war brought many new problems, but it did not help to solve the old ones.

[25] *Manila Bulletin*, July 23, 1941.
[26] *Report and Recommendations of the Joint Philippine-American Finance Commission*, H.R. Doc. 390 (Washington, July 8, 1947), p. 11.

CHAPTER THREE

POSTWAR RELIEF AND REHABILITATION

THE Philippine economy, struggling toward independence, could ill afford its wartime setbacks. Furthermore, because of complicated economic and political factors, it proved impossible to take advantage of the opportunities for basic economic reconstruction presented by the task of postwar rehabilitation.

The Philippine Islands, twice fought over and occupied by Japanese forces for more than three years, were among the foremost victims of World War II. A United States congressional report declared:

Official reports, photographic evidence, and statements of those who have seen the ruin and destruction are unanimous in asserting that, of all the war-ravaged areas of the world, the Philippines are the most utterly devastated from the standpoint of the ratio of functional construction still intact to functional construction damaged or destroyed, the effect of destruction on functional economy, social facilities of the nation, and the effect of war damage on the capacity of the nation to rebuild and repair.[1]

There were three major phases of destruction in the Philippines. In 1941–42 damage was done in the initial attack by the Japanese and in demolition of facilities by the retreating Americans. During the period of occupation there was sabotage by guerrilla forces and by the Japanese in retaliation. Finally, during the liberation, damage was done by United States bombings, by the Japanese forces in retreat, by guerrilla fighting, and by combat artillery fire in re-entering the major areas.

The damage in the first phase of Japanese conquest was relatively small, and confined mainly to major military objectives, such as Manila, Cebu, Davao, and Zamboanga. There was widespread destruction during the occupation period, but this was primarily in small villages and rural areas where the Filipino opposition operated, and along the main Japanese supply lines, which were subject to guerrilla action. It was in the final phases of the war, during the reconquest by United States forces, that the greatest devastation of the Philippines occurred.

In addition to actual property damage, the Philippines suffered severe economic disruption as a result of three years of "co-prosperity." Japanese economic policy during the war was not based on any long-term plan; as con-

[1] *Rehabilitation of the Philippines*, Report from Congressman C. Jasper Bell, chairman, House Committee on Insular Affairs, to accompany S. 1619 (Washington, 1945).

querors who had major battles still to fight they sought as much loot for as little expenditure as was possible. Only minimum standards of living were allowed for occupied peoples, although Japan hoped to avoid revolts which would require large troop garrisons. Philippine metal ores were important to the Japanese, since they were needed for war production in the home islands. Sugar and many other agricultural products, however, could more easily be obtained elsewhere in the Japanese Empire; the shortages of shipping facilities and of "trade goods" were obstacles to commerce in foodstuffs. As a result, sugar plantations fell into disuse and Japanese propaganda and organizing efforts were directed to increasing food production for local consumption. At the same time the standard of living in the Philippines was reduced, consumer goods were unavailable, and real wages fell. Inflation was widespread just before the liberation, when Japanese control mechanisms broke down.

Attempts were made by the occupying Japanese forces and by the puppet Philippine government to control various phases of the economy.[2] On February 22, 1942, standards of wages were established for use by public employment offices: the daily wage for unskilled labor in Manila was 40 cents for an eight-hour day for men and 30 cents for women, with rates outside the city set at 80 percent of the Manila figures. Luxury articles faced a sales tax of 35 percent and "semiluxury" articles a tax of 20 percent. An energetic food production campaign was inaugurated, and in May 1942 an executive order sought to have food grown on all idle lands. In March 1944 all able-bodied men and women between sixteen and sixty were required to register for one day a week of compulsory, unpaid agricultural labor. Prices were relatively stable during the first year of the Japanese occupation, but as the military prospects of Japan declined and the submarine blockade was established, they increased at an accelerating rate.

The Americans who reconquered the country in 1944 were concerned primarily with military goals; the Philippines was a way station on the road to Japan. The urgent needs of 18 million Filipinos for food, housing, clothing, and medical care, however, could not be ignored. These matters were of major concern to the Philippine government in exile, which had sat in Washington during the war years. Headed first by President Manuel Quezon, and upon his death in 1944 by the former Vice-President Sergio Osmeña, a small group of Filipinos acted as a holding body for Philippine interests during the war and tried to maintain a voice in the over-all Pacific political strategy.

President Osmeña waded ashore in Leyte in October 1944, together with General Douglas MacArthur, to begin the difficult task of re-establishing Philippine authority in the Islands. Not the least of the problems was to be the relations with the Filipino leaders who had remained in the country during the war and occupied posts of varying degrees of collaboration with the Jap-

[2] Lora S. Weston, "Co-Prosperity Fails in the Philippines," *Far Eastern Survey*, January 31, 1945, pp. 22–26.

anese. But before tackling the political questions, there was the immediate task of relief for millions of homeless and hungry Filipinos.

In the initial period after the reoccupation, the United States undertook emergency relief work. This developed into quite a substantial program, in terms of both dollar expenditures and physical volume of goods, including food, medical supplies, clothing, seed, and other commodities. In addition, a good deal of transportation equipment was turned over to the Philippine government and to private enterprise. The Army Civil Affairs Program also co-operated in setting up schools and hospitals in devastated areas. As the civilian relief program drew to a close, the Commonwealth government, on August 8, 1945, reported that approximately 200 million pounds of food had been issued up to July 31 of that year. Some of this food had been issued as direct relief to indigents but the great bulk of it had been sold through stores to individual Filipinos.

The relief needs of the Filipinos after the liberation were most urgent. On February 28, 1945, one day after the re-establishment of the Commonwealth government in the Islands, President Osmeña cabled to Governor Lehman, then Director-General of UNRRA: ". . . within this ruined capital city we find ourselves face to face with problems of staggering proportions. Thousands and thousands of families are without shelter and in rags, millions are facing hunger and starvation."

Although the responsibility of UNRRA for Philippine relief was as yet undetermined, the Director-General agreed on March 30, 1945, that one million dollars' worth of emergency relief supplies should be offered for particularly devastated areas there. This was accepted on May 12 by the Philippine government, and an initial shipment of foodstuffs, medical supplies, and contributed used clothing was sent at the end of June. Much later, on September 14, almost seven months after the re-establishment of the Commonwealth, the first shipment of UNRRA goods was received in Manila harbor. A second shipment was received later in the month, and by September 30, 1945, UNRRA had shipped to the Philippines about 5,500 tons of supplies, of which about 4 million pounds was used clothing. A second emergency program of $2 million was authorized in November 1945, followed by a third program of $3 million in March 1946, and a fourth program of $5 million, plus suitable clothing, approved in August 1946. Over half of all allocations were for food; other major categories were clothing, items such as seed and farm implements for agricultural rehabilitation, medical supplies, and shipping charges. In addition to relief work, UNRRA made a survey of agricultural conditions and food prospects, in co-operation with the Philippine Department of Agriculture. Another phase of the UNRRA program was the repatriation of 6,680 Chinese from the Philippines.

There was no question that the Filipinos were in desperate need after the war. The inadequacies of the UNRRA emergency operations were apparent when set against the Philippine estimate that a relief program of over $100 million was actually required. But both the international agency and the Philippine government faced a major dilemma in their attempts to grapple with the relief problem.

UNRRA's resources were limited, and in allocating its funds it had to ask not only whether relief was needed, but also who should foot the bill. The position of UNRRA, understandable in view of the circumstances, was "not to deplete its avaliable resources for the relief and rehabilitation of any area whose government is in a position to pay with suitable means of foreign exchange." An UNRRA subcommittee which investigated the financial position of the Philippines advised, after considering the balance-of-payments position and domestic and overseas assets, that "the Philippines be considered at the present time in a position to pay with suitable means of foreign exchange for essential relief and rehabilitation imports."[3]

One factor had been omitted, however, and that was the semicolonial status of the Philippine government. While it was true that the Philippine balance-of-payments position was sound, most of the foreign exchange of the country was tied up in large currency reserves, held in the United States, which were not available for relief purposes because the Philippine government did not have the right to alter its currency rate, which was tied to the United States dollar. Careful controls might have made it possible to enlarge the scope of Philippine relief operations, but it should be recalled that the country was emerging from long years of occupation, and from the devastation of the military campaign to eject the Japanese. The knowledge that assets were held for their government in distant vaults was no comfort to the hungry and ragged Filipinos. The UNRRA emergency aid did little to ease the desperate need. The Filipino citizen, as a result, was a victim of the myth that abundant foreign exchange must necessarily mean prosperity, and of the difficulties of balancing current needs against assets available only in the future.

Following the liberation of the Philippines, attention turned from immediate problems of relief to longer-range questions of rehabilitation and reconstruction. Even in the early stages of the conflict, before victory was in sight, the need for postwar rehabilitation of the Philippines had been foreseen. In June 1943 the United States Congress had approved a joint resolution amending a section of the Tydings-McDuffie Act and providing for the establishment of a joint Philippine-American commission on rehabilitation, including nine Americans and nine Filipinos. According to the congressional resolution, this group was to "investigate all matters affecting postwar economy, trade, finance, economic stability and rehabilitation of the Philippine Islands" and to formulate recommendations for future trade relations between

[3] Statement of the UNRRA Subcommittee, M. Valensi, chairman. This policy was upheld by the Director-General at the Fifth Council Session in Geneva in August 1946. See Operational Analysis Paper No. 50, *UNRRA in the Philippines, 1946–47* (Washington, April 1948), pp. 47–51.

the United States and the Philippine Republic. The group, however, met in joint session only a few times, and it proved impossible to reconcile the divergent views of its Filipino and American members, in particular on the question of free trade. Hence no progress was made.

Consideration of future policy on the Philippines was also the subject of an Interdepartmental Committee on Philippine Affairs, representing all major departments of the United States government concerned with the Islands, including State, War, Navy, Treasury, Agriculture, Interior, and the Tariff Commission. The views of this group were also highly divergent, and no firm policy resulted from its deliberations.

After the reconquest of the Islands the question of reconstruction became urgent, and several official missions and reports paved the way for action. Inevitably, the problem of rehabilitation and reconstruction in the Philippines became intertwined with that of future Philippine-American relations. Some voices even urged the postponement of independence, at least until the country had recovered from the effects of the war.

Senator Millard E. Tydings, known for his long-standing interest in the Philippines, headed a group which surveyed war damage. Reporting in the Senate on June 7, 1945, he described a picture of devastation and chaos. He recommended that the independence policy stand; that loans be made to aid the Philippine government through the emergency period; that a gift, of perhaps $100 million, be extended for reconstruction and rehabilitation purposes; and that a trade program for the Islands aim at economic as well as political freedom for the Philippines.[4] Some of his recommendations were embodied in later legislation.

In the wartime program of the Reconstruction Finance Corporation some thought had been given to the problem of compensation for war damage. Shortly after the Pearl Harbor attack, the War Insurance Corporation was created by the RFC, with a capital of $100 million, to "provide reasonable protection against losses resulting from enemy attacks." This protection, given to continental United States on December 13, 1941, was extended on December 22 to property owners in Alaska, Hawaii, the Philippine Islands, Puerto Rico, and the Virgin Islands. An act of March 27, 1942, however, terminated on July 1, 1942, the free insurance protection of the War Insurance Corporation.

In June 1945 a special investigating mission was sent to the Philippines by the War Damage Corporation to estimate losses and prepare recommendations on handling claims. From June to September the mission conducted a block by block survey of Manila, Cebu, Bacolod, Iloilo, and Zamboanga, and a general survey of Baguio, San Fernando, Dagupan, Tarlac, Pampanga, Lingayen, and Malolos. Loss to buildings was based on 1939 assessed values and on in-

---

[4] Senator Millard E. Tydings, *The Philippine Islands*, Remarks in the United States Senate, 79th Cong., 1st sess., Doc. 53 (Washington, June 7, 1945).

formation from officials. Personal property loss was based on information from Chambers of Commerce, government officials, and industrial experts.

As a result of this investigation it was estimated that the total loss to private, public, and church properties in the Philippines was approximately $800 million. The city of Manila was found to be 50 percent destroyed. A summary of wartime losses prepared by the War Damage Corporation may been seen in the table below.[5]

Public property	$195,347,595
Catholic property	125,000,000
Other church property	14,000,000
Private property (including automobiles)	464,420,000
	$798,767,595

Other estimates have been made of war damage. For example, the Census Office of the Philippines put war losses at $305 million for government and $990 million for private parties, totaling $1,295 million.[6]

Compensation for war damage in the Philippines was considered in Congress along with other phases of rehabilitation and reconstruction. The Tydings bill, S. 1488, introduced in the Senate in October 1945, originally proposed $100 million in compensation. It was first discussed before the Senate Committee on Territories and Insular Affairs on October 22, 1945. In his testimony at the hearings John D. Goodloe, general counsel of the War Damage Corporation, defined the limits of responsibility recognized by the United States. He declared that, in the opinion of counsel for the Reconstruction Finance Corporation, neither the United States government nor the War Damage Corporation was legally committed to compensate for war damages in the Philippines, since the question was then still pending in the federal courts. As a result of official statements, the United States was morally committed to pay war damages in the Islands for the period up to July 1, 1942, but not in excess of "reasonable protection" and up to the proposed $100 million limit.[7]

Several controversial points were raised in the hearings. Total war damage in the Philippines had been estimated at from $700 million to more than a billion dollars, and the proposed limit of $100 million was criticized, particularly by Filipino representatives, as too meager a sum. One question was

[5] *Survey of War Damages in the Philippines*, Report of the Special Investigating Mission sent to the Philippines in June 1945, by the War Damage Corporation and completed in September 1945, 79th Cong., 1st sess. (Washington, 1945), p. 3.

[6] José Apostol, *Some Effects of the War on the Philippines*, Philippine Paper No. 2, Institute of Pacific Relations, Tenth Conference (1947), p. 18.

[7] *Philippine Rehabilitation Act of 1946*, Hearings before the Committee on Territories and Insular Affairs, U.S. Senate, 79th Cong., 1st sess., on S. 1488, October 22, 23, 24, 29, and 30, 1945 (Washington, 1945), pp. 10–20.

whether the obligation which had been recognized for the period from December 7, 1941, up to July 1, 1942, did not entail full compensation for claimants, regardless of the percentage paid to those suffering losses in the later periods. In answer it was said that it would be an impossible technical problem to draw a fine enough line between earlier and later claims, and that, disregarding the technical time limit, persons who suffered as a result of war damage in the later period were as deserving as those who had lost property earlier. The proposed legislation had restricted payments to "natural persons," and the advisability of compensating for public properties and institutional losses was raised in the discussions. In addition, arguments for compensation for obligations incurred by the resistance forces were presented to the Committee by Tomas L. Cabili, Filipino legislator and former resistance leader.

Five amendments to the rehabilitation bill were proposed by representatives of the Philippine government. It was recommended that damage to both public and private property be compensated, that payments be made for resistance activities, and that corporations controlled by enemy aliens be excluded from benefits. It was also suggested that payments to small property owners be limited to $1,000 and that the sum of one billion dollars be appropriated, in lieu of the $100 million proposed by Senator Tydings.

As a result of both Senate and House action, the Rehabilitation Act for the Philippines, which was finally approved on April 30, 1946, differed in many respects from the original proposal of Senator Tydings. The law provided for the establishment of a Philippine War Damage Commission of three members appointed by the President, one member to be a Filipino. The commission was authorized to compensate for losses incurred from December 7, 1941, to October 1, 1945, resulting from one or more of the following:

1. Enemy attack
2. Action taken by or at the request of the military, naval, or air forces of the United States to prevent such property from coming into the possession of the enemy
3. Action taken by enemy representatives, civil or military, or by the representatives of any government co-operating with the enemy
4. Action by the armed forces of the United States or other forces co-operating with the armed forces of the United States in opposing, resisting, or expelling the enemy from the Philippines
5. Looting, pillage, or other lawlessness or disorder accompanying the collapse of civil authority determined by the commission to have resulted from any of the other perils enumerated in this section or from control by enemy forces[8]

Instead of the modest provisions of the original proposal, which would have set a maximum of $500 for individual payments, the law as finally passed allowed claims equal to the actual cash value of losses or the cost of repair and

[8] Philippine Rehabilitation Act of 1946 (Public Law No. 370, 79th Cong., 2d sess.), p. 2.

replacement, whichever was less. It was provided, however, that payments of large claims be reduced by 25 percent of the amount over $500. A total of $400 million was authorized for compensation for private parties.

Four classes of private claimants could qualify for compensation under the rehabilitation law: (1) individuals who were citizens of either the United States or the Philippines, or of a nation not an enemy of the United States which grants reciprocal war damage payments to resident Americans; (2) individuals who served in the armed forces of the United States or the Philippines, or in the merchant marine; (3) any church or other religious organization; and (4) any unincorporated association, trust, or corporation, but excluding any corporation wholly owned by the Commonwealth.

As assistance in reconstruction, a maximum of $100 million worth of surplus property was to be transferred to the Commonwealth government without compensation. In addition, $120 million was authorized for allocation to various agencies to restore and improve public property and essential public services. Other sections of the Rehabilitation Act outlined measures for improving roads and harbor facilities, public property and public health, inter-island commerce, air navigation, weather information, fisheries, and coast and geodetic survey. Technical training of Filipinos in the United States was provided, and co-operation between American officials and Philippine government authorities in the Islands was proposed. Five million dollars was authorized in the act for the restoration of United States property in the Philippines.

Section 601 of the Rehabilitation Act, under Title VI, was inserted on the recommendation of the House Committee on Insular Affairs. It stated:

No payments under Title I of this Act in excess of $500 shall be made until an executive agreement shall have been entered into between the President of the United States and the President of the Philippines, and such agreement shall have become effective according to its terms, providing for trade relations between the United States and the Philippines.[9]

In other words, rehabilitation was to be tied to trade and any payments over $500 were to be conditional upon Philippine acceptance of United States trade legislation. The author of the proposed trade bill was Congressman C. Jasper Bell, chairman of the committee which recommended that this condition be inserted in the rehabilitation measure. Between October 1945 and April 1946, therefore, the original rehabilitation proposals had been expanded, the kinds and numbers of claimants had been extended, and the amount appropriated had been multiplied by five. But a joker had been added: if the Filipinos wanted all this, they must also take the companion measure under discussion, the Bell Bill, which was to become the Philippine Trade Act of 1946.

The Philippine War Damage Commission, formally organized on June 5, 1946, faced a formidable task. Out of approximately 3 million Filipino families,

[9] *Ibid.*, p. 15.

about one third had suffered property losses. At the outset more than a million individual claims for compensation were expected, as well as 100,000 claims of corporations and about 1,000 from government units and agencies. Not only was it necessary to investigate the validity of each claim and the degree of damage, but also the title to the property, original cost, and replacement value. About four years had been allotted to the commission to complete its assignment, which meant processing about 1,000 claims a day.[10]

The difficulties of setting up field operations for this type of agency should not be underestimated; there were problems of language, of securing publicity, and of recruiting personnel in the face of disrupted communications, transportation, and living facilities. Even considering these factors, however, the initial pace was leisurely. The first payment, made on December 6, 1946, was $1 million, presented to President Roxas as an advance payment on a government claim. Private property claims were not accepted until March 1, 1947, and the initial payment on such claims was not made until April 18, 1947, almost a year after the Philippine Rehabilitation Act became effective.[11] By the end of 1947, the first full year of operations, approximately 8 percent of the total authorized in the act for public claims, and just over 3 percent of the sum allocated for private claims, had been paid out.

The activities of the commission moved into high gear in the following year.[12] By February 29, 1948, the last day for filing private claims, 1,256,602 applications with a claimed value of $1,215,055,684 had been submitted. Of these 80 percent were for claims of $500 or less. A report of the chairman of the Philippine War Damage Commission early in 1949 declared that about 3,000 claims were being liquidated each working day, and an average of about $3 million was being paid out each week. As of February 18, 1949, the commission had liquidated 617,647 claims and paid out $116,829,000. In addition, $48.4 million of the funds authorized for payment of public property claims had been awarded to the Philippine government, and payments already made amounted to $29.3 million. This was in keeping with the policy of paying funds on public projects only if reconstruction work was already in progress.

While increasing the amount of money in circulation in the Philippines, the war damage payments did not necessarily increase economic stability, as there were limits to the ability of the economy to absorb such a cash influx. Frank Waring, chairman of the Philippine War Damage Commission, speaking in Manila on December 10, 1948, commented:

Unfortunately, the Philippine government has been unable to utilize the funds as fast as the Commission has awarded them. The Commission has approved

---

[10] U.S. Philippine War Damage Commission, *First Semiannual Report for Period Ending December 31, 1946* (Manila, 1947), p. 4.

[11] *Manila Bulletin*, December 13, 1947.

[12] John Snure, Jr., "Paying the War Damage Claims," *Philippines Commerce* (Manila), December 1948, pp. 15–16.

more than 1,000 projects and I regret to state that work has been started on less than 50 percent of them. This means that of the funds thus far awarded, nearly 60 million pesos is awaiting action by the Philippine officials to provide jobs for their citizens.[13]

The commission completed its work in advance of the termination date set by Congress (April 30, 1951).[14] It had considered some 1,248,901 claims for compensation, and had paid out a total of more than $388 million. Compensation for damage to public property included approximately $55.3 million. This went for the reconstruction of public structures, such as hospitals, municipal waterworks, schools, and government buildings. Four United States agencies—the Bureau of Public Roads, the Army Corps of Engineers, the Public Health Service, and the War Damage Commission—administered the funds for project repair.

Although the Rehabilitation Act had provided for payment on claims over $500 up to 75 percent of the total, prorata allowances had provided for only 30 percent of such claims up to 1950, and the balance of available funds allowed a possible additional 15 percent, bringing the total compensation on larger private claims up to an estimated 45 percent. As a result, a bill[15] was introduced into the United States Congress to provide an additional $100 million for rehabilitation, which would permit compensation up to the full 75 percent figure. This measure had the strong support of the National Foreign Trade Council and the Philippine-American Chamber of Commerce, as well as of other business groups with prewar Philippine interests. It was opposed, however, by the Bell Mission Report in 1950 on the ground that any further appropriations would be better spent on direct project aid, rather than on compensation for individuals or corporations. In the end, no action was taken on the bill.

Another phase of the rehabilitation program was the provision for the transfer of surplus war materials to the Philippine government. The handling of this assignment developed into one of the major scandals of the postwar period, with widespread charges of looting, graft, and corruption. Feelings on the subject ran high in the spring of 1947, when, goaded into action by Philippine "Congressional disclosures and a barbed press,"[16] President Roxas ordered an investigation of surplus disposal. By August it was estimated that property roughly valued at $300 million (procurement cost), out of an allotment originally worth $435 million which had already been transferred, had been lost through pilferage and looting during the previous two years. This was confirmed by the Philippine Surplus Property Commission, which esti-

[13] Frank A. Waring, "Pro and Con of Protectionism, an American View," *Philippines Commerce* (Manila), December 1948, p. 9.
[14] "President Truman Lauds Work of War Damage Commission," *Bataan*, May 1951, p. 14.
[15] H.R. 7600, 81st Cong., 2d sess.
[16] *New York Times*, April 30, 1947.

mated losses as high as 70 percent of money value.[17] Responsibility was not clearly fixed, the magazine *Bataan* going so far as to report that "Philippine Commission representatives said that they hoped the United States Government would make good the difference between the represented value and the presentation value," but admitting that no additional funds were available, and that an appropriation from the United States Congress would be required.[18]

Some money was eventually realized from the surplus sales, but far less than had been expected. The Surplus Property Commission, which had charge of disposing of an estimated $630 million worth of movable surplus goods and $55 million of fixed installations (procurement cost), with a write-off value of $100 million, reported that by May 1948 approximately $36 million in gross sales had been realized. The operations moved slowly as time went on, in part because of the saturation of the local market, the inability of surplus items to compete with imported consumer goods, and the fact that heavy equipment was not fitted to local needs. It was, therefore, deemed necessary to market surplus items elsewhere; ironically enough, some of it found its way back to the original supplier. According to the chairman of the Surplus Property Commission, Arsenio N. Luz, "Almost the only country which at present is absorbing much of the local surplus goods is the United States itself."[19]

Actual disposal of surplus property in black markets and in private deals continued, the final amounts realized by the government being only about $40 million. Accusations on surplus property irregularities were made on February 21, 1949, against the politically powerful Senate president, José Avelino. Senator Avelino, titular head of the Liberal party, was charged with personal graft in general and specifically with selling approximately $250,000 worth of surplus property to Chinese buyers. In answer he contended that his accusers had acted from political motives, and that the "rump" Senate which had been called by supporters of President Quirino was illegal, since it lacked the required quorum.[20] The charges and the way the matter was handled reflected the political dissension between two rivals for party power (Avelino and President Quirino), and the internal weaknesses of the administration. As a result the need for reform in government was sharply raised as a major public issue.

The record of the surplus transfer, in itself an admirable scheme, showed how rehabilitation efforts could be frustrated by lack of effective controls. Although undoubtedly a good part of the surplus allotment was unsuitable

[17] *Ibid.*, August 6, 1947.

[18] "Philippine Government Takes Steps to Guard War Surplus Depots in Islands," *Bataan*, September 1947, p. 19.

[19] Arsenio N. Luz, "The Problem of Surplus Disposal," *Philippines Commerce* (Manila), May 1948, p. 9.

[20] *New York Times*, February 22, 1949.

for Philippine needs, there is no question that inadequate guarding of valuable materials, widespread looting, and reported black-market operations substantially reduced the over-all value of the transfer to the Philippine government. Dissipation of the property had important economic consequences, for it meant that the surplus material could not play as significant a role as it might have in Philippine reconstruction or in future industrial development.

While the relief and rehabilitation record left much to be desired, it was probably not very different from a number of other experiences in devastated areas in the period of postwar confusion and emergency. Of more lasting significance were arrangements for the Philippine-American trade relations in future years.

CHAPTER FOUR

THE BELL BILL BEFORE CONGRESS

IN spite of years of study, both before and during the war, and repeated investigations and recommendations, the drafting of legislation governing Philippine-American economic relations after independence proved to be a prolonged and controversial process. Before the Bell Bill was enacted into law, to become the Philippine Trade Act of 1946, it went through five versions and seven months of bitter debate. The original recommendation for a twenty-year period of free trade was considerably watered down in the final bill. Filipino supporters of the legislation, such as Brigadier General Carlos P. Romulo, then Resident Commissioner in the United States, frankly stated that the bill was not written as the Filipinos would have wished, but that it was the best that could be obtained under the circumstances.

At the congressional hearings on the Bell Bill in Washington, extending from October 1945 through April 1946, high officials from the United States Departments of State, Treasury, Commerce, and Agriculture, and from the Tariff Commission, protested vigorously against one or another provision of the proposed measure. Amendments were offered, some were accepted but more were rejected, and new and controversial sections were added as the seemingly endless discussion proceeded. Finally, on April 30, 1946, two months and four days before the scheduled date for Philippine independence, the legislation was approved.

The first version of the Bell Bill (H.R. 4185), introduced in Congress in October 1945, had the support of Philippine President Osmeña and Commissioner Romulo. According to its author, Congressman C. Jasper Bell of Missouri, "For the first 20 years of their independence this bill would mean Philippine free trade; that is the basis upon which the principles of the bill are founded, which will guarantee to investors of America and to the investors in the Philippines that they can safely invest private capital and that it can be done, not only safely, but with a reasonable profit. . . ."[1]

In describing the original proposals Paul V. McNutt, then United States High Commissioner to the Philippines, called it primarily a rehabilitation bill rather than a tariff bill and gave it his full backing. According to its provisions reciprocal free trade between the Philippines and the United States would have

---

[1] *Philippine Trade Act of 1945*, Hearings before the Committee on Ways and Means, House of Representatives, 79th Cong., 1st sess., on H.R. 4185, H.R. 4676, H.R. 5185, Executive Session (Washington, 1946), p. 12.

continued for a period of twenty years, under an excutive agreement. Absolute quotas were provided for sugar, cordage, coconut oil, tobacco products, and embroideries, and Congress was given the power to establish additional quotas in the future on any commodities which might come into substantial competition with similar United States products. Allocation of quotas was for the most part based on production in the Philippines in 1940. Export taxes were reciprocally prohibited, and there were several preferential restrictions relating to internal revenue taxes. Among other provisions protecting American investments were the stipulation that citizens and corporations of the United States should enjoy in the Philippines all the rights of Filipino citizens and corporations, and that the peso remain tied to the dollar at the existing rate of exchange.

Supporting the bill in principle, although favoring some minor amendments, General Romulo discussed in his testimony the most-favored-nation principle and concluded that because of the circumstances of the case, no criticism could properly be leveled at the special treatment provided for the Philippines. He pointed out that the trade concessions granted to Cuba had not been claimed by other nations under the most-favored-nation clause because they were conditioned on the granting of a naval base and other rights to the United States, and no other nation could, or wished to, meet these conditions. "This principle," according to General Romulo, "may well be applied to the Philippines and with greater justification."[2]

The first major witness to present significant criticism of the proposed bill was E. G. Martin, general counsel of the United States Tariff Commission. On October 16 Mr. Martin pointed out that the legislation would institute "radical changes" in existing Philippine tariff and quota policies. Recalling that on April 20, 1945, the chairman of the Filipino Rehabilitation Commission had requested advice from the State Department on the Commonwealth's proposal to inaugurate a twenty-year period of free trade, Mr. Martin stated that this recommendation had been considered by an Interdepartmental Committee on Economic Foreign Policy, including representatives from the Departments of State, Treasury, War, Navy, Interior, Agriculture, Commerce, and Labor, the Tariff Commission, and the Foreign Economic Administration. "That committee," said Mr. Martin, "recommended that no trade program with the Philippines should be entered into which provided for free trade for as long a period as 20 years; and it recommended a trade program which it believed appropriate in the circumstances."[3] The details of the interdepartmental program were never made public.

The uncertainty of House committee members on the sponsorship of the legislation before it was apparent in the questions put to Mr. Martin. For example, Congressman Robert W. Kean, of New Jersey, said, "It does not

[2] *Ibid.*, p. 55.
[3] *Ibid.*, p. 61.

seem to me that we should pass this Bill if the Executive Committee, consisting of representatives from every department of the Government, has made a recommendation contrary to the Bill," while Congressman Harold Knutson of Minnesota asked, "What is this story that comes to me that only the Interior Department is in favor of the Bell Bill?"[4]

On the following day, October 17, the House committee heard the statement of Senator Millard E. Tydings of Maryland, chairman of the Senate Committee on Territories and Insular Affairs, and sponsor of the Philippine Independence Act of 1934.

Senator Tydings was outspoken in his criticism of the free-trade provisions. "If you give them 20 years' free trade you will be exactly in the same position 20 years from now that you are in today," he said.[5] Commenting on the wishes of the Filipino members of the Rehabilitation Commission, he said that their position "is for unlimited free trade in the American market. That is what they want. They do not want any limitation of 20 years, 50 years, 100 years or a thousand years."[6] Senator Tydings referred to his own proposal for gradually increasing tariff rates and to the possibilities for real independence for the Philippines. When questioned on the position of Mr. McNutt, he said:

I have no right to quote the Governor, but I think that fundamentally he is opposed to Philippine independence, and if you would ask him he would tell you so. The truth of the matter is that most of the people, outside of the Filipinos, who favor this bill are fundamentally opposed to Philippine independence. Many of them have told me so. I do not like to mention names. Their whole philosophy is to keep the Philippines economically even though we lost them politically.[7]

As a result of his testimony, it was apparent that further compromise was needed to secure administration support, and except for a few brief statements, the hearings were adjourned until November 14.

Following a White House conference on the Bell Bill, attended by the President, the Secretary of State, Assistant Secretary of State Will Clayton, Acting Secretary of the Interior Abe Fortas, Senator Tydings, and Representative Bell, a compromise measure was reached (H.R. 4676), and it was expected that administration support would follow. The new proposal, the second version of the Bell Bill, included only two major changes.

Instead of free trade for twenty years, the revised bill proposed eight years of free trade following independence; during the next twenty-five years the tariff would be stepped up at the rate of 4 percent a year. In all, this allowed thirty-three years for adjustment. Another important change was the provision that United States citizens doing business in the Philippines were to be taxed at the same rate as Filipinos. This section of the measure was prefaced

[4] *Ibid.*, p. 74.
[5] *Ibid.*, p. 84.
[6] *Ibid.*, p. 93.
[7] *Ibid.*, p. 90.

by the clause, "Notwithstanding any existing provision of the Constitution and statutes of the Philippine Government," and the wording drew lively discussion from the congressmen at the hearings. Congressman Walter A. Lynch of New York asked whether this meant that we would pass a law which would supersede the Philippine Constitution. Congressman Bell answered, "Of course, we would not contemplate that the Philippine people would do anything contrary to their Constitution, but would contemplate that they, as a people, have the power to amend their Constitution, and, if there should be anything prohibiting this sort of agreement, they would undertake to make such amendment as might be necessary."[8] He went on to say, "Of course, the broad purpose of this bill is to help the Filipinos to get on a sound financial basis. . . . We are the great source of capital investment and this bill was designed so that American capital could and would flow into the Philippines. . . ."[9]

Although interdepartmental agreement on the proposed legislation was ostensibly reached at the White House conference, a succession of witnesses and of statements from the Departments of Agriculture, Treasury, State, and Commerce indicated that the support was far from unanimous, and that many government experts on Philippine affairs felt the bill was inadequate in most respects.

Dr. Harry D. White, then Assistant Secretary of the Treasury, testified on two monetary provisions of the Bell Bill. These stated that the currency of the Philippine government would remain tied in a two-to-one ratio with United States currency, and that neither the United States nor the Philippine governments would impose any restrictions on exchange between the two countries, nor raise any barriers to trade and financial negotiations. Dr. White objected to the lack of flexibility of the provision, and warned that the price level which might eventually result in the Philippines from existing fiscal arrangements might make it very difficult for Filipinos to export to other countries, and would make it extremely expensive for them to import commodities from overseas. He suggested that changes in Philippine-American financial relations be permitted subject to the approval of the President of the United States.

In evaluating the question, Congressman Wilber D. Mills of Arkansas said to Dr. White: "As I understand the purpose of section 21 and section 22 [the fiscal arrangements] we are attempting in the language there to safeguard the value of capital that may go from the United States to the Philippines for a period of 33 years, so that when the capital decides to revert to the United States it may come to the United States without depreciation."[10] In reply Dr. White spoke of the dangers of maintaining an unrealistic rate of exchange,

[8] *Ibid.*, p. 135.
[9] *Ibid.*, p. 136.
[10] *Ibid.*, p. 176.

and said: "The very essence of sovereign monetary systems is that they may get out of line with each other. Now, if you protect the loss against exchange by fixing that rate of exchange so that it cannot be altered, you may be subjecting the country to economic conditions which would be bad for the whole country."[11]

Quotas, tariffs, and preferential treatment were discussed by the next witness, Leroy D. Stinebower, deputy director of the Office of International Trade Policy of the Department of State. Referring to the trade preferences, Mr. Stinebower recalled that on March 16, 1945, the Interdepartmental Executive Committee on Economic Foreign Policy had gone on record against any prolonged period of free trade with the Philippines, and President Roosevelt had approved its position. The bill under discussion, said Mr. Stinebower, represented a compromise between the recommendations of the Interdepartmental Committee and the provisions of the first Bell Bill, for twenty years of duty-free trade. He pointed out that too long a period of free trade might encourage the Philippines to establish or rehabilitate only those industries which could exist on the basis of subsidy or preferences, and that even the proposed eight-year period might have this effect to some extent. Discussing the over-all foreign economic policy of the United States, Mr. Stinebower said:

In the current conversations with the British we are asking for the reduction and eventual elimination of Empire preferences. The present and future efforts and leadership of the United States in this direction would be jeopardized if this Government were to abandon its policy of gradually eliminating preferences in our trade relations with the Philippines and maintain a system of preferences inconsistent with the international programs which we are advocating.[12]

Although the tariff preferences were accepted as a compromise measure, the State Department suggested specific modifications of other provisions of the Bell Bill. It proposed that the bill be amended to permit imports in excess of quotas, provided that full duty be paid on the excess imports, since, as Mr. Stinebower said, absolute quotas were contrary to the commercial policy of the United States government. Also inconsistent with established policy, according to the State Department witness, was the provision that additional quotas might be imposed, if Philippine production costs were 20 percent below United States costs for similar articles. "It is essential," he said, "that no discriminatory quota formula be applied to any particular country; our policy with respect to quotas should be practiced on a basis of equality to all countries."[13]

Mr. Stinebower also objected to the section which would exempt from a processing tax and any other internal revenue tax both Philippine coconut oil and oil produced from Philippine copra and rendered unfit for human con-

---

[11] *Ibid.*, p. 177.   [12] *Ibid.*, p. 183.   [13] *Ibid.*, p. 184.

sumption. This represented a discriminatory tax preference for the Philippine produce which would have jeopardized efforts to obtain equality of tax treatment for American exports abroad. The proposed legislation would prevent the Philippines, during the next thirty-three years, from reducing duties on imports from third countries unless the Philippine duty was higher than the general United States duty on such articles, in which case they could be reduced to the level of the latter. This provision would obviously tie the Philippine tariff to that of the United States. According to the witness, "It is the view of the Department that this unilateral restriction on Philippine tariff autonomy would be inconsistent with Philippine political independence; it might also create an unfortunate precedent for establishment of similar arrangements by other powers with respect to their former dependencies."[14]

A fourth State Department proposal related to the section providing for equal rights for American nationals in the Philippines, which, according to Mr. Stinebower, would require from the Philippines more privileges than the United States would be able to grant to a foreign power. It was felt that this matter could be handled more appropriately in a comprehensive treaty of friendship, commerce, and navigation. In addition, the State Department raised some questions regarding currency arrangements, a matter already discussed by Dr. White of the Treasury.

Following this testimony, the Congressional hearings on the Bell Bill were not resumed for three months, until February 15, 1946. At that time a third version of the measure was proposed, H.R. 5185. Of the points made by Mr. Stinebower, the limitation on Philippine tariff autonomy in relation to third countries had been dropped, and currency changes could be made "with agreement" of the American President. The substance of the legislation remained, however, with regard to tariff preferences, absolute quotas, allocation of quotas, currency relations, and equal rights for American nationals. The time for decision was growing short, for legislation had to be enacted before the independence date. A letter from President Truman to the committee urged action, and High Commissioner McNutt appeared again to seek approval of the third version of the bill.

Commissioner McNutt spoke frankly of the critical situation in the Islands and the importance of its export trade, saying:

When you say trade in the Philippines, you mean the national economy. It is a trading economy. And I might and should say here and now that we, the United States, managed it that way. We are responsible for the sole dependence of the Philippines on the American market. Our businessmen and our statesmen in past years allowed the Philippines to become a complete economic dependency of the United States to a greater degree than any single State of the Union is economically dependent on the rest of the United States.[15]

Admitting that this was a compromise bill and that he would have pre-

14 *Ibid.*, p. 185.   15 *Ibid.*, p. 199.

ferred a twenty-year free trade period, Mr. McNutt spoke of his extended efforts to get support for its enactment, and of his visits to the heads of various government departments, at the request of the President. He complained that although he had obtained the support of the Secretary of State, after his conversations, "apparently some of those in the lower echelons of the Department had gotten to him,"[16] because the department subsequently recommended further changes.

The suggestions of the Department of State were further presented by Winthrop G. Brown, chief of its Division of Commercial Policy. Mr. Brown reiterated the Department's objections to absolute quotas. He also spoke against the equal rights provision, in the following exchange with Congressman Knutson:

MR. BROWN: . . . It seems to the State Department that we are asking too much there. We are asking more than we give the citizens of the Philippines in our own legislation. We are asking more than we could possibly ask the Philippines to give to other countries. And we don't feel that we should ask for exclusive, preferential treatment for our citizens in the Philippines. . . .

CONGRESSMAN KNUTSON: In other words, you are afraid American citizens might get some benefits that all the rest of the world would not have?

MR. BROWN: Well—

CONGRESSMAN KNUTSON: Yes or no?

MR. BROWN: In this particular case, yes.

CONGRESSMAN KNUTSON: Well, that is what I thought. Of course, it would be a crime to give American citizens any better treatment.[17]

A final point made by the State Department representative was that all reference to Cuba had been omitted from the bill. Existing special arrangements between the United States and Cuba are usually noted in other treaties as an exception to provisions for equal treatment. This could mean, in effect, that at the end of the specified period the Philippine tariff would be the same as the Cuban, and a preferential position would thereby be retained by the Philippines, in relation to other foreign countries.

Another section of the proposed legislation provided that the Philippine government was not to impose any processing or other internal revenue tax on articles coming into the Philippines by or for the official use of the United States government or any department or agency thereof, and this was to be reciprocal on articles entering the United States for the official use of the Philippine government. In explaining this provision to the committee Mr. McNutt said, "That section was placed in there because it is contemplated we will have both Army and Navy bases, which will mean the importation of a great deal of goods."[18]

16 *Ibid.*, p. 204.   17 *Ibid.*, p. 221.   18 *Ibid.*, p. 245.

Although speaking in support of the Bell Bill, General Romulo declared, "Of course, if I would have written this Bill, I would have written it differently. I would have had free trade in perpetuity, no quotas, the currency would not be as it is, the rights of American citizens would be in the Treaty of Friendship."[19]

Before the House hearings closed two more critics from government agencies were heard and several memoranda were presented, reiterating criticisms made previously. The position of the Department of Commerce was expressed in a letter from Henry A. Wallace, then Secretary of Commerce. He protested against the imposition of absolute import quotas, the embargo on edible coconut oil from the Philippines, and the authority of Congress under the bill to impose further quotas on unspecified commodities. Objecting also to the allocation of quotas in the Philippines, Mr. Wallace asserted in his letter that "the establishment of dates prior to Pearl Harbor for the purpose of determining the identity and quantitative interest of the allottees will inevitably result in legislating benefits to business interests which collaborated with the occupying forces."[20] He also criticized the bill's provision for special treatment of American nationals, and the inflexibility of the proposed monetary arrangements.

The final United States government witness at the House hearings was Earl B. Wilson, director of the Sugar Branch, Department of Agriculture. His position was that sugar quotas should be omitted from this bill and considered with general sugar legislation later in the year. Congressman Paul H. Maloney of Louisiana said that domestic cane-sugar producers would prefer a smaller sugar quota, or, if the present quota were to remain, that it be measured in terms of short and not long tons. (The use of short tons would reduce imports by 204 million pounds annually.)

On March 26, 1946, the House finally passed H.R. 5856, the fourth draft of the Bell Bill. Sugar quotas were stated in short tons, and a preferential period of twenty-eight years was allowed, with duties increasing annually by 5 percent after the first eight years. The bill then went to the Senate.

Hearings before the Senate Committee on Finance opened on Tuesday, April 2, and members heard a strong plea from Commissioner McNutt to restore the original long-ton sugar quotas. This was also urged at the Senate hearings by Harry B. Hawes, United States representative of the Philippine Sugar Association, and by General Romulo. On the other hand, use of the short ton was supported by C. J. Bourg, vice-president of the American Sugar Cane League.

Although most of its recommendations had been rejected by the House committee, the State Department tried again at the Senate hearings to force reconsideration of objectionable sections of the Bell Bill. William L. Clayton,

[19] *Ibid.*, p. 246.   [20] *Ibid.*, p. 289.

Assistant Secretary of State for Economic Affairs, supported the basic features of the bill and the principle of declining preferences, but went on to state:

There are, however, several provisions of the Bill which cause me much concern. Certain of its clauses are clearly inconsistent with the basic foreign economic policy of this country and conflict directly with the proposals for expansion of world trade and employment which were developed by the Departments of State, Commerce, Agriculture, and the Treasury, the Tariff Commission, and other agencies, and which were published to the world by this Government last December. . . . Other provisions seem to me clearly inconsistent with our promise to grant the Philippines genuine independence.[21]

Referring to the imposition of absolute quotas, Mr. Clayton called these "one of the most vicious of trade restrictions." He recommended that the internal tax preference on Philippine coconut oil be eliminated, since it was inconsistent with United States economic policy. He also opposed the section of the bill requiring that equal rights be given American nationals, stating that this provision was not, and could not be, made reciprocal. American laws frequently discriminate against foreign nationals; for example, there are limitations on leasing public domain, operating broadcasting stations and power plants, and owning real property. Mr. Clayton pointed out that existing rights of Americans were fully safeguarded by both the Tydings-McDuffie Act and the Philippine Constitution, and that the effect of the Bell Bill would be not so much to protect existing rights as to guarantee future privileges. He said the United States should assist the Filipinos, rather than demand special privileges from them. The allocation procedure, which was based on 1940 production, was also criticized by Mr. Clayton, who said:

Not only does this deprive the Philippine government of a sovereign prerogative, but it has the effect of giving prewar producers a virtual monopoly for 28 years of most important Philippine exports. It would enable them to prevent the investment of capital by new American enterprises in these important export industries, and new Philippine producers would not be able to compete freely in their own country. . . . These provisions should be eliminated. The United States should not take advantage of the Philippines' need for special tariff treatment, accentuated by the tribulations of our common war effort, to obtain such special privileges.[22]

Commissioner McNutt, in answer to Mr. Clayton, reviewed the lengthy history of the proposed legislation, and asked for action in view of the urgency of the situation in the Philippines. Concerning the independence issue, he said:

Even those who have felt that independence was unwise at this time have come to the conclusion that the matter has gone so far that it would be necessary for

---

[21] *Philippine Trade Act of 1946*, Hearings before the Committee on Finance, Senate, 79th Cong., 2d sess., on H.R. 5856 (Washington, 1946), pp. 49, 50.

[22] *Ibid.*, p. 65.

them to try independence, and that with our wholehearted support and effort to help them. If they should not be satisfied, then, as a sovereign people, they could come back to the United States and ask to reestablish political ties in some form or another.[23]

Mr. McNutt suggested that absolute quotas would have the effect of forcing diversification of production. In reply Mr. Clayton quoted the section of the bill which, at any later date, would permit the imposition of absolute quotas on any articles then thought to be in substantial competition with similar American products. He said, "I submit, Mr. Chairman, that that is not for diversification in the Philippines, that is for the protection of the United States interests and, so far as I am aware, that is a provision that is not in the law with respect to importations from any other country in the world."[24]

As the final witness before the Senate committee, General Romulo spoke freely of the deficiencies of the bill.[25] He avowed that the legislation would "to a very great extent, tend to restore the status quo as it existed before the war and that this status quo had its evils as well as is benefits." He expressed displeasure with the quota provisions, indicating that the Filipinos had accepted them "under protest, only because it has thus far been apparent that the sentiment of the House was in favor of such quotas." He urged that the sugar quota be expressed in long tons, and underlined the lack of reciprocity in the provisions for special rights for American nationals in the Philippines. In summing up, General Romulo said, "since we cannot have perfection then let us have action."

Action was finally achieved, though few were entirely satisfied with the result. Because of the pressure of time—the date for independence was approaching—there was little discussion of the legislation on the floor of either the House or the Senate. With the restoration of long tons for the sugar quota as a minor concession to Philippine interests, a fifth version of the Bell Bill was finally passed by Congress, and became the Philippine Trade Act of 1946.

[23] *Ibid.*, p. 96.
[24] *Ibid.*, p. 99.
[25] *Ibid.*, pp. 127–42.

CHAPTER FIVE

THE PHILIPPINE TRADE ACT ANALYZED

THE Philippine Trade Act of 1946 established a pattern for future economic relations between the United States and the independent Philippine Republic. Underlying the act was the assumption that Philippine economic revival depended on restoring trade with the United States and stimulating a flow of American investment into the Islands. Hence free trade was continued, though on a temporary and gradually diminishing basis; special privileges were granted to American investors; and the Philippine currency was tied to the American dollar. Philippine-American economic relations thus retained a quasi-colonial character.

The Trade Act represented a compromise between the divergent viewpoints of two American economic groups which had traditionally been concerned with Philippine affairs. Mercantile and investing groups sought closer ties with the Islands, while domestic agricultural producers, who feared Philippine competition, advocated severance of preferential relations. On the one hand, the act sought to encourage the investment of new American capital, by property and tax safeguards, by free convertibility of a stable currency, and by a protracted period of free trade with gradually declining preferences. On the other hand, in the interests of American producers, absolute quotas on Philippine goods were continued, and might be extended to any commodities which might at some future time come into competition with American products.

From the American standpoint, therefore, the act represented a compromise between conflicting economic interests. From the Philippine standpoint it also represented a compromise, between the immediate advantages of hastening economic recovery by restoring the prewar American market—which loomed large in a country whose economic life had been prostrated by war—and the disadvantage that the Philippine economy was still bound closely to that of the United States, as in the colonial period, and that limitations were placed on the Philippine Republic's freedom of action in fixing its economic policies. This was a real dilemma to which no easy answer was possible. An answer might have been found in a program of developing Philippine industries with American aid. In 1946, however, attention was centered on the immediate need for economic recovery.

Another conflict of interests existed between established firms in the Islands, whether Philippine or American, and newcomers. Both groups received concessions in the Trade Act. Specific guaranties were given to the prewar producers by allocating quotas on the basis of 1940 production and exports, as well as by the prolonged free-trade period. But the legal position of prewar American businessmen in the Philippines was already protected under the Independence Act. Therefore the much debated section of the Trade Act which required that Americans should enjoy equal rights with Philippine citizens in matters of property, operation of a business, and taxation was designed to satisfy the new business interests with capital to invest, rather than the established prewar firms.

Five major topics were covered in the Trade Act: tariffs, absolute and duty-free quotas, allocation of quotas in the Philippines, special rights for Americans, and financial ties.

Reciprocal free trade was established from the effective date of the act until July 3, 1954; from that date until July 3, 1974, gradually increasing duties were specified for imports into each country from the other. From July 4 to December 31, 1954, the duty would be 5 percent of the full tariff; for the year 1955, 10 percent; and thereafter through 1972 the duty would increase by 5 percent annually. For the period from January 1, 1973, to July 3, 1974, full duties would be paid.

The act continued the preference of 2 cents a pound for Philippine coconut oil in the United States processing tax. It further provided (Title III, Section 322) that "No export tax shall be imposed or collected by the Philippines on articles exported to the United States." This provision affected only the Philippines, as the United States was already prohibited from imposing export taxes by its own Constitution.

Absolute quotas were fixed on seven products, as follows:[1]

Sugar (including not more than 50,000 long tons of refined sugar)	850,000 long tons
Cordage	6,000,000 pounds
Rice	1,040,000 pounds
Cigars	200,000,000
Tobacco	6,500,000 pounds
Coconut oil	200,000 long tons
Buttons of pearl or shell	850,000 gross

Instead of being subject to increasing duties, cigars, tobacco, coconut oil, and buttons were given decreasing duty-free quotas. For example, 200 million duty-free cigars could be admitted annually from 1946 through 1954. The amount would decrease by 10 million in each subsequent year, so that by 1964 only 100 million duty-free cigars would be admitted, while another 100 million could be sent to the United States on payment of full customs duty. By

[1] Philippine Trade Act of 1946 (Chapter 244, Public Law No. 371), Title II, Sections 211–14.

1973 only 10 million cigars could be admitted duty-free, and 190 million with full duty. Duty-free quotas would disappear by 1974.

Further trade restrictions might be imposed at the discretion of the President. The act stated:

. . . whenever the President of the United States, after the investigation by the United States Tariff Commission . . . finds, with respect to any Philippines articles (other than those for which quotas are established . . .) that they are coming or likely to come into substantial competition with like articles which are the product of the United States, he shall so proclaim, and in his proclamation shall establish the total amount of such Philippine articles which may in each of specified periods be entered, or withdrawn from warehouse, in the United States for consumption. . . .[2]

The act thus carried a warning to Philippine manufacturers to avoid production for export of articles which might compete with American products. This was contrary to the avowed American policy of seeking reduction of trade barriers throughout the world, as well as to the economic doctrine that the location of industries should be determined by natural advantages. These restrictions were aimed, moreover, at a former colony which the United States had promised to aid in making the difficult transition to independence.

The Trade Act, while furnishing some protection for American producers, served to prolong the former preferential relationship for twenty-eight years. Although in the short run these arrangements appeared beneficial to the Philippines, they encouraged the continuation of the prewar situation in which the Philippine economy had suffered from overspecialization and from too great reliance on the American market—conditions not compatible with economic independence.

The act provided an allocation procedure for each of the commodities under quota restriction. Annual quotas would be granted to producers and manufacturers operating in 1940, on the basis of their activities in that year. A plan such as this would of course restore to prominence those firms which were dominant before the war. In a memorandum describing the principal interests involved in the allocation of quotas, inserted in the record of the congressional hearings on the Bell Bill by Congressman Daniel A. Reed of New York, the narrow control of major industries was discussed.[3] The memorandum stated that only three cordage firms would receive almost the entire cordage allocation: the Elizalde rope factory would receive about 50 percent, and the rest would go to the Johnston Pickett Rope Company, owned by Elizalde, and the Manila Cordage Company, a subsidiary of the Tubbs Cordage Company of San Francisco, which also owned the Portland Cordage Company and the

[2] *Ibid.*, Title V, Section 504.

[3] *Philippine Trade Act of 1945*, Hearings before the Committee on Ways and Means, House of Representatives, 79th Cong., 1st sess., on H.R. 4185, H.R. 4676, H.R. 5185, Executive Session (Washington, 1946), pp. 140–43.

Western Cordage Company in California. Three tobacco companies accounted for about 90 percent of tobacco exports before the war. These were the Helena Cigar Company, owned by Freider Brothers of Cincinnati, about 40 percent; Tabacalera, a Spanish firm, about 30 percent; and the Insular Company, Philippine-owned, about 20 percent.

In 1941 there were approximately 24,000 sugar planters in the Philippines and forty-six mills in production. Only six or seven, however, were really large exporters; the rest exported their products through other enterprises, such as the Philippine National Bank, Warner Barnes, Tabacalera, Kaerr and Company, and Smith Bell Company. The sugar quota allocation in 1940 was divided about equally, half going to the forty-six sugar mills or centrals, and half to the 24,000 small planters. Of the total quota of 50,000 tons of refined sugar, over 84 percent was refined by the Insular Sugar Refining Corporation, owned by the government-controlled National Development Corporation.[4]

Three shell button factories in Manila shared in prewar production, the Manila Button Factory with 32 percent, the Philippine Button Corporation with 56 percent, and the Shell Craft and Button Corporation with 12 percent.[5] There were two major coconut oil mills, the Philippine Refining Company with 44 percent of the business and Spencer Kellogg and Sons with 27 percent.[6]

Economic power in the Philippines has always been highly concentrated. The provisions of the Trade Act encouraged monopolistic control by giving the few prewar firms practically exclusive rights to export of major commodities.

In an attempt to safeguard the country's resources from future foreign control, the Constitution of the Philippines, ratified in 1935, had provided:

All agricultural, timber, and mineral lands of the public domain, waters, minerals, coal, petroleum and other mineral oils, all forces of potential energy, and other natural resources of the Philippines belong to the state, and their disposition, exploitation, development, or utilization shall be limited to citizens of the Philippines, or to corporations or associations at least 60 percentum of the capital of which is owned by such citizens, subject to any existing right, grant, lease, or concession at the time of the inauguration of the Government established under this Constitution. . . .[7]

The protection of existing American rights was apparently satisfactory to United States interests at the time the Constitution was under discussion, but in 1946 it was felt that future as well as existing American business required protection. Section 341 of the Philippine Trade Act, therefore, stated:

The disposition, exploitation, development, and utilization of all agricultural, timber, and mineral lands of the public domain, waters, minerals, coal, petroleum

---

[4] *American-Philippine Trade Relations*, Report of the Technical Committee to the President of the Philippines (Washington, 1944), p. 47.
[5] *Ibid.*, p. 146.   [6] *Ibid.*, p. 80.
[7] Constitution of the Philippines, 1935, Article XII, Section 1.

and other mineral oils, all forces and sources of potential energy, and other natural resources of the Philippines, and the operation of public utilities, shall, if open to any person, be open to citizens of the United States and to all forms of business enterprise owned or controlled, directly or indirectly, by United States citizens.[8]

Insertion of this provision, the so-called parity clause, made it necessary to amend the Philippine Constitution, an action which called for a nation-wide referendum. Not only did the provision come into conflict with Philippine law when it was passed by the United States Congress, but no effort was made to extend reciprocal rights to Filipinos in the United States. The American Constitution has reserved to the states those rights not specifically allocated to the national Congress. Thus the states, rather than the federal government, are empowered to regulate the ownership of property and the right to operate such enterprises as public utilities. No reciprocity existed in the parity clause of the Trade Act, nor would any have been possible under the American federal system.

Another restrictive provision in the Trade Act was in Title III, Section 342, which declared:

The value of Philippine currency in relation to the United States dollar shall not be changed, the convertibility of pesos into dollars shall not be suspended, and no restrictions shall be imposed on the transfer of funds from the Philippines to the United States, except by agreement with the President of the United States.[9]

With the peso thus irrevocably tied to the dollar, the Philippine Republic was not free to manage its own currency as changing conditions and national needs might dictate, and price fluctuations and business cycles in the United States would inevitably be reflected in the Philippines. Nor could the Philippines impose exchange controls or regulate the flow of capital in periods of financial stringency.

As stated earlier, two important prewar problems of the Philippines were overspecialization in a few agricultural products for export, and lack of industrialization. The prolonged period of preferential trade provided in the Trade Act encouraged the re-establishment of specialized agricultural production, which had been disrupted during the Japanese occupation. Trade preferences and privileges to American investors tended to encourage the development of extractive industries, such as mining, rather than manufacturing for the domestic Philippine market. It was, indeed, argued that the tapering off of tariff preferences would encourage eventual diversification of new capital investment. Yet the continued preference given to American products in the Philippine market and the possible imposition of new American quotas on Philippine exports circumscribed the possibilities of new economic development.

[8] Philippine Trade Act of 1946, Title III, Section 341.
[9] Ibid., Title III, Section 342.

Moreover, the act offered special privileges to American nationals and corporations in the Philippines, and sought to assure American investors of a stable currency and the right to withdraw their funds at any time. Although the Philippines undoubtedly needed new capital, these provisions made the country almost entirely dependent on the United States for investment funds, and tended to strengthen American control over Philippine industry.

In short, as it gained political independence, the Philippine Republic was still far from possessing economic sovereignty. The United States, on the other hand, retained some of the economic and military advantages of a colonial power, while it was relieved of the burden of administration and of direct responsibility for Philippine welfare.

CHAPTER SIX

ATTITUDES OF AMERICAN BUSINESS

IF so many United States experts and government agencies were opposed to one or another section of the Philippine Trade Act, then who exactly supported it? Some approval was forthcoming from those who felt that, while no panacea, the act was an acceptable compromise. Certain rehabilitation benefits would accrue to the Philippines from continued preferential entry of their products into the American market, and this was considered essential to economic recovery. From the American business point of view the act satisfied various groups. Domestic agricultural interests which sought to prevent Philippine competition, business groups with assets in the Islands, and those who hoped to invest new capital, each received some consideration.[1]

A perusal of the list of several hundred registered lobbyists contained in the Congressional Directory for 1947 failed to reveal a single firm or organization which described itself as being primarily concerned with Philippine affairs. Several trade and business associations did, nevertheless, exert considerable influence on legislation.

At the congressional hearings on the Bell Bill, business interests remained for the most part in the background. At the House hearings only one individual representing organized business, J. S. McDaniel, secretary of the Cordage Institute and Cordage and Twine Industry Council, was heard. The circumstances surrounding the calling of Mr. McDaniel to the executive sessions of the committee were of interest.

On November 4, 1945, when the proposed progressive tariff rates were under consideration, Congressman Charles L. Gifford of Massachusetts asked whether the various interests concerned had been or would have an opportunity to be heard, stating that he had received an appeal that very morning from an industry that might be affected. The following testimony ensued:

MR. McNUTT: Mr. McDaniel is in Washigton and, if you gentlemen will excuse me, I will have him on the phone in 2 minutes.

MR. GIFFORD: I am really much interested in cordage, others are interested in sugar. Now, those interests that have had this sprung upon them very quickly— are they going to be heard?

[1] Several methods were used by the author in an attempt to obtain an objective estimate of the attitude of American business on Philippine policy. Testimony presented at legislative hearings was studied, a representative sample of trade journals and business publications was analyzed, personal interviews were held, and the views of about thirty trade associations and commercial firms were sought by letter and questionnaire.

70

MR. McNUTT: Well, Mr. McDaniel represents all of the cordage interests.

MR. GIFFORD: I know that.

MR. McNUTT: Let me get Mr. McDaniel on the phone.

MR. GIFFORD: That is only cordage, but don't pick on me particularly. There are the sugar interests and the cigar interests.

MR. McNUTT: May I suggest that the original Bell Bill had more unanimous support on the part of business interests concerned than any Bill I have ever seen having to do with the Philippines. It is the first time I have ever seen such unanimity of opinion upon the part of all concerned. . . .

Mr. Chairman, I have just talked to Mr. McDaniel, who is acting really as chairman of a group of interests that he represents, who are interested in this matter, and he has asked to appear and I told him that I would recommend to the chairman and to the committee that he appear here this morning in the executive session. I have asked him to come down. So you will find the statement of Mr. McDaniel in support of the Bell Bill, and my position is his.[2]

The character of Mr. McDaniel's testimony, however, was indeterminate.[3] After some discussion he said, "I have never seen the Bill. The Bill as quoted to me was not that way," and, later, "I am sorry, Mr. Chairman, not having seen the Bill I misunderstood its contents." He spoke, however, of the need for some kind of immediate action, indicating that he had spent the last six months in Washington working on the problem of Philippine legislation.

Another evidence of business support was introduced into the House hearings in the form of letter and resolution from the Philippine-American Chamber of Commerce, in favor of the original Bell Bill.[4] In a letter from Louis R. Glavis, representing the Cigar Manufacturers Association of America, attention was drawn to the problem of equating dates for internal revenue taxes in the two countries.[5]

The Senate hearings saw somewhat more active interest on the part of business representatives. The action of the House in changing the sugar quota from long to short tons resulted in controversy between spokesmen for domestic and for Philippine interests. Harry B. Hawes appeared before the Senate committee to represent the Philippine Sugar Association. At the time he was also legal adviser to the Philippine Commonwealth and counsel for the Cordage Institute of America. He stated that the House Ways and Means Committee, "in its worthy and commendable effort of securing unanimous agreement," had substituted the word "short" for "long" in sugar tonnage.

[2] *Philippine Trade Act of 1945*, Hearings before the Committee on Ways and Means, House of Representatives, 79th Cong., 1st sess., on H.R. 4185, H.R. 4676, H.R. 5185, Executive Session (Washington, 1946), pp. 147–48, 150.

[3] *Ibid.*, pp. 153–58.

[4] *Ibid.*, p. 119.

[5] *Ibid.*, p. 292.

Mr. Hawes vigorously objected to this, saying that it would place a heavy burden on Philippine trade. Interpreting the change as a direct concession to the Cuban sugar interests, Mr. Hawes said, "Must we take this life blood of trade from the Filipinos at this eleventh hour and give it to Cuba who does not need it? . . . We all desire Cuba to be rich, to prosper, to expand, to be happy and do not want to take anything from her, but we should not reach clear across the world and take from the bleeding Philippines $168,000,000 to hang on a Cuban Christmas tree."[6]

Arguments in favor of a short-ton quota were presented by C. J. Bourg, vice-president of the American Sugar Cane League, who represented the Louisiana sugar industry at the hearings. Explaining his appearance before the committee, Mr. Bourg said:

When this Bill was prepared we were not consulted, and we did not feel that we should have been consulted. But in order that there be no misunderstanding of our position I asked for an interview and I went to his [McNutt's] office and explained to him that we had nothing to suggest, no objections to make. After that there were certain considerations which we discussed and which we felt were proper considerations.[7]

After some further discussion of the size of the sugar quota, the question of absolute as against tariff quotas arose. The patchwork nature of the bill was illustrated in the subsequent testimony:

SENATOR WALSH: Is not the absolute quota in the long run more beneficial to the domestic industry than the tariff quota?

MR. BOURG: Yes.

SENATOR WALSH: Is not that one of the reasons why some persons had put in here the absolute quota, so as to protect the domestic industry? It is a protection of the domestic industry, isn't it?

MR. BOURG: Yes, sir.

SENATOR JOHNSON: It gives a stability to it?

MR. BOURG: Yes; but I do not think we would ever dare to advocate it ourselves.

SENATOR WALSH: I understand.

SENATOR LUCAS: Who did advocate it?

MR. BOURG: Governor McNutt said that he and Mr. Bell and Mr. Hester and others drew up this bill.

SENATOR LUCAS: They probably had the local folks in mind when they wrote this bill.

MR. BOURG: I am glad of that.

SENATOR VANDENBERG: They probably wanted to pass it.[8]

---

[6] *Philippine Trade Act of 1946*, Hearings before the Committee on Finance, Senate, 79th Cong., 2d sess., on H.R. 5856 (Washington, 1946), pp. 79–81.

[7] *Ibid.*, p. 105.   [8] *Ibid.*, pp. 106–7.

One minor repercussion was that, while the discussion on long versus short tons for sugar continued, a communication was sent to the Senate Finance Committee by the National Renderers Association. Commenting on the possibility that sugar might be expressed in terms of short tons whereas the coconut oil quota was in long tons, the association stated that "in the interests of consistency, we would like to recommend that both limitations be expressed in short tons."[9] This suggestion was not followed, however, for the long ton was restored for sugar and retained for coconut oil. In the interests of the domestic oil and fats producers, the association recommended that the clause allowing for possible future quotas be amplified to include products not only like but also interchangeable with or usable as substitutes for those of the United States. In explanation, F. B. Wise, secretary-treasurer of the National Renderers Association, said in his letter, "In other words, we are not asking that a quota on Philippine copra be placed in the bill at this particular time but we do feel, nevertheless, that consideration of a copra quota at some future date should not be bargained away for a period of 28 years by the use of a limiting word."[10]

With reference to cordage and twine, a memorandum from the Cordage Institute to the Senate committee reaffirmed support of the absolute quota on cordage. Two major reasons were given: the need for protection against the competition of Philippine-made cordage, and the fact that the Bell Bill, together with the Philippine Rehabilitation Bill, would help reconstruction in the Philippines and "enhance the production of Manila fiber (abacá), the raw material grown in the Philippines and essential to the production of rope in the United States.[11]

The testimony discussed above was the sum of business opinion offered at the congressional hearings on the Bell Bill. The comparatively resigned position of the domestic and Cuban sugar interests in the conflict around the bill reflected market conditions at the time, as well as the general political climate of opinion. From several editorials in *Sugar*, an important trade journal, during and after the deliberations on the bill, the point of view of the industry became apparent. One editorial stated:

The question arises how far this country should go in encouraging the newly independent (July 4, 1946) Philippine Commonwealth to return to dependence on a one-crop economy based on an assured position in the U.S. market. Do the people of the Commonwealth really profit from so artificially maintained an industry? Is it sound economic development for that nation to rely on supplying a market 7,000 miles distant? . . .

The sugar industry in Cuba is a going concern; the prosperity of that country depends on a large and active sugar industry. The Philippines, on the other hand,

9 *Ibid.*, p. 85.
10 *Ibid.*, p. 86.
11 *Ibid.*, p. 83.

are about to embark on a politically independent career. Her sugar industry is in ruins. Her economy may take any direction that her leaders deem desirable. Would it not be wiser to encourage a diversified economy designed to supply the needs of her own people and of her natural markets in the Far East? Financial assistance as provided in the Tydings Bill must be forthcoming. But to grant political independence while withholding economic independence is to grant a very questionable return to a brave and loyal ally.[12]

Three reasons for the domestic and Cuban sugar stand were discernible. One was the strong moral position of the Filipinos, whose wartime losses meant that generous treatment would be expected. Second, it was well recognized that the Philippine sugar industry was badly hit, and production was not likely to be resumed in normal amounts for several years. In the third place, the strong demand, world-wide shortages, and high market prices assured domestic sugar interests of a favorable position for some time and made it difficult for them to cry discrimination.

There was ample evidence to illustrate this. For example, in the April 1946 issue of *Sugar* an article date-lined Washington discussed the visit of Mr. McNutt and said that the "House Ways and Means Committee, to which the [Bell] Bill was referred, has been marking time—on request of administration forces—until the deal for the purchase of Cuba's 1946 sugar crop had been consummated." It went on to say:

Little opposition to this proposal [the Bell Bill] for getting the Islands on their feet is expected from domestic producers, inasmuch as their quotas are not affected. However, Cuba has had an eye on the Philippine quota, hoping it would be added to her own when the Islands are cut loose in July. She would like to have at least part of it, but the backers of the Bell Bill are not greatly concerned over opposition that may develop from that quarter.[13]

An article in the same periodical, the following month, stated the industry's belief that the eight-year duty-free sugar quota allowed under the bill—850,000 tons—was an academic figure, inasmuch as it was far more than the Philippines would have available for export.[14]

Cuban reaction to the sugar provisions of the Trade Act was expressed by Senator José Manuel Casanova, president of the National Association of Sugar Mill Owners, who said the quota arrangement was "in perfect accord with the present spirit of the people of the United States, to offer the people of the Philippines some compensation in appreciation of the great sacrifice and suffering experienced as a result of the war. We have nothing to say with respect to this." He went on, however, to speak of the importance of Cuba as a supplier of the United States in both wars and said Cuba "has an equal right to special treatment by which we may be assured in peace time of a sugar quota equivalent to not less than 40 per cent of the total sugar consumption of the

[12] *Sugar*, March 1946, p. 27.   [13] *Ibid.*, April 1946, p. 30.   [14] *Ibid.*, June 1946, p. 26.

American market."[15] A story date-lined Havana, May 15, 1946, in the same publication stated, "Only reasons of emergency and the moral considerations before stated can go counter to the sane economic reasoning that the logical outlet for Philippine sugar should be its natural markets in the Orient."[16]

The position of the cordage industry had already been made clear at the legislative hearings. It was further expressed in comment on the Philippine situation in *Cord Age*, official trade publication of the cordage, twine, and allied industries, which stated:

Of strategic importance to the United States in its quest for security in the atomic age, and of vital significance to the American cordage industry as the largest source of its raw material, the Philippines have been given the benefit of new laws designed to ease and promote their reconstruction from the ravages of the Japanese invasion.

Part of the benefits to be derived from the reciprocal trade and rehabilitation assistance will be the reconstruction of the Philippine abacá industry for supplying the raw material without which American cordage consumers cannot obtain adequate supply of Manila rope. . . .

Philippine independence is somewhat qualified, of course, by such factors as the islands' economic dependence upon the United States, and the necessity for the United States to maintain army, navy and air bases in the islands for their security as well as that of this country. . . .[17]

Those sections of the Trade Act which referred to competitive agricultural products, therefore, held no threat for the established interests. The moral obligation involved, the devastated condition of the Philippines, the lack of real competition, and the generally prosperous American economic picture, with high world prices and over-all shortages, meant that domestic agricultural interests, if not satisfied, were at least placated. A more significant role in Philippine policy was to be played by business interested in current and future investment. For this group the two most important sections in the bill were that establishing equal rights for new business, and that which tied the Philippine currency to the American dollar.

American business comment during 1946 was mainly applause of the Bell Bill, but it was felt that prospective investors would wait until after March 1947, the date of the parity referendum in the Philippines, before risking their capital. There was a good deal of unwarranted optimism at this time on the amount of investment that could be expected. For example the *Far East Trader*, newsletter on business conditions in Asia, said in September 1946, in a discussion of prospective United States investments: "Business, as well as official, circles hum with talk that the Bank of America, backed by millions of dollars, will be the first to come here. U.S. interests reportedly have in-

[15] *Ibid.*, June 1946, p. 29.   [16] *Ibid.*, p. 35.   [17] *Cord Age*, July 1946, p. 7.

dicated to Malacañan that they want to harness the Maria Cristina falls in Mindanao for economic purposes, and that smelting plants will likely be constructed by U.S. capital to develop the rich Surigao iron deposits."[18] The anticipated investment was not forthcoming, however; Maria Cristina remains unharnessed, and the Surigao iron deposits undeveloped.

Another optimistic picture of conditions in the Philippines and of opportunities for business was presented in *Barron's National Business and Financial Weekly*. The Trade Act was supported and the parity provisions explained in the following terms:

In view of the sacrifices that the American taxpayer is making, and to help remove the blight that the Filipinos are always on the receiving end, provisions were made for U.S. citizens to enjoy equal rights with the Filipinos to own or control, directly or individually, any business enterprise that has to do with natural resources and public utilities. American interests controlled most of the utilities in the Philippines before the war, and the new constitution had called for a drastic cut in foreign holdings. The other spur to American business in the Philippines is the guaranty that the dollar exchange standard of the legal ratio of two pesos to one dollar will be maintained.

. . . the overall economic and political outlook for the Philippines more than justifies confidence in the independent Republic of the Philippines as a bastion of democracy in the Orient, and an assurance of American security in the Pacific.[19]

Under the headline, "New Era Opening in the Philippines," a leading story in the financial section of the *New York Times* in March 1947 interpreted business opinion as follows:

If Western capitalism is to help shape the future of the Orient American citizens and American capital can join in the test unhandicapped, at least so far as the Philippine Islands are concerned. This is the meaning that the financial district is reading into the outcome of the plebiscite by which the new Philippine Republic last week accorded to American citizens rights paralleling the constitutional guarantees assured to the Filipinos themselves.[20]

Speaking just after the plebiscite vote, John W. Haussermann, president of the Benguet Mining Company, called the approval of the act encouraging to American capital. Declaring that industrial and agricultural development would both enhance Philippine living standards and help achieve a self-supporting economy, Mr. Haussermann indicated that Benguet had spent a million dollars since the war in putting its mines back in working condition. The report of his speech stated:

With economic independence thus reared upon the foundation stone of political

[18] *Far East Trader*, September 25, 1946.
[19] Ralph Masiello, "Chances for Success of New Philippine Nation Good," *Barron's National Business and Financial Weekly*, September 2, 1946, p. 9.
[20] Paul Heffernan, "New Era Opening in the Philippines," *New York Times*, March 16, 1947.

independence—according to the Haussermann vision—the islands could still in fact remain a lasting American outpost in the Pacific, culturally a testimonial to American institutions, and, economically, a neutral free zone—or warehouse—for American products destined for less-developed parts of the East.[21]

Widespread approval was given by American business to the Philippine law exempting necessary new industry from taxation for a four-year period. An article in the trade publication *Steel* applauded this tax exemption. Reporting on the attitudes of Filipinos to new investments, it stated, "Washington representatives of the Islands hail their country as a new 'western frontier of U.S. business men.'" In encouraging American businessmen, the Filipino spokesmen, according to this report, had produced a map and pointed out that Manila or any one of half a dozen other Philippine cities was a good location for serving a large part of the Orient.[22]

In addition to industry associations and journals, there were also groups concerned with general trade promotion in the Philippines. The Far East–America Council of Commerce and Industry, an association of several hundred firms organized to promote trade between the United States and the Far East, established a Philippine-American Trade Council, chaired by Paul V. McNutt, former ambassador to the Philippines.[23]

The National Foreign Trade Council was also interested in Philippine affairs as they affected American businessmen. For example, the council made certain proposals to further private investment and trade in the Islands, such as restoration of tax incentives to American business in the Philippines by amending Section 251 of the United States Internal Revenue Code. In the existing situation American companies paid not only the 12 percent income tax imposed by the Philippine government, but an additional 26 percent to meet the 38 percent United States tax. According to the council, companies of other countries operating in the Philippines were exempted from corporate taxes of their respective governments, and so were American companies operating there for twenty-five years prior to Philippine independence. A restoration of such exemption, in the opinion of the council, would enable American companies to proceed with rehabilitation of properties and would attract new capital. In addition, the council proposed a co-ordinated program of economic aid, a treaty between the two countries defining a legal framework for reciprocal rights, a treaty to avoid double taxation, and the extension of the expiration date of the amounts payable on larger claims under the Rehabilitation Act.[24]

While Philippine policy was of peripheral concern for some of the better-known business groups, it was the focus of interest for the Philippine-American

[21] *Ibid.*

[22] "New Island Republic Offers Four Year Tax Exemption to American Firms," *Steel*, November 4, 1946, p. 75.

[23] *New York Times*, December 29, 1947.

[24] Press Release, National Foreign Trade Council (New York), June 28, 1949.

Chamber of Commerce, the main organization in this country which has represented American business interested in the Philippines. The Chamber was formed "to foster and promote trade, commerce, mutual welfare and other business relations between the United States and the Philippines, and their respective peoples, and to serve those persons and organizations having financial, trade, business and professional interests in either or both countries."[25]

The roster of the Chamber in 1948 included 141 members, over half of whom had major business interests in the Philippines, the rest having nominal or indirect connections. Among the members were trading firms, banking and business organizations, and individuals. The list of officers and directors included officials from such important firms as Standard Vacuum Oil Company, National City Bank of New York, Goodyear Tire and Rubber Export Company, General Foods Corporation, General Mills, Inc., Philippine Refining Corporation, and Texas Oil, Ltd.

The Chamber has informed and advised its members primarily on Philippine-American trade relations, but it has also been concerned with legislation. For example, in the report of the board of directors presented to its annual meeting on January 15, 1947, C. A. Richards, president, spoke of the Chamber's interest in both the Trade and the Rehabilitation acts. He said:

> Prior to their enactment, the Chamber was very active in the building up of various sections contained therein. The views of the Chamber concerning many controversial items were conveyed to Committees of Congress by groups of directors. The Board vigorously protested the attempt on the part of certain interests to decrease the allocation in the Bell Bill of sugar from 850,000 long tons to short tons. The Senate restored the quantity to long tons. Recommendations made by the Board concerning legislation were well received. Harmonious relations were maintained with the representatives of the Philippine Government in Washington at all times.
>
> As to the Bell Bill, the Board at all times supported the contention of the Philippine Government that free trade should be maintained for a period of 20 years. The bill as passed granted free trade for eight years. The Board felt that this period was too short but it was the longest that our Congress was willing to grant.[26]

Other matters on which action has been taken by the Chamber included recommendations on export licenses and controls, air mail, parcel post service, taxation, and patent laws.

In addition to its concern with United States policy, the Chamber has also shown an interest in Philippine actions affecting business operations. For example, in a communication to the Division of Philippine Affairs in the De-

[25] Certificate of Incorporation of the Philippine-American Camber of Commerce, as amended December 14, 1945.

[26] *Annual Report of the Board of Directors*, Philippine-American Chamber of Commerce, January 15, 1947.

partment of State, on February 21, 1947, Philippine legislation on bank deposits was discussed. The Chamber stated:

The Chamber has received a reliable report that a House bill has been introduced in the Philippine Congress to the effect that any banking institution in which 60 per cent was not owned by Filipinos would be prohibited from having savings accounts. The report also indicates that Congressman Roy of the Banking Committee is not only in favor of the bill but wishes to amend it to prohibit the affected banks from having any deposit accounts, savings or commercial.

The Philippine-American Chamber of Commerce wishes to go on record as being unalterably opposed to the passage of such a bill.

We are of the opinion that at this stage of Philippine rehabilitation, a change in the banking system now in effect would have disastrous results and discourage the investment of American capital so badly needed.

Whether the Philippine Government is right or wrong in desiring to have more complete control over the banking system, we earnestly believe that this is not the time to make a change.

It is requested that our views be transmitted by cable to the Philippine Government.[27]

Two pieces of legislation, one Philippine and one American, received particular attention from the Chamber in 1948 and 1949. The first was the Philippine Flag Law (Commonwealth Act No. 138), which gave a 15 percent advantage to a bidder of Philippine nationality in Philippine government agency purchases. In comparing this with the United States Flag Law, the Chamber pointed out that that American legislation merely grants priority to United States goods in government purchases, whereas the Philippine law in effect penalizes the government because the 15 percent leeway might force prices upward. From the Filipino point of view, however, the question might be raised as to which if any Philippine products could actually endure price competition with American-made goods, at least until the Philippine industrialization program was well under way.

The Chamber also expressed interest in the problem of taxation of American business in the Republic. When the Philippines became independent, exemption from U.S. corporation taxes, which had been granted in 1921 to American corporations and individuals doing business in American possessions, automatically ended. Businessmen in the Philippines maintained that this put them at a disadvantage with respect to other foreign firms operating there, whose tax burden at home might be lighter than that of United States nationals.

An attempt to amend Section 251 of the Internal Revenue Code in this respect was made in the 80th Congress by Representative W. Sterling Cole of New York. The essence of his bill, H.R. 4208, was that the provision for tax

[27] *Weekly Bulletin to Members*, Philippine-American Chamber of Commerce, February 24, 1947, p. 3.

exemption in "possessions of the United States" in the Code be extended to include the words, "or, effective July 4, 1946, the Republic of the Philippines." Hearings on the proposal were held by the Ways and Means Committee of the House, but the measure was not reported out of committee. In the report of their board of directors, the position of the Philippine-American Chamber on this matter was clearly stated. "While the Bill was under consideration," the report commented, "Secretary of the Treasury Snyder went on record as being opposed to its passage. However spokesmen for the Chamber and the National Foreign Trade Council placed arguments in the hands of Congressman Cole in an attempt to offset the objections of the Secretary of the Treasury."[28]

American business opinion on Philippine policy, however, was by no means unanimous. Older American firms which had been long established in the Islands were critical of the parity provisions of the Trade Act, which were actually designed to attract new capital, rather than to safeguard old investments. This group may also have been more aware of Filipino reactions to the Trade Act, and more concerned with maintaining good will for foreign business in general. The position taken by the American Chamber of Commerce in the Philippines, composed of United States firms operating in the Republic, must therefore be distinguished from that of the Philippine-American Chamber of Commerce, with headquarters in downtown New York. For example, an editorial in the *Journal of the American Chamber of Commerce* for July 1946 took a strong position in opposition to the parity clause, stating:

One of the provisions of the Philippine Trade Act which has particularly aroused the ire of Filipinos, and rightfully so, is that which requires the Republic of the Philippines to allow Americans equal rights with Filipinos in the acquisition and development of natural resources. The question is not whether such provision is wise or not. The question is simply one of justice as between nations. The United States has granted independence to the Republic of the Philippines and has no right to impose a provision of this nature. To Americans in the Philippines the provision is a source of considerable embarrassment. The then High Commissioner McNutt made clear on one public occasion that the provision did not originate with Americans in the Philippines, and was never asked for by them as a group or individually. In the interest of preserving the respect and friendship of the Filipinos, the fullest possible publicity should be given to this fact. In the interests of honesty and fair-dealing, the government of the United States should voluntarily abrogate the invidious provision at the earliest moment.[29]

In spite of this opposition from established American business in the Philippines, the parity provision was passed. The Americans hoped for a new frontier for investment in the Islands, and the Filipinos hoped that benefits would percolate down to the Philippine economy.

[28] *Annual Report of the Board of Directors*, Philippine-American Chamber of Commerce, January 19, 1949.
[29] *Journal of the American Chamber of Commerce* (Manila), July 1946.

CHAPTER SEVEN

PHILIPPINE SENTIMENT

WHAT may seem to be a minor question of foreign economy policy on Capitol Hill can become a major political issue in the country affected. Unfortunately, too little overseas opinion on United States policy has been reported in the American press, particularly from Far Eastern countries. Filipino reactions to the American economic policy expressed in the Trade Act, however, can be documented from Philippine publications, public statements, and newspaper and periodical comments. Although views of Filipinos on this issue were by no means unanimous, a strong current of nationalist sentiment underlay most of the discussion at the time.

In a story headlined "Anti-Americanism in the Philippines," the *Far East Trader* commented:

Most U.S. citizens regard our Philippine policy as generous and enlightened. . . . Thus it is a shock to find the P.I. President forced to use his full power of persuasion and political pressure in order to get his people to accept the Bell Trade Bill. . . . No amount of argument seems to convince a considerable segment of P.I. opinion that the U.S. is not an imperialist nation bent on exploiting the Islands. . . . It is a sad condition, and not a little provoking. . . . But the principle of U.S. good will to the P.I. apparently will only be proved to this dissident group by time, and not by words.[1]

The rise of nationalism in southeast Asia during and after World War II made it necessary for Western countries to re-examine their relations with colonial areas and to seek new arrangements to safeguard economic interests. In some cases nationalist forces clashed in open warfare with former rulers, in others negotiation and bargaining were undertaken. In the Philippines the United States held an unusually favorable position. Co-operation during the war with guerrilla forces had been outstanding, and the loyalty of the majority of Filipinos to American wartime goals had been proved. Thus an inside track was available to both military and civilian American advisers in the postwar period. The way was open for a reintroduction of American economic interests, not through conquest but through co-operation with selected Filipino leaders. The Philippines needed and wanted help. One of the major questions, however, was whether the proposed United States economic policy was designed to serve Filipino as well as American interests, and the degree to which these interests could be reconciled.

[1] *Far East Trader*, June 26, 1946.

American economic policy became a matter of vital concern in the Philippines on three occasions during a period of one year. These were the presidential elections in April 1946, the discussion of the Trade Act in the Philippine Congress (especially in June 1946), and the nation-wide discussion of parity beginning in September and culminating in the referendum on March 11, 1947.

Two major issues, the Trade Act and the national elections, developed concurrently in the spring of 1946. Although American economic policy was widely discussed, the issues were not sharply defined. The rival candidates at the April elections were Manuel Roxas, former president of the Senate, and Sergio Osmeña, who as Vice-President had succeeded to the presidency on the death of Manuel Quezon in August 1944. Two major parties entered the election contest, the newly formed Liberal party, backing Roxas, and the old Nacionalista party, supporting Osmeña, who was also backed by a coalition group including the prewar Popular Front and the newly organized Democratic Alliance. This last body included the Hukbalahap, the National Peasants Union, the Commission on Labor Organization, the Civil Liberties Union, and the Communist party, which had merged with the Socialist party before the war. A bitterly fought contest resulted in the election of Roxas, who received 1,333,392 votes against 1,129,996 for Osmeña. Of fifteen senators elected nine were from the Liberal wing and seven were Osmeña supporters.

Although many of the election issues were local, American policy and American reactions were felt in the Philippines. The question of collaboration with the Japanese was raised with regard to Roxas. A significant move in the electoral conflict was General MacArthur's public approval of full participation by Roxas in postwar political activity. On the other hand, Washington commentators reported a good deal of pro-Osmeña sentiment in official circles. Officially, however, the United States maintained a hands-off attitude, leaving the issues to the Filipino voters.

Roxas conducted a whirlwind campaign, sparing no opportunity to travel and to speak. His forceful oratory, his far-reaching promises—including restoration of peace and order in thirty days, full payment of back pay, redemption of guerrilla currency, speedy rehabilitation, clean administration, and voting rights—the endorsement of his candidacy by Mrs. Quezon, and the denial by High CommissionerMcNutt of the charges that no American aid would be forthcoming if Roxas were elected, all won votes.[2] In one speech Roxas declared, "I am fighting in this election because we must save this country from chaos, corruption, and Communists."[3] In his election-eve appeal, Roxas made no mention of the Bell Bill but spoke of the rehabilitation needs of the Philippines and said that, if elected, he would seek financial aid from the United States.[4]

[2] Philippines Daily News, April 21, 1946; Star Reporter (Manila), April 27, 1946.
[3] Manila Post, April 10, 1946.
[4] Philippines Daily News, April 21, 1946.

Osmeña refused to campaign or to participate in the political discussion that seethed about his office. In his only political speech, at a rally held in Manila, he discussed rehabilitation needs, saying that there were differences of opinion with respect to certain provisions of the American legislation but that he was certain that fairness and justice would prevail in the end. The firmest opposition to the proposals was shown by the Democratic Alliance, which stated, "The chief beneficiaries of the Bell Bill are the sugar centrals and coconut oil refineries, a big majority of which are owned by American vested interests."[5]

As the election date approached, the implications of the Trade Act and the related rehabilitation measures became more evident, and there began the polite passing of responsibility for supporting what looked like unpopular legislation. The *Philippines Daily News* commented as follows:

Caught sleeping on the job, Malacañan has ventured forth on a campaign of face-saving by shifting the blame for its mishandling of the Bell trade bill question to Resident Commissioner Romulo, who, long before President Osmeña came out against the measure, had praised it as a piece of legislation acceptable to the Filipinos.

. . . suddenly, aroused by local public opinion against the latest changes in the trade relations bill, the Cabinet passed a resolution registering its opposition to the measure, using the very words and phrases the press had been hurling at it. And it was only then that President Osmeña seemed to have made up his mind, and gave out a feeble statement opposing the bill.[6]

On the other hand, inaction was also criticized, and an editorial in the *Manila Post* said that both followers and opponents of Roxas could not understand why he had not taken a stand on the Bell Bill.[7]

Most controversy was aroused with regard to the proposed Tydings amendments, which would have permitted the United States government to maintain any agencies or instrumentalities in the Philippines after independence, in addition to real properties. A report for the Philippines in the *Far East Trader* of April 10, 1946, declared:

Strenuous opposition to the Independence Act amendment introduced in the U.S. House and Senate last week is mounting rapidly here. President Osmeña, usually mild in his statements dealing with U.S. relations, is rallying the people against the amendments which he said would "nullify Philippine freedom." . . . The office of Foreign Relations earlier called the amendments "the most sweeping attempt of the U.S. government to establish extraterritoriality rights in the Philippine Islands.[8]

[5] Press statement, March 5, 1946, quoted in Ira Gollobin, "Philippine Election Coalition," *Far Eastern Survey*, April 24, 1946, pp. 120–21.
[6] *Philippines Daily News*, April 10, 1946.
[7] *Manila Post*, April 11, 1946.
[8] *Far East Trader*, April 10, 1946.

The major point at issue was the future disposition of the rich holdings in Davao, including coconut and abacá plantations, which were formerly Japanese property but were retained at the end of the war by the U.S. Alien Property Custodian. Widespread Philippine protest resulted in subsequent modification of the proposed amendents.

A few days before the Trade Act was passed by the United States Congress, the Filipino people went to the polls and elected Roxas as President. The *Manila Chronicle* interpreted the results as meaning "That the present administration, by demonstrated incapacity to dissipate confusion and formulate decisions on problems of national importance, cannot be trusted at this critical period to achieve those results which will answer with any measure of adequacy to the popular demand for an honest and efficient government . . ."[9]

The point of view of the opposition was expressed in another editorial in the *Philippine Press*, addressed to the outgoing President Osmeña, which said:

The price for the Presidency was the granting of back-pay, and the yielding to the imperialist demands of a former ally and friend in exchange for immediate but temporary benefits and aid. You [Osmeña] would not bankrupt the country for a handful of government employees, you would not mortgage your country's independence for American relief with strings attached. And so you must go. Another man was prepared to pay the price, make the proper alliances, enter into the necessary agreements, promise all. "For the ultimate good of the Filipino nation" he had done it once and gotten away with it. He was ready to do it again. He will be the President of the Philippine Republic.[10]

Expressing gratification at the results of the election, Roy Howard, publisher of the United States Scripps-Howard newspapers, said in an interview in Manila at the time that the returns would be well received in the United States. He further said that, with regard to the charge that Roxas was guilty of treasonable collaboration with the Japanese, the American attitude was, "If he's good enough for General MacArthur, he should be good enough for the United States."[11] In his first broadcast to the United States as President-elect, Roxas appealed for United States aid and for American capital to assist in the task of reconstruction.[12]

In the meantime, the Trade and Rehabilitation acts had been passed in Washington. There was little indication in the congressional hearings or in the American press of the mixed feelings in the Philippines. All that was said was that the Filipinos desired action. The fact was, however, that the legislation touched off a year-long debate in the Philippines on the merits and demerits of American policy. Strong language and deep feeling were expressed

[9] *Manila Chronicle*, April 27, 1946.
[10] *Philippine Press*, April 27, 1946.
[11] *Manila Post*, April 30, 1946.
[12] *Manila Times*, April 29, 1946.

in Philippine publications. One critical comment, for example, in the *Star Reporter*, April 11, 1946, stated:

What the Indiana transportation magnate-politician Paul V. McNutt fondly described as "an historic victory for the people of the Philippines" does not necessarily mean the triumph of the Filipino masses. . . .

The American interests which are bound to get the lion's share of the 850,000 long tons of sugar that may be exported yearly to the United States duty free are the Pampanga Sugar Mills, the San Carlos Milling, the Hawaiian-Philippines, and the Bogo-Medellin. This concerns only the American sugar interests here.

There are other American firms which are favored under the Bell free trade bill, including the Manila Cordage company, the Tubbs Cordage company, the International Harvester company, the Philippine Refining company, the Spencer Kellog, Philippine Manufacturing company, Agusan Coconut company, the Philippine Button corporation and the Shell-craft and Button corporation.[13]

A columnist in the *Philippine Press* declared, "Japan is occupied. So we are told anyway. The Philippines is supposed to be quote liberated unquote. Why not slap the Bell Bill on the Japs?"[14] The *Manila Chronicle* said in editorial comment that the basic decision was up to the people, but that "The Bell Bill will certainly benefit almost exclusively already vested interests here, and these are almost exclusively American and foreign."[15]

A good deal of the discussion centered on the controversial parity provision, which would give equal rights to American nationals. There was some speculation on the origin of this proposal. The *Manila Post* reported:

That the amendment is advocated by American businessmen who fear discrimination was admitted yesterday by Commander Julius C. Edelstein who, speaking as the High Commissioner's spokesman at a press conference yesterday, said of the provision, "That was put in the bill by some Congressmen at the request of American businessmen as a condition of investing money in new enterprises and rehabilitating old ones in the Islands."[16]

On the other hand, the *Evening Herald* declared:

To insinuate then that imperialistic motives prompted the backers of the Bell Bill is highly unjustified. While we recognize that imperialists plague the world, let's not show ingratitude to those who sincerely have been working for our national revival. . . . Let's accept the Bell Bill now and ask for amendments later if it is necessary.[17]

A prominent role in the discussion was taken by Mr. McNutt, then High Commissioner. Reporting to the Philippine Bar Association on his trip to

13 *Star Reporter* (Manila), April 11, 1946.
14 *Philippine Press*, April 15, 1946.
15 *Manila Chronicle*, April 18, 1946.
16 *Manila Post*, April 21, 1946.
17 *Evening Herald* (Manila), May 3, 1946.

Washington to seek action on the Bell Bill, he said he had never worked harder in his life. Describing his activity, Mr. McNutt said:

We used every contact, every stratagem, every trading point we could through those long weeks of negotiations, deliberation, committee hearings, legislative drafting and re-drafting of that trade bill. We buttonholed senators and congressmen in their offices, at their homes, at social gatherings. . . . We had, perhaps, the most active and persistent lobby any bill has ever attracted. . . . We met obstacles at every step, objections from many quarters. Many individuals and groups had different ideas on how best to accomplish the goals most of us were agreed upon. . . . We succeeded in neutralizing almost all the domestic sugar interests, which was a major accomplishment in itself. It took many hours of conferences and arguments, pleas and appeals to patriotism and citations of the economic facts of life. . . .[18]

In discussing the parity provision Mr. McNutt said the Philippines must create a middle class and encourage small business, and that such was the intention of the equal rights section. Declaring that big business needed no encouragement to invest in the Philippines, he maintained that the small businessman, the American engineer, consultant, oil driller, sponge iron manufacturer, and expert woodworker were the people needed in the Islands, and the ones for whom the equal rights provision was inserted in the Bell Bill.

In his inaugural address President Roxas spoke of friendship and gratitude to the United States and said, "I find no dream of empire in America."[19] The new Congress of the Philippines, however, met after the elections in a tense atmosphere and once again the close tie between political and economic policy was seen. The Osmeña administration, on leaving office, had prepared for the incoming President a memorandum outlining detailed objections to the Bell Act. This was criticized as a political move, designed so that the outgoing party could not be blamed for the unpopular legislation.[20]

The first sessions of the Philippine Congress were marked by the refusal of the ruling faction to seat ten minority representatives, including seven members of the Democratic Alliance in the House and three Nacionalista senators, Diokno, Vara, and Romero, on the ground that a report from the Commission on Elections said that voting in disputed districts "did not reflect the true and free expression of the popular will." A turbulent meeting was followed by a walkout of the minority congressmen, and the issue was unresolved.[21] On the other hand, when the opposition representatives raised the question of collaboration on the part of certain majority congressmen, both houses took the stand that indictment for treason was not sufficient ground to deprive a member of his seat and representation.[22]

[18] *Manila Bulletin,* May 10, 1946.
[19] *Evening News* (Manila), May 28, 1946.
[20] *Star Reporter* (Manila), May 16, 1946.
[21] *Sunday Times* (Manila), May 26, 1946.   [22] *Manila Bulletin,* May 27, 1946.

With several congressmen unseated, a constitutional question arose as to the legality of certain controversial legislation. The Philippine Constitution, like the American, required more than a simple majority vote to legislate on specified matters. The question raised was whether this meant a majority of "congressmen elected" or "congressmen seated." If, as the minority asserted, it meant "congressmen elected," then some of the controversial measures would not in fact have been able to secure the necessary votes for ratification, had the full complement of elected congressmen actually been seated and able to vote.

It was unfortunate that the proposed Trade and Rehabilitation acts were not fully and openly discussed in the Philippines until after passage in Washington, so that the Filipinos were confronted with a *fait accompli*. In fact, one of the most frequent arguments for ratification in the Philippines was that the acts had already been passed in the United States Congress, and it was therefore too late to do anything about them.

Despite his adverse memorandum, Osmeña participated with Roxas in a joint appeal for acceptance of the Trade Act by Congress and by the Filipino people on the ground that it was the best legislation that could be secured and "the wisest and most expedient course . . . at the present time."[23] This was countered by a statement from the Democratic Alliance which called the Trade Act "non-reciprocal and one-sided," and declared, "It is claimed by its imperialist backers that the Bell Bill will rehabilitate Philippine economy. Undoubtedly, it will do even more. It will develop Philippine economy. But it certainly will not be Filipino economy. It will be American economy in the Philippines."[24]

After a brief visit to Washington, Roxas and McNutt, on their return to Manila, held a joint press conference and urged the Filipinos to accept the Trade and Rehabilitation acts, suggesting that any provisions prejudicial to the interests of the Filipinos could be altered in future negotiations.[25] Commissioner of Foreign Relations Vicente G. Sinco took exception to this view, declaring that it was still possible to work for amendment of the acts and correction of imperfections before July 4.[26]

The Nacionalista party, after a three-hour caucus, went on record as being unanimously opposed to the Trade Act, contrary to Osmeña's personal position. They stated that the legislation would "condemn the Filipino people to slavery."[27] On the other hand, Roxas' Liberal party made every effort to promote favorable sentiment. The legal experts of the administration ruled that the act was a piece of "simple legislation" and not a commercial pact or treaty. Therefore, they concluded, it required only a simple plurality vote and not

23 *Manila Daily Bulletin*, May 23, 1946.
24 *Star Reporter* (Manila), May 23, 1946.
25 *Manila Chronicle*, May 23, 1946.
26 *Star Reporter* (Manila), May 24, 1946.
27 *Manila Times*, May 24, 1946.

approval by a two-thirds vote. This was challenged by minority groups.[28] Ten civil and labor bodies wired their opposition to the act to certain United States congressmen. Those protesting included the Civil Liberties Union, the Philippine Lawyers' Guild, the Commission of Labor Organizations, the Philippine Veterans' Association, the Society of Economists, Statisticians and Accountants, the Philippine Writers' Association, the Congress of Youth Organizations, the Philippine Students' Union, the National Peasants Union, and the Philippine Newspaper Guild.[29]

In his message to Congress on the future of trade and economic relations with the United States, President Roxas recalled that the Trade Act had had the support of the Osmeña administration. With reference to the equal rights section, he said, "If I could, I would remove it, not because of the alleged dangers it holds for us . . . I believe these to be non-existent . . . but rather because of the manner and form in which it is included." He continued, "The equal rights provision was not designed as a protection for American interests already here—it is intended to reassure potential investors that the Philippines are a safe area for enterprise, safe against discrimination for the next 28 years. . . . I do not propose to sacrifice the national welfare on the altar of pride."[30] Roxas went on with a spirited defense of the other provisions of the act. He said the currency tie put the Philippines "within the magic and charmed circle of standard value, the dollar area," and that the absolute quotas would force industrial diversification. Furthermore, he indicated that no financial aid could be expected from the United States if the Trade Act were not accepted.

At public hearings held by the Committees on Foreign Relations of the Philippine Senate and House, the Trade Act was both assailed and defended by various witnesses.[31] A third point of view was presented at the hearings by Senator Alejo Mabanag, who said the Philippines had little to lose and everything to gain by delaying acceptance of the Trade Act with a view to amending it. Referring to the excess of imports over exports, he deplored impatience, saying that if the Filipinos were to postpone action and work for amendment, they could meanwhile collect tariff duties on American imports.[32] The Philippine Youth party suggested postponement of action for a six-month period.[33] On the other hand, the board of directors of the Chamber of Commerce of the Philippines formally supported the administration stand.[34] Editorial comment in the *Manila Times*, which favored the Bell Bill, stated that "the Act emerges as an effort on the part of the U.S. to legislate not for, but in behalf of the Philippines. Some interests, some individuals, will profit. That is in the

[28] *Evening News* (Manila), June 11, 1946.
[29] *Ibid.*, June 15, 1946.
[30] *Manila Times*, June 22, 1946.
[31] *Sunday Times* (Manila), June 23, 1946.
[32] *Manila Times*, June 24, 1946.
[33] *Ibid.*, June 25, 1946.
[34] *Ibid.*, June 26, 1946.

nature of things. But it is the people of the Philippines who will profit most.
And, in the last analysis, it is the people of the Philippines who will have the
last word in the ultimate application of even the most objectionable of the
objectionable provisions of the Act."[35]

The Committee on Foreign Relations of the House reported favorably on
accepting the executive agreement embodying the Trade Act. In a dissenting
opinion, however, Congressman Felixberto Serrano, member of the committee,
made several noteworthy points. Speaking for the minority, he said in part:

The Bill, in the language of the President, "provides the basic blueprint of our
economic recovery" without which, in his opinion "we are immediately faced by
disaster." On the other hand, other quarters no less profoundly concerned in the
welfare and salvation of our people, view the Act as a curtailment of some of the
essential attributes of our sovereignty and as a bid for the exploitation of the patri-
mony of the nation in exchange for doubtful trade preferences therein proffered. . . .

I cannot understand how a measure which took six months for the various
Committees of the United States Congress to consider . . . should be pressed to,
for immediate action by, the Congress of the Philippines after only two days of
hurried public hearings and hardly two hours of deliberation in this Committee.
. . . On the other hand, if immediate action is, for reasons I cannot understand,
deemed necessary, I believe the only action consistent with our self-respect and
dignity as a people and with the bare essential requirements of self-preservation,
is to recommend rejection of the measure. In the first case, we can immediately
provide for a *modus vivendi* by enacting a law embodying the purely trade provisions of the Act until such time as a formal treaty can be concluded between the
United States and the Philippines on the basis of a mutually satisfactory formula
of such trade relations. In the second case, we can immediately send a mission
to the United States to present the views of our people on the controversial features
of the Act to which we trust full sympathetic consideration will be accorded by
both responsible officials of Washington and the American people as a whole.[36]

On the eve of independence, after an all-day and all-night session in the
Senate and a continuous eighteen-hour debate in the House, and amid mixed
cries of "Faith in America" and "Economic Slavery," it was finally voted to
authorize the Executive Pact.[37] The Philippine Congress, however, in a con-
current resolution, declared that the Bell Act "contains imperfections and
inequalities."[38]

This was only the beginning of the controversy. The next hurdle was the
amendment of the Philippine Constitution to allow equal rights for Americans, as required by the American legislation. Not only was debate continued

[35] *Ibid.*, July 3, 1946.
[36] Philippine *Congressional Record*, House of Representatives, June 29, 1946, Appendix,
pp. 14–16. Concurring in the foregoing resolution were Congressmen Cipriano Primicias, Justiniano
Montano, Floro Crisologo, and Lorenzo Teves.
[37] *Manila Times*, July 3, 1946.
[38] *Sunday Times* (Manila), July 21, 1946.

but issues became sharper and language more specific. Only in rare instances was there real approval of the Trade Act; most of the support was based on a "lesser evil" argument and on grounds of expediency. For example, Gil J. Puyat, president of the Chamber of Commerce of the Philippines, in an article in the Chamber *Journal* pointed out five objections to the Rehabilitation and Trade acts. These were: (1) that war damage payments were tied to acceptance of the Trade Act; (2) that the bulk of war damage would go to foreigners; (3) the equal rights provision; (4) the imposition of absolute quotas; and (5) the pegging of the peso to the dollar. Mr. Puyat felt, however, that these objections did not carry enough weight to warrant rejection of the legislation. He said:

When the objectionable provisions were first discussed in Congress, the Chamber of Commerce of the Philippines was among the first organizations here that opposed them. We made our stand known to the administration at that time. We communicated our views to our resident commissioner and we also wired some influential Americans. . . . However, in spite of our opposition, the provisions were retained in the laws which were finally enacted. Part of the local press has recently charged that the Chamber of Commerce has reversed its stand. There has been no such change. . . . The Chamber of Commerce of the Philippines finally resolved to support the administration in the conviction that the advantages [of the Acts] outweigh the disadvantages and that it will prove possible to secure revisions to the laws which will make them more favorable to us. This the Chamber has done as a matter of economic expediency. Now we can work for the improvement of the Acts and the elimination of the objectionable provisions. If we fail, we must not forget that provision which enables either government to cancel the agreement . . . in case it finds the arrangements entered into are not satisfactory. . . .[39]

On the other hand, a statement by the Philippine Lawyers' Guild, introduced into the United States *Congressional Record*, said, "Through their chief agent and spokesman in these Islands, High Commissioner (now Ambassador) Paul V. McNutt, American business interests succeeded in railroading the Bell Act through the U.S. Congress. This law, falsely labeled as 'Reciprocal' is so onerous that if carried into full effect it will inevitably reduce the Philippine Republic to nothing better than its Jap-puppet predecessor."[40] The guild reported that on the very day that the news of President Truman's signing of the bill had been published, a parade and demonstration of protest had been held in Manila, attended by some 50,000 peasants and city workers, members of about twenty-three civic groups.

The next step in the political treadmill was to secure Philippine congressional approval of the parity provisions, and to follow this with a nation-wide

[39] Gil J. Puyat, "A Filipino Looks at the Rehabilitation and Trade Acts," *Journal of the American Chamber of Commerce*, July 1946.

[40] *Congressional Record*, 79th Cong., 2d sess., August 2, 1946, Appendix, p. A4858.

referendum amending the Constitution. The issue was again warmly debated in the Philippine Congress. Senator Tomas Confesor, opposition leader, branded the resolution as a dangerous precedent which placed the integrity of the Republic in jeopardy. He asked what the Filipino attitude would be if Russia or China or Great Britain demanded the same privileges.[41] President Roxas denied reports of American influence, saying, "There is no truth whatsoever to any reports that the U.S. Government used pressure or have evinced any unusual interest in our political and legal deliberations concerning the equal rights amendment. . . ."[42] Approval of the equal rights provision was secured from President Osmeña, who wired the minority group in Congress to rally behind the measure for patriotic reasons. Opposition in the Nacionalista party, as a result, was most effectively split.[43]

Approval of a national plebiscite on a constitutional amendment squeezed narrowly through Congress on September 18, by a vote of 68 to 18 in the House and 16 to 5 in the Senate.[44] The government held that this was two votes over the three-quarters majority needed for ratification in the House, and just exactly sufficient votes in the Senate. The Philippine Constitution, however, specified that constitutional amendments could be proposed by a vote of three fourths of "all the Members" of the Senate and of the House of Representatives, voting separately,[45] and the government calculation allowed for only seated members. If a percentage of all elected members had been taken, including those not seated, passage would have required 18 votes in the Senate and 73 in the House. The legality of the vote on the amendment, therefore, was challenged by the minority party.

One of the arguments used in the Congress by supporters of the legislation was that it was up to the people to decide, and therefore the correct procedure was to pass the amendment and let the nation-wide referendum proceed. There were, however, a few unexpected repercussions. For example, Congressman José Topacio Nueno of Manila, one of the ranking members of the House majority, announced that, although he had voted for the amendment in Congress, he would go before the people and urge its defeat. He said he had surveyed his own district and found the people against the proposal, and declared, "I have done my duty to the party by voting in favor of the bill in Congress, so that it may be taken to the people for final decision. It is now my turn to discharge my duty to the people, and in obedience to their decision, I will oppose this parity constitutional amendment at the coming plebiscite."[46]

From another point of view entirely Dr. José Laurel, former puppet Presi-

[41] *Manila Post*, September 12, 1946.
[42] *Manila Courier*, September 17, 1946.
[43] *Manila Bulletin*, September 18, 1946.
[44] *New York Times*, September 19, 1946.
[45] Philippine Constitution, Article XIV, Section 1.
[46] *Evening Herald* (Manila), September 26, 1946.

dent, criticized parity on grounds of Philippine nationalism.[47] Luis Taruc, Communist guerrilla leader and elected but unseated congressman, criticized Roxas as a puppet of American imperialism and blasted Laurel for "justifying his previous policy toward the Japanese fascist government." In a letter to the Philippine *Liberty News*, Taruc wrote from central Luzon, where he was in hiding, "We are not anti-American, but we are against un-American practices."[48]

In the midst of the violent controversy, some voices were heard urging forbearance and asking that long-term values be not lightly thrown away in return for short-term gains. The *Sunday Post*, in editorial comment, said the arguments for the Trade Act and large-scale investment were based on the faulty premise that industrial development should be hurried "at any cost, in any event." The article pointed out that industrialization was not an unmixed blessing, but brought problems as well as gains. It cautioned, "There is an influential section of the people which believes that it is a far more practical nationalism to make haste slowly in the matter of disposing of and developing natural resources."[49]

Mrs. Osmeña, wife of the former President, urged the minority congressmen to fight the equal rights amendment and to make a determined stand against the administration.[50] Alarmed at the extent of opposition to parity, congressional leaders were reported to have sought ways of checking the antiparity feeling. The *Manila Times* stated, "Reports pouring in at administration headquarters in Manila were said to be disclosing the daily gains which opponents of the proposed amendments are making not only in Manila but also in the provinces. . . ."[51]

Pro-Roxas quarters attributed this sentiment to an extended anti-American whispering campaign. On the other hand, spokesmen for the minority party expressed fears that a 6-million-peso appropriation allocated for the reassessment of provincial real estate would indirectly be used by the majority party to gain rural support for the Trade Act.[52] A *liga Filipina* to "defend the Philippine Constitution from unwarranted changes" was formed and sought support on a nonpartisan basis. In a straw vote conducted by the *Manila Post* well in advance of the voting date, results were heavily against the parity provisions. For example, on November 17 the paper reported 82,156 No votes and 36,747 Yes votes.[53]

In a speech before the University of the Philippines, President Roxas predicted that failure to approve parity would lead to "national disaster and chaos," including unemployment, postponement of plans for industrialization, loss of revenue, lack of rehabilitation payments, and Filipino-American mis-

---

[47] *Manila Courier*, October 5, 1946.
[48] *Liberty News* (Manila), October 11, 1946.
[49] *Sunday Post* (Manila), October 13, 1946.
[50] *Manila Chronicle*, October 17, 1946.
[51] *Manila Times*, October 14, 1946.
[52] *Star Reporter* (Manila), October 23, 1946.
[53] *Sunday Post* (Manila), November 17, 1946.

understanding.[54] A different view was taken by Jaime Hernández, former Secretary of Finance under Osmeña, who was described as "obliquely" assailing the Trade Act, having said, in effect, that under parity Filipinos would become mere laborers working for American capital.[55]

While most of the discussion was on the economic merits of the legislation, a good deal of resentment appeared in the press against the privileges taken by American military personnel in the Philippines. Instances of discrimination, of places marked "Filipinos Keep Out," were frequently cited and seemed to the Filipinos to be an unhappy omen for the future of "equal rights." The *Manila Chronicle* said in its editorial columns, "At the rate the U.S. Army is taking over Philippine territory, Filipinos will soon live like Indians, on reservations. . . . It seems that there is no need of amending our Constitution to grant Americans 'special rights' in this country. They are making themselves at home even without it, and driving us out into the backyard of our own house."[56]

The administration embarked on an all-out selling campaign, and high officials conducted extensive pro-parity speaking tours all over the Philippines. President Roxas went on a tour of several important provinces in the south during a nine-day air trip.[57] Vice-President Quirino motored to the northern provinces, accompanied by high officials. Senate President José Avelino undertook a southern tour.[58] The speech of Roxas in Iloilo city was reported in the press under the headline, "No Parity, No Money, Says President." The President discussed three reasons why parity should be approved. These were: (1) that Americans were not ruthless exploiters; (2) that the granting of equal rights was in keeping with the foreign policy of the Republic; and (3) that American capital was badly needed for rehabilitation and reconstruction.[59] Senator Eulogio Rodriguez, Sr., president of the Nacionalista party, disagreed. He said that the Philippines was entitled to preferential treatment by virtue of its war effort and that American capital would come to the Philippines with or without parity rights.[60]

Aside from the effusive speeches of political leaders, there was considerable discussion on the question from Filipinos all over the country. A review of the unsolicited letters, both pro and con, published in the *Philippines Free Press*, widely read weekly magazine, gave an interesting picture of average reactions.[61] Some typical comments on the pro side were as follows:

As long as we take our military and economic alliances with the United States seriously and stand behind democracy as opposed to communism, there is no need

[54] *Manila Bulletin*, November 2, 1946.   [55] *Manila Chronicle*, November 20, 1946.
[56] *Ibid.*, November 27, 1946.   [57] *Evening News* (Manila), December 4, 1946.
[58] *Manila Post*, December 5, 1946.
[59] *Manila Courier*, December 8, 1946.
[60] *Manila Post*, December 11, 1946.
[61] "Free Press Readers React to Parity," *Philippines Free Press*, January 11, 1947.

for shouting intruder. We are still part of America insofar as economic and defense schemes are concerned. [From Gulion, Palawan.]

If we are immune to hunger, cold and disease, then there is no need of parity. Is not our present need for economic reconstruction greater than all objections to the parity measure? [From Caloocan, Rizal.]

I am going to vote for parity because it will give us work. [From Samar.]

In these days of want and hunger, sentimental outbursts cannot help us a bit. The needs of the belly the heart cannot fill. [From Bauan, Batangas.]

Similarly revealing comments were offered on the con side:

Parity is a decent term for economic prostitution. [From Malaybalay, Bukidnon.]

Gratitude is one thing and the preservation of personal and national dignity is another. Parity is unfair. Americans will get the lion's share of our resources. [From Polangui, Albay.]

There are absolutely no means by which we can reconcile parity with the preamble to our Constitution. [From Manila.]

Whatever prosperity may accrue, will be prosperity for the Americans and poverty for the rank and file of Filipinos. [From Manila.]

In an editorial anticipating the success of the parity amendment, the *Free Press* said: "Should the expected be realized and the Pros triumph, there should be little or no humiliation in it for the Antis. They have put up a gallant fight but the odds were against them from the beginning. They had to cope with a high-pressured administration machine, and it seems to have been fated that they should take its dust."[62]

When the vote was finally taken, parity won by a large majority. Commenting on the landslide vote, an Associated Press dispatch stated:

Filipinos voted by an overwhelming margin . . . to sacrifice some economic independence for the next twenty-seven years in return for millions of American rehabilitation dollars. . . . However, opponents saw in the heavy stay-away vote a form of "silent rebuke." Only an estimated 40 percent of three million persons registered voted, with such men as former President Sergio Osmeña abstaining. A Roxas administration follower observed, however, that voter apathy is "always evident in a landslide."[63]

There was a widespread impression, even after the vote, that acceptance of parity had been a prerequisite to future American aid. For example, the *Settlement Advocate*, a periodical on rural problems, published on the same page which announced the parity vote a prominently displayed box which said, "Ambassador Joaquin Elizalde arrived in Manila this week with a loan

[62] *Philippines Free Press*, March 8, 1947.
[63] *New York Herald Tribune*, March 12, 1947.

for $75 million from the U.S. Reconstruction Finance Corporation. The check was signed a few hours after the news of parity ratification was relayed to the United States."[64]

On March 14, 1947, shortly after the parity vote, a ninety-nine-year agreement was concluded for United States military bases in the Islands. Under the terms of the agreement fifteen bases were agreed upon, ten of them to be auxiliary training and service establishments. The other five were to be major centers consisting of one important Army and four Navy operating areas, including three fleet centers and one naval air center. Jurisdiction within the bases was granted to the United States government, except when an offense was committed in which both parties were Philippine citizens. In addition to the fifteen bases mentioned, seven additional areas were designated as possible future sites. To meet Filipino objections, it was agreed that no permanent operating bases be established in the centers of population, particularly in Manila.[65]

Although this far-reaching argreement was not signed until over eight months after independence, the basis for it had been laid long before that date. The Tydings-McDuffie Act of 1934 provided for the retention of American naval reservations and fueling stations in the Philippines after independence. According to Manuel Roxas,[66] in 1943 the Commonwealth government in exile had held a series of conversations in Washington on the future of the Philippines, including military relations with the United States. At that time the Filipinos were said to have agreed to the establishment of United States Army, Navy, and Air Force bases in their country after liberation. This agreement was incorporated in a Joint Resolution of the United States Congress, approved by the President on June 29, 1944, providing for additional bases after independence and giving authority to the President of the United States to establish such bases. This policy was adhered to by the Philippine Congress on July 28, 1945, in a resolution which authorized the Philippine President to carry on such negotiations. These began informally in May 1946, but the final agreement was not signed until after the parity referendum was completed.

Just as the bases agreement meant that a certain amount of authority was traded for a certain kind of security, so the acceptance of parity meant that a degree of economic sovereignty had been temporarily renounced in the expectation of economic prosperity. The next major question was the extent to which the administration could make good on its campaign speeches. The great economic problems of agricultural reform, employment, effective taxation, and progress toward industrialization remained. New capital was needed to

[64] *Settlement Advocate* (Manila), March 1947, p. 6.

[65] *Statement of the Philippine Government on the Occasion of the Signing of the Agreement by the Philippine Republic and the United States Concerning Military Bases* (Manila, March 14, 1947).

[66] *Special Message of His Excellency, President Manuel Roxas to the Senate on March 17, 1947* (Manila).

aid in development, but foreign investment would have to be geared to the needs of the economy so that it would benefit the Filipino people as well as the American investors. To achieve such a result, the government would have to be keenly responsive to popular needs and have majority support from all important sections of the urban and rural population.

In an editorial entitled "Great Expectations," the *Philippines Free Press* said that this phrase, borrowed from Dickens, seemed applicable to the parity question. It asked: "Assuming that the plebiscite goes as generally anticipated, and American capital is given the privilege of equality with Filipino capital in developing the country's resources and acquiring franchises for public utilities, will the roseate dreams of the plentitude of such capital be realized?"[67] The editorial went on to discuss some of the internal factors which made capital timid. To these could have been added the opportunities at the time for domestic investment in the United States, and the growing interest in other fields for investment and trade, such as Europe and Latin America. Extremely appropriate as a summary of the press and periodical discussion of the parity issue was the crucial question asked by the *Free Press*: "Great Expectations— will they be realized?"

[67] *Philippines Free Press*, March 8, 1947, p. 10.

Chapter Eight

POLICY IN OPERATION: 1945-47

EVEN while discussion on Philippine legislation in the United States Congress lagged, action on day-to-day problems in the Islands had to proceed. Every effort was made, even immediately after the liberation, to move "back to normal" and restore activity in the Philippines to something resembling its prewar status. In fields where private enterprise was unable to operate, government agencies took over, with the understanding that responsibility would be assumed by business as soon as possible. Emphasis in American policy was twofold: to see that desperately needed commodities were sent to the Philippines, and to facilitate the shipment to the United States of Philippine raw materials in short supply there.

American troops entered Manila on February 3, 1945, and about one month later, on March 5, the first cargo from the liberated Philippines arrived in San Francisco. It consisted of a load of hemp, taken from a Japanese ship ready to sail from Manila harbor.[1] The restoration of economic activity, however, was not so speedy or spectacular. On March 21, 1945, a $60 million program for marketing essential consumer goods in the Philippines was announced, under the authority of the United States Commercial Corporation, a unit of the Foreign Economic Administration. It was planned that 500,000 tons of food, clothing, hardware, drugs, chemicals, and seed would be shipped to the Philippines following an initial six-month period of United States Army relief. The United States Consulate General was opened in Manila on March 27, 1945. On May 5 it was announced that a contract had been signed between the United States Commercial Corporation and the Copra Export Management Company[2] for the purchase of copra in the Philippines. Steps taken in the United States to facilitate normal trade included the licensing of commercial exports to the Philippines on May 28, 1945, and the resumption of limited commercial cargo shipping services. The first commercial ship which brought civilian goods to the Philippines arrived there on August 23, 1945.

Up to September 1, 1945, limited rehabilitation activity in the Philippines

[1] *Christian Science Monitor*, March 7, 1945.

[2] The Copra Export Management Company was a Philippine corporation formed by representatives of five prewar companies engaged in the copra export trade. Additional concerns could also participate. This joint corporation assumed responsibility for procurement on account for the U.S. Commercial Corporation, and acted as its agent in all copra transactions. It was to function only where normal trade could not be conducted, and to dissolve when conditions warranted.

was carried on by the United States military authorities. After that date the Foreign Economic Administration undertook to supply essential civilian goods until such time as normal trade could be re-established. At the same time it arranged for the procurement from the Islands of badly needed staples, such as copra and abacá. As private traders steadily increased the flow of shipments of civilian goods, the activities of the United States Commercial Corporation were curtailed.[3]

The extent of commercial trade could be seen from export and import data for 1945.[4] United States figures indicated that imports of Philippine copra, abacá, and rubber, and a small amount of bristles amounted to the meager sum of $791,000 for that year. The value of average annual imports of all products for 1938–40 was approximately $92 million. Exports from the United States to the Philippines in 1945 were valued at $40 million, over half of which was shipped in November and December. This included approximately $16 million worth of foodstuffs, $4 million of textile products, and $4 million of chemical products, chiefly drugs and medicines. Prewar exports had averaged $93 million annually.

The slow development of activities for real rehabilitation in the Philippines over the spring, summer, and fall of 1945, coupled with the urgent needs, led President Truman to issue, on October 26, eleven directives which called for reports or action on major outstanding questions.[5] The presidential statement included a request to High Commissioner Paul V. McNutt for a prompt investigation of agrarian unrest in the Philippines, to be undertaken with the co-operation of the Commonwealth government. Having indicated that the guerrilla armies "reportedly did good work against the enemy," but, because they did not disband, "constitute a special problem which threatens the stability of the government," President Truman declared, "their legitimate claim to fair treatment and the assistance they rendered in resistance to the enemy required that they be not dealt with in a ruthless manner."

Having noted that "Reports have appeared in the press which indicate that a number of persons who gave aid and comfort to the enemy are now holding important office in the Commonwealth Government," President Truman requested the Attorney General to investigate collaborators and recommend appropriate action. He also ordered the War Department to assist in the training and equipment of a Philippine Constabulary, on a nonmilitary basis, to help maintain order. Other presidential memoranda to the Secretaries of Treasury and War, and to the Veterans Administration, the Export-Import Bank, and the War Shipping Administration sought information on currency, purchasing power, the postion of veterans, business conditions, and available shipping

[3] *Foreign Commerce Weekly*, February 23, 1946, p. 44.

[4] *Ibid.*, April 27, 1946, pp. 3–4.

[5] Text of President Truman's Philippine letters, *New York Herald Tribune*, October 27, 1945.

tonnage in the Philippines. A directive was issued to the Surplus Property Administrator to make surplus medical supplies available without cost to the Commonwealth government, and to the Alien Property Custodian to vest title to all former enemy property in the Philippine government, rather than in the United States Army. Finally, a directive to the Reconstruction Finance Corporation authorized the United States Commercial Corporation to continue operations and, where necessary, to sell goods on credit terms not exceeding two years.

These eleven directives indicated the major needs, and showed what phases of American activity in the Philippines were of particular importance at the time. They were followed, in December 1945, by a statement from Ambassador Edwin Pauley recommending extensive reparations for the Philippines.[6]

The domestic picture in the Philippines at the beginning of 1946 was far from encouraging. Major national issues had to be faced, including the presidential election, the collaboration question, agrarian unrest and violence, and the approach of political independence. Demand for both consumer and producer goods was still extremely high. Very heavy orders placed at the end of 1945 were reflected in extensive shipments from the United States in January 1946, valued at $30 million, half of which was food and textiles.[7]

The expansion of imports brought the cost of living down slightly, but price ceilings for both imported and domestic commodities were not enforced and black markets operated openly.[8] The average cost-of-living index for a wage earner's family in Manila in 1945, based on 1941 as 100, was 693. During the year the index had risen from 560 in March to a high of 752 in July, and fallen to 669 in December. In the last month of 1945 food cost over eight and a half times what it did in 1941, and clothing over ten times as much. The average daily wage in Manila had risen from 2.3 pesos for skilled laborers in 1941 to 5.3 pesos for the period from July to December, 1945. For common laborers the daily wage rose from 1.2 pesos in the prewar year to 3.5 pesos in 1945. Neither increase, however, was adequate to meet the inflated costs.

The sugar industry had suffered major damage as a result both of wartime destruction and of years of neglect under Japanese rule.[9] After the war the Philippines was forced to import sugar for its own use. In addition, a good part of what was available domestically was being diverted to local distillers for use in the manufacture of alcoholic beverages. This sugar was sold, as would be expected, at extremely inflated prices.

Of the main prewar crops, copra and abacá production revived more quickly than did sugar. Tobacco production in March and April, 1946, was estimated

[6] *New York Herald Tribune*, December 12, 1945.

[7] *Foreign Commerce Weekly*, April 27, 1946, p. 4.

[8] J. Bartlett Richards, "Philippine Independence Faces Crippled Agriculture, Industry," *Bataan*, July 1946, pp. 22–27.

[9] *Foreign Commerce Weekly*, January 25, 1947, p. 30.

at about 40 percent of prewar levels. The 1945–46 rice crop was estimated by UNRRA and the Philippine Department of Agriculture and Commerce at 70 percent of prewar. There were serious losses of livestock during the war. Other industries were slow to resume activity, except those directly related to United States Army needs. Of thirty-seven small sawmills operating at the end of 1945, all but nine were run by or for the Army. Inadequate rail and inter-island shipping, general inflationary conditions, and political uncertainties hampered the reconstruction program of the early postwar period.

There was growing labor unrest in the early months of 1946, with large and recurring strikes in all basic fields of activity, including transport, communications, and manufacturing. The first large strike of 1946 was on the Manila Railroad, operated at the time by the United States Army. Transportation was tied up from January 15 to 30, when substantial concessions were finally made to labor, including an increase in the basic daily minimum rate from 2.16 to 4 pesos ($1.08 to $2.00). A strike threat in the Philippine Refining Company was settled by a decision of the Court of Industrial Relations granting an 80 percent wage increase. Strikes occurred in the Elizalde rope factory and the Manila Electric Company, among others. In general, workers sought a minimum daily wage of 5 pesos a day and often settled for about 4 pesos. This represented three times the basic prewar rate, but still did not compensate for the higher cost of living.[10] Of some importance was the waterfront strike, in February 1946, which involved Filipino and American workers, United States Army and Philippine government authorities, and both CIO and AFL pressure. It resulted in an over-all wage increase of about 50 percent on the docks.[11]

On July 4, 1946, political sovereignty was transferred from the United States to the Philippines, and the promise of independence was fulfilled. The date, however, did not serve as a turning point for the economy of the country and in many respects foreign economic relations continued as before.

Two exclusive purchasing agreements concluded by the United States with the new Philippine Republic on August 8, 1946, although of brief duration, underlined the continuing economic tie between the two countries. Under the abacá agreement the U.S. Reconstruction Finance Corporation had the exclusive right from August 8, 1946, to June 30, 1947, to purchase the exportable surplus of the Philippine fiber. The RFC was to advance $2 million to rehabilitate the former Japanese abacá plantations in Davao; in partial repayment 10 percent was to be deducted from the purchase price of all abacá fiber bought by the RFC. In a companion agreement, the Philippine government undertook to sell the entire exportable surplus of copra and coconut oil to the U.S. Commodity Credit Corporation for one year beginning July 1, 1946, at

[10] *Ibid.*, May 18, 1946, pp. 33–34.
[11] Jack Silver, "Philippine Labour Rouses Itself with Strikes: Union Leaders Encouraged by Outlook," *Bataan*, May 1946, pp. 17–19.

the specified price of $103.50 per long ton for copra and 7⅛ cents per pound for coconut oil. The Philippine government agreed not to place any restrictions upon production or export of these products to the United States, which was to handle all purchases for foreign customers.

Commodities purchased under these agreements came into the United States under price ceilings set by OPA regulations, effective domestically. Political developments in the United States, and the impending congressional elections in the early fall of 1946, however, severely weakened the structure of price control. Increasing American prices for Philippine products, coupled with widespread resale abroad at highly inflated figures, meant that purchase agreements at low fixed prices could not continue for long. On November 18, 1946, just over three months after its effective date, the exclusive purchasing agreement for abacá was terminated and controls over both the price and the destination of the fiber were lifted. This was followed by an initial price advance of about 40 percent, and a subsequent period of fluctuations. The copra agreement was similarly terminated late in 1946,[12] and in May 1947 copra was selling for $250 a ton. Thus these two agreements were abruptly abrogated, not because of their exclusive and restrictive character, but rather because they could not work in a period of spiraling prices.

Both Manila and Washington faced numerous administrative and technical problems in implementing some of the provisions of the Trade Act. In some cases confusion resulted from the inexperience and understaffing of the newly established Philippine agencies; in others it was due to lack of foresight in drafting the legislation in the United States. An example of confusion in commercial operations was the attempt to implement the provision that defined "United States articles" as those products containing not more than 20 percent of foreign material.[13] The provision that goods with more than this amount should be treated as foreign goods was applied equally to commodities coming to the United States from the Philippines, and going there from the United States. Difficulties of administration, however, were all on one side. While Philippine products such as abacá and copra created no problems entering this country, to determine the origins of raw materials in a product such as an American automobile entering the Philippines was obviously a very different matter. Another problem was the handling of drawback on duties already paid. These commercial matters took time to work out, and in the early period of independence they produced many technical difficulties which slowed down the resumption of trade.

Further problems arose from the attempt to provide equal treatment for United States and Philippine enterprise and trade. One example of this was the conclusion of an international air transport agreement between the two countries, which provided for the full "five freedoms" of the air based on the

---

[12] *Foreign Commerce Weekly*, January 25, 1947, p. 31.
[13] *Ibid.*, p. 33.

principle of complete reciprocity.[14] This would circumscribe attempts of the Philippine government or Filipino business to provide special privileges for their own airlines, which could scarcely compete with well-established United States facilities. This again raised the question of how an underdeveloped country could find a way to efficient industrialization without some measure of protection.

By the end of 1946 there was improvement in some phases of the Philippine economy, particularly foreign trade, in some aspects of agricultural production, and to a certain degree in wage rates. Industrial production and construction lagged behind. The circulation of Philippine currency in 1946 reached "record breaking amounts,"[15] and controls were ineffective. Financial difficulties and lack of seed, fertilizer, and equipment postponed any substantial expansion in the sugar industry. The tobacco crop for 1945–46 was abnormally low, being estimated at 17,170,000 pounds. The two export crops of the 1946 season were abacá and copra. Abacá production approximated 110 million pounds for the year, or about 28 percent of the prewar output. The output of copra averaged 60,000 tons a month in the latter part of 1946.

There was little industrial activity in 1946. Four factories produced soap and vegetable lard, cigars were manufactured on a limited scale, a number of small sawmills operated, a large brewery and two soft-drink bottling plants functioned in Manila. Mineral output was negligible. Building costs were about four times prewar and supplies particularly hard to get. The cost-of-living index for a Manila family (1941 = 100) was 462 in December 1946, as compared with 669 for the previous December. Food was the most inflated item, costing 5.7 times as much as in 1941. The sharpest drop was in clothing prices, from 9.8 times 1941 figures in January 1946 to 3.7 times in December. Wages had risen slightly to 5.52 pesos a day for skilled and 4.21 for unskilled workers, but they still lagged behind living costs.

According to the Philippine Bureau of Census and Statistics, Philippine exports in 1946 were valued at over 106 million pesos, not including re-exports worth over 22 million pesos. A report of the United States commercial attaché, however, suggested that the figure should be closer to 140 million pesos, because large amounts of copra loaded on United States Army ships were not included in the bureau's figures, which also omitted data on ores and metals.[16] Of the Philippine valuation of exports at 106 million pesos, over 76 million, or about 75 percent, went to the United States. According to the commercial attaché's data, goods worth 110 million pesos, or about 80 percent of the total, went to the United States. The leading export was copra, which accounted for over 78 million pesos, according to Philippine figures. Significantly absent from the

[14] New York Times, November 5, 1946.
[15] Foreign Commerce Weekly, January 25, 1947, p. 30.
[16] Report of J. Bartlett Richards, commercial attaché, on "Philippine Foreign Trade," April 15, 1947, based on figures from the Philippine Bureau of Census and Statistics.

export list were the prewar commodities of sugar, gold, embroideries, and pineapples.

Imports in 1946, according to the Philippine statistics, amounted to almost 592 million pesos, of which over 515 million, or 87 percent, came from the United States mainland and the Territory of Hawaii. The main imported commodities were grains, tobacco, textiles, and metals.

In a candid report on the "State of the Nation" for 1946, Dr. Leon Ma. Gonzáles, director of the Philippine Bureau of Census and Statistics, indicated that, while some progress was made, on the whole reconstruction was not rapid and planning for future development not vigorous.[17] He pointed out that the Filipinos planted smaller crops than formerly; for the first half of 1946 only a little over 1.5 million hectares of rice were planted, about four-fifths the prewar acreage. Corn production for the same period was about 60 percent of the prewar; livestock and poultry were sadly depleted.

Some progress was reported in the building industry, which accounted for an estimated 50 million pesos' worth of construction and repair during the year. Industrial production, however, was very slow. In the cigar and cigarette industry average monthly production in 1946 was only 15 percent of prewar; in the distilling industry the total yearly output hardly equaled the average monthly production in 1941. Textile production for the first eight months of 1946 was only about one-fourth that of a similar prewar period, cement production was about 30 percent of prewar, and the manufacture of shoes had fallen drastically.

Of particular interest were Dr. Gonzáles' comments on employment. He reported that by the end of 1946, nearly two years after liberation, the United States Army was still the biggest employer of labor in the Philippines. In November 1945 there were 230,000 Filipino civilians working for the Army. This number gradually decreased and by October 1946 was less than 90,000. Commenting on the employment situation in 1946, Dr. Gonzáles stated:

There is no glossing over the fact that the unemployment problem in the country is not only great but acute as well. The President was fully conscious of this when, on his election, he urged the people to join hands with him in the war against the twin specters of inflation and unemployment.

In addition to those who are gradually crossed out of Army payrolls, there are an estimated 400,000 guerrillas in Manila and the provinces who have not been inducted into the Army and are thus considered displaced persons. Also the paring down of Philippine Army personnel to peace-time strength will add about 100,000 more unemployed. The acuteness of the situation is indicated clearly by the fact that over 50,000 job seekers were registered in the Department of Labor from August to October 1946.

[17] Dr. Leon Ma. Gonzáles, Statistical Report on the "State of the Nation," 1946, released by the Philippine Embassy, Washington, D.C.

There are no available data as to the exact number of persons out of work in Greater Manila area, but it is conservatively estimated at 145,000. These are the men and women who roam the city streets and storm the gates of big firms looking for jobs.[18]

In addition, wage rates did not go up in proportion to living costs. According to Dr. Gonzáles, real wages at the end of 1946 were "only about half of the wages paid before the war." The situation of the city wage earners, however, could not be considered as typical of the country as a whole, because agricultural wages were not included in these cost-of-living statistics.

For a rural economy like the Philippines, where much of the income was distributed in kind, an approximation of national income was particularly difficult to make. The Joint Philippine-American Finance Commission[19] estimated net national product in the Philippines at 2.8 billion pesos in 1946, the equivalent of 863 million at 1938 prices, as compared with an actual 1938 net national product of 994 million pesos. If both estimates are measured in terms of 1938 prices, the amount of goods and services produced in 1946 was 15 percent less than in 1938. If one allows for a 1938–46 population increase from 16 to 18.5 million, actual output per capita in 1946 was 24 percent below that of 1938. Another estimate, "Goods and Services Available for Philippine Consumption and Investment," which took account of imports as well as national product, indicated that goods available for consumption in 1946, figured at 1938 prices, approximated those available in the prewar year. This did not include such items as rural house construction and boat building. But the "prosperity" that this estimate suggested could be traced to two unstable and short-term factors: exceptionally high prices for copra and large United States expenditures.

In the field of business Dr. Gonzáles noted extensive business activity in 1946, wtih average monthly investment almost 332 percent above prewar. In 1946 a total of 808 corporations with a paid-up capital of over 21 million pesos and 447 partnerships with a paid-up capital of 24 million pesos was registered. About three-fourths of the stock corporations were Filipino-controlled, while Chinese firms predominated in the partnerships.

While the flurry of business activity appeared to be a sign of prosperity, an analysis of the fields which attracted capital was disappointing. It showed that the emphasis was on rapid turnover, rather than on long-term capital invest-

---

[18] *Ibid.*, p. 5.

[19] *Report and Recommendations of the Joint Philippine-American Finance Commission,* H.R. Doc. 390 (Washington, July 8, 1947), pp. 14–16. For details on the techniques of estimating used, see *ibid.,* Appendix IV, "The National Income," pp. 100–5. An approximation of national income has been obtained by analyzing the gross national product, or all the goods and services produced including replacement costs. From that total, depreciation was subtracted. Other income, for which no payments were made or services rendered, was then added.

ment. This was revealed in the following figures, for the first six months of 1946:

CONSOLIDATED PAID-UP CAPITAL OF NEWLY REGISTERED STOCK CORPORATIONS
AND PARTNERSHIPS, ACCORDING TO KIND OF BUSINESS,
JANUARY–JUNE, 1946

Business	Number	Amount of Capital (*pesos*)
General merchandise	217	7,562,626
Import and export	110	2,250,493
Transportation	44	1,516,248
Lumber	51	1,270,895
Construction	21	883,420
Cinema	20	813,150
Manufacturing	18	785,261
Real estate	5	638,250
Agriculture	18	539,105
Brokerage	19	491,100
Motor supplies	6	364,850
Dry goods	7	360,200
Broadcasting	2	335,000
Educational	25	308,157
Financing	2	300,000
Other	135	3,415,259
Total	700	21,834,014

Source: *Yearbook of Philippine Statistics, 1946* (Manila, 1947), pp. 342–46. Data from Securities and Exchange Commission.

According to this data, 45 percent of new investment capital in the period cited was in the fields of general merchandise and imports and exports. More new money went into "cinema" than into manufacturing, more was absorbed by brokerage activities than by motor supplies. This was not a complete picture, for it included only newly registered firms, but the problem of directing capital to necessary and productive industry was obvious. This illustrated how impossible it was to measure the effect of a high level of current business activity on long-term development, without considering the character and direction of investment.

In 1947 evaluation of the economic situation differed, depending on whether the desired goal was reconstructing the past, stimulating present activity, or planning for future stability. Many businessmen reported excellent progress toward rehabilitation. C. A. Richards, a director of the export division of the Interchemical Corporation and president of the Philippine-American Chamber of Commerce at the time, told that body that "The Philippine Government has taken energetic steps to put the economy of the country on a sound basis."[20]

[20] *New York Times*, January 22, 1948.

He commented favorably on the expansion of Philippine trade, the increase in government revenues, the balancing of the budget, improvement in enforcement of law and order, measures to eliminate black-market activities, and a better balance between demand and supply of consumer goods.

In studying the period from April through August, 1947, a U.S. Department of Commerce analysis reported "unmistakable signs of a trend toward the pattern of basic economy long characteristic of the Philippines."[21] This meant a return to concentration on a few export crops and a high level of imports, particularly of consumer goods.

By 1947 trading activity in the Philippines was at an all-time high. Imports, however, were more than double exports, and only heavy dollar receipts and inflated prices for copra gave the Philippine economy its look of prosperity. Imports reached 1,022.7 million pesos; in money terms this was nearly three and a half times the prewar peak, and 42 percent over the 1946 level. Foodstuffs were the leading item, followed by textiles; together they accounted for about one-half of total imports. Philippine exports amounted to 531.1 million pesos (including re-exports of 45.1 million), over four times the 1946 figure. Of this total, however, copra alone amounted to 354.4 million pesos; coconut products and abacá together accounted for over 90 percent of the total value of all exports.

In addition to the striking imbalance of exports and imports, there was an interesting shift in the movement of goods. Commodities continued to come from the United States, to the extent of 87 percent of all imports in 1946 and about 85 percent in 1947. Exports, however, shifted in destination. In 1946 some 72 percent of Philippine goods went to the United States; by 1947 this had dropped to 57 percent.

Copra was by far the leading agricultural product of 1947; production totaled 1.1 million tons, as compared with 650,000 tons in 1946. Prices were very high, but unsteady, reaching $250 per long ton, f.o.b., in March 1947, falling to $135 in July, and rising again by the end of the year. Abacá production in 1947 was 796,000 bales, as compared with 392,000 in the previous year. All of the 1946–47 sugar crop of 84,571 tons was used to fill domestic needs. The sugar crop for the 1947–48 season, however, was approximately 400,000 tons. Tobacco had not recovered from wartime damage, and production rose very slowly. The rice crop reached 1.3 million metric tons, which was somewhat under prewar production. Needs, of course, were greater because of increased population. The numbers of livestock were low; the 1948 cattle population was estimated at about 60 percent of prewar.

Industrial production continued to be slow in 1947. In the Manila area, for example, the Manila Electric Company reported that industrial consumption of electric power in December 1947 was less than half of that in October 1941.

<hr>

21 *Foreign Commerce Weekly*, October 11, 1947, p. 16. See also Appendix Tables I to IV.

Twenty of the forty-one prewar sugar centrals were in operation in 1947; saw-mill capacity about equaled that of 1941; two rope factories produced only one-half of what three had done in 1941. Cigar factories operated at only a fraction of the prewar rate, producing about 60 million cigars, mainly for domestic consumption, as compared with an annual prewar output of over 300 million. The embroidery industry functioned at about one-quarter of prewar production.

The government-financed National Development Company was not very active in 1947. Its operations were confined to a textile mill and the Cebu Portland Cement Company. Three gold mines were in operation in that year, producing gold valued at about 4 million pesos (at the official rate), as compared with about 60 million pesos before the war. Some refractory-grade chromite was mined, but no copper and negligible amounts of manganese.

In 1947, 6,952 building permits were issued, an increase over the 1946 figure of 5,359, while construction expenditures rose from 47,527,000 pesos in 1946 to 88,264,000 in 1947. This did not mean, however, that building activity was taking place in the most essential areas. Reports from American Embassy officials stated that the south port area was the scene of intensive renovation, in which American traders and businessmen played a prominent part, and which included the repair of a number of downtown office buildings and hotels and many retail stores. But this report added:

In the north port area, however, new construction was at a standstill and in the very center of Manila many streets remained all but impassable. Students of the University of the Philippines assembled in ruins, and most Government offices were in quarters which precluded efficient operation. Throughout the city impro-vised shelters of squatters and the homes of most lower-wage white-collar workers remained run-down and crowded.

The year witnessed a flourishing growth of high-priced construction of dwell-ings in the suburbs of Manila, particularly in Quezon City, and it was reported that, in the southern islands, there was a substantial increase in the number of new warehouses, places of entertainment, and houses in Cebu. . . .[22]

Transportation, particularly inter-island shipping, was somewhat improved in 1947. Of the 5,035 bridges destroyed by the war, about 3,000 were replaced with temporary structures, but only two spans were permanently rebuilt. There were 7,167 miles of national roads open to transit at the end of the year. Through service was operating on the government-owned Manila Railroad main line south of the city; but there were serious fiscal problems, and opera-tions were conducted at a substantial deficit. In May 1947 the airlines of the Far East Air Transport, Inc., were taken over by the Philippine Air Lines,

[22] This statement and data on conditions in 1947 were taken from the *International Reference Service*, U.S. Department of Commerce, Office of International Trade, *Economic Review of the Republic of the Philippines, 1947* (Washington, December 1948).

which made about fifty airplanes available for domestic use. International flight facilities were greatly expanded and in August PAL was granted an American Civil Aeronautics Board permit to fly the trans-Pacific route on a regular schedule.

The number of commercial broadcasting stations increased from two to six in 1947, including an outlet of the Philippine Department of Foreign Affairs and a short-wave relay station for the Voice of America.

Although the superficial aspect of the Philippine economy was that of an active trading community, neither production figures nor the character of industrial planning gave much promise of steady development. Many observers were concerned about the economy's lack of balance and uncertain future. For example, M. Z. Landicho, Manila staff correspondent of the magazine *Bataan*, wrote:

The postwar export boom of the Philippines which so far has been financed largely through the sales of copra products and by the "pipeline" from America, is in the final analysis a program arranged by the United States to accelerate the economic recovery of our devastated area. But accelerating the return of prosperous trade predicated on artificial, high prices of a few export commodities and the mere underwriting of recovery during the transition to peace time economy is not an adequate solution to world economic stability.

At the present time, trade and industry in this country are thriving, but there are indications that serious lack of balance is gradually developing, apart from the danger of inflation. . . . During this postwar era, when the Philippines is now the "arsenal of copra industry," these raw materials are considerably being expanded. In the meantime, according to an observer, "the economy that takes shape in this rapid expansion will be unbalanced. It will be an extreme example of a temporary concentration on export commodities and capital outlays far in excess of any conceivable long-run trend."[23]

The cost-of-living index for Manila, based on 1941, fell to 379 in March 1947. There were reports of heavy inventories, such as a *Foreign Commerce Weekly* dispatch which stated that "inventories of consumer's essential supplies (rice, textiles, flour and canned milk) were heavy—stocks of flour and milk, troublesomely so."[24] A comment in the *Far East Trader* in March 1947 reported:

Eyebrows were lifted in Manila last week at the first signs of a "buyers' market" in the Philippines—or anywhere else in the Orient, for that matter. . . . Manila department stores held "bargain sales" with dry goods marked down 20 percent and more, and canned goods, shoes, and other items reduced to clear. . . . Trade observers think this may be the signal for declines in still other commodities where the supply is beginning to meet the accumulated demand.[25]

[23] M. Z. Landicho, "Unemployment Is No Real Problem in P.I., but Shortage of Capital for Development Is," *Bataan*, September 1947, p. 5.

[24] *Foreign Commerce Weekly*, October 11, 1947, p. 16.

[25] *Far East Trader*, March 5, 1947.

It was unlikely, however, that the supply had met the real need of the Filipinos for food, textiles, and other consumer goods. More likely it had met the "economic demand," or "desire plus ability to pay."

Although United States military expenditures and war damage payments meant there was more money in circulation, the ultimate effect on the economy was not apparent. For example, the Department of Commerce reported: "It is noted that much of the past two years' money income from United States military expenditure, which entered the community at the 'grass roots' level, has found its way into the stronger hands of the merchant and investing class."[26] Industrial unrest continued in 1947; fifteen strikes were sponsored by the Congress of Labor Organizations by midyear. In May 1947 seven strikes which involved about 5,000 workers occurred concurrently, including a dispute in the textile mills. In June there was a strike involving 3,500 men in the shipyards.[27]

While there has been agreement on the need for foreign investment in the Philippines, there have been differences of opinion on where the money should go. One American correspondent, Robert P. Martin, reported from Manila: "American capital wants quick and profitable returns. Sugar centrals, coconut oil refineries, mines—not fertilizer plants, processing industries, textile factories—are objectives of American interest."[28] The country, he said, was dollar-rich on the consumer level, but faced widespread unemployment in the sugar-producing and mining areas, and as the United States Army scaled down its construction, unemployment would increase. According to Mr. Martin, "the overall economic picture is superficially bright." But he went on to say:

The falseness of this prosperity, however, is revealed by official government figures on rehabilitation and industrialization. . . . The key to sound employment of Philippine resources lies in the dollars expected to be spent by the U.S. here during the next few years. These dollars are now being used for luxury and non-essential imports. Last year only 10 percent of imports was in capital goods. The Philippines is sounder than most Asiatic countries, but the government is not utilizing its wealth properly. . . . New riches go into consumption rather than investment. Sound taxes, domestic borrowing and encouragement of private saving would provide the government with a large part of the funds it now wants to borrow abroad.[29]

[26] *Foreign Commerce Weekly*, October 11, 1947, p. 16.
[27] *Ibid.*, p. 18.
[28] *New York Post*, December 12, 1947.
[29] *Ibid.*

CHAPTER NINE

POOR LITTLE RICH COUNTRY:
THE FINANCE COMMISSION REPORT

Two years after the war ended it was evident that, despite extensive American grants for rehabilitation and trade arrangements designed to cushion the shock of independence, Philippine economic recovery had been slow and spotty. United States grants and military expenditures in the Islands had stimulated a feverish business activity, the benefits of which were very unevenly distributed. Available funds were being used to make quick commercial profits rather than for long-term productive investment. Little progress had been made in laying the foundations for a sound economy. Philippine finances were being sustained only by a flow of dollars which would soon come to an end. A superficial prosperity concealed the fundamentally precarious economic position of the new state. The continued insurgency of the Hukbalahap reflected both Communist activity and an acute agrarian problem.

This situation was of concern not only to thoughtful Filipinos but also to the United States, which still felt some responsibility for the welfare of its former ward. Moreover, the development of the cold war was by this time pushing the United States into a position of leadership in strengthening the power of the western world—military, political, and economic. As the Philippines was a key point in United States Pacific defenses, the internal stability of the country was a matter of direct interest to the American government.

Since the most immediate threat to Philippine stability appeared to lie in the field of government finance, this topic became the subject of study in 1947 by a joint commission representing both countries, whose report was a milestone in postwar Philippine-American relations. The work of the commission can best be understood against the background of earlier Philippine financial history, both before the war and in the immediate postwar period.

Before the war the Philippine peso, which was freely exchangeable for 50 cents (U.S.), was for all practical purposes a dollar bill cut in half. This convertibility ensured the security of foreign investments and promoted overseas trade. But it did not meet the basic need for national development. The main financial problems faced by the Filipino people have been those associated with the distribution of national income, budget appropriations, and the tax and revenue structure. In these terms it was possible after the war to describe the Philippines as the "poor little rich country" of the Far East. There were budget deficits because of low corporate tax rates, inadequate tax collections, and poor use of funds. On the other hand, there was a stable currency because of large dollar reserves and the high level of postwar United States disbursements.

As a result of its former ties with the United States, the Philippine Republic had a "hard" currency, one of the few in the postwar world, and in the early postwar years there was no lack of dollar exchange. Furthermore, the Bell Act not only pegged the peso to the dollar for twenty-eight years, but prohibited any alterations in the exchange mechanism without the agreement of the President of the United States. This served as a kind of guaranty to investors of American money in the Philippines, in the possible event of capital withdrawals (until the flight of dollars in 1949 necessitated exchange controls). The monetary situation just after independence, however, did not differ in any substantial way from that existing when the Philippines was under American sovereignty.

The foundation of the currency system was the Philippine Gold Standard Act of 1903, which sought to establish a form of the gold standard that would function automatically, without the need to circulate gold coin or maintain a gold reserve.[1] This was accomplished by continuing the circulation of the silver peso, but maintaining it at parity with a theoretical gold peso of 12.9 grains, a unit with a gold content exactly half of what was then the United States dollar. The Gold Standard Fund, consisting of silver coins held in the Treasury in Manila and dollar deposits in United States banks, was used to maintain parity. Adjustment proceeded in the following manner: the Insular Treasurer sold drafts on dollar deposits of the Gold Standard Fund in exchange for pesos and held the pesos in Manila, while the depository banks in the United States could sell drafts on the Manila part of the fund in exchange for dollar deposits in the States. This should have meant automatic adjustment of money in circulation. In addition, the Silver Certificate Reserve, consisting of silver pesos against which certificates had been issued, was established to maintain parity of the silver certificate with the silver peso.

This scheme broke down, partly because currency circulation was not contracted as planned, and partly because large amounts of the Gold Standard Fund were invested in the Philippines in nonliquid loans. In a revision of the currency system in 1918, the Gold Standard Fund and Silver Certificate Reserve were combined into a single Currency Reserve Fund. Further difficulties were encountered, and from 1919 to 1921 the Philippines was practically on a paper standard. Evidently there had been repeated violations of the intent of the legislation, and the Philippine National Bank had acquired nearly the entire dollar balances of the currency reserve, which had been dissipated by the sale of drafts. Paper currency had been used to expand loans and invest-

[1] Discussion of the background of the currency system is based on George Luthringer, *The Gold Exchange Standard in the Philippines* (Princeton, 1934), a comprehensive study of prewar fiscal problems in the Philippines.

ments, leaving in its wake inflation and instability. In 1922 there was a large Insular government bond issue to restore the depleted reserves, and the currency law was revised to something very closely resembling the original provisions of the 1903 act. A separate Gold Standard Fund and Treasury Certificate Fund were established; the latter could consist in part of bank deposits in the United States, and certificates could be issued against the silver peso. Thus the Philippine currency system was both conservative and inflexible.

Under this plan currency reserves in the Philippines were excessive. According to the law, Treasury certificates had to be backed by a 100 percent dollar reserve. In addition, the Gold Standard Fund, which was the adjustment mechanism, had to include reserves for not less than 15 percent of Philippine currency, either in circulation or available therefor. This included both coin and Treasury certificates, even though the latter were already fully secured by dollar deposits. On December 31, 1932, for example, the total currency of the Philippines in circulation or available therefor was 101.5 million pesos, of which 72.2 million was actually in circulation. Total cash reserves amounted to 123 percent of money in circulation or available therefor, and 173 percent of money actually in circulation. United States currency and bank deposits amounted to 102 percent of money in circulation or available therefor, and 143 percent of money actually in circulation.[2]

At the time of the United States monetary devaluation in 1934, Philippine deposits in American banks amounted to about $56 million. The Secretary of the Treasury was authorized to establish a Philippine credit for almost $24 million, which represented the increase in value of the gold equivalent of the Philippine Gold Standard Fund and Treasury Certificate Fund on balance on January 31, 1934, less interest.[3]

Thus the Philippine government in the Commonwealth period had a stable, conservative currency, closely tied to the American dollar. This was the position at the beginning of the war.

In spite of the years of occupation and the wartime devastation, the Philippine government was able to retain control over its currency reserves, since the United States served as banker for the country. In a speech in April 1943, Jaime Hernández, then Auditor General of the Philippines under the Osmeña regime, indicated that the Commonwealth government would be as sound financially at the end of the war as it was at the beginning. He said:

It was very fortunate for the Philippines that, when the war broke out, most of the funds of the Philippine Government were on deposit either in the Treasury of the United States or in depository banks in this country. It was fortunate, too,

[2] *Ibid.*, p. 234.

[3] The measure authorizing this action, Public Law No. 419, 73d Cong., was passed by a vote of 188 to 47 by the House of Representatives on June 14, 1934, and unanimously by the Senate on the preceding day.

that when the Japanese captured Manila, they were not able to seize any sizable amount of the Government funds left in the Islands. The Philippine Treasury certificates or paper money were taken to Corregidor, and after they had been properly recorded and accounted for, they were destroyed by burning. The Government gold bullion, which Japan would have made any sacrifice to obtain, was taken out of Corregidor in a submarine and brought to the United States, where it is deposited to the credit of the Philippine Commonwealth. Most of the securities and bonds owned by our Government, as well as the Coconut Oil Excise Tax Fund which the United States was refunding to the Commonwealth, are also on deposit in the Federal Treasury of the United States.[4]

The ratio of currency reserve to outstanding note issue in the Philippines was indirectly augmented because of the destruction and loss of bills during and after the war. Currency circulation in 1946 was estimated at about 800 million pesos, backed by over $400 million of reserve.

The background of the currency situation has been reviewed in some detail, as it is an important part of American-Philippine relations. As both keeper of funds and guardian of policy, the United States undoubtedly conserved substantial resources for the new government and placed the Philippines in the enviable position of being one of the few war-torn countries with monetary resources. However, one of the most urgent needs facing the new government after the war was to secure current operating funds. How to meet the budget was uppermost among fiscal problems. Reserves accumulated in the United States and accounts which were available from the coconut oil tax helped the hard-pressed government.

From the time that civilian government was restored in February 1945 until June 30, the end of the fiscal year, Commonwealth expenditures were estimated at 23.3 million pesos, of which more than half was budgeted for the Department of Instruction and Information. Revenues for the same period were estimated at 1.8 million pesos.[5] Visible assets of the government in October 1945 were 163 million pesos, including 26 million on hand, 7 million anticipated income, and 80 million from the coconut oil excise tax.[6] This last amount had been released on November 9, when President Truman signed a bill unfreezing Philippine funds from excise and coconut oil taxes held in the United States Treasury.[7]

In addition, over 50 million pesos were anticipated from the Philippine Amendment to the Exchange Standard Fund. The former provision, which had called for reserves against Treasury certificates, already backed 100 percent by dollar deposits, was abolished, and the reserve requirement of the Exchange

[4] Statement of Jaime Hernández, Office of War Information broadcast, San Francisco, April 3, 1943.

[5] *Foreign Commerce Weekly*, July 14, 1945, pp. 26–29.

[6] *Ibid.*, December 22, 1945.

[7] *New York Times*, November 10, 1945.

Standard Fund was set at only 15 percent. Thus one of the overprotective aspects of the Philippine currency system was discontinued, and the funds released provided badly needed income for current government expenditures.

The extent to which prewar assets and reserves held in the United States helped the Philippine government in the first postwar years can be seen from the budget figures.[8] In fiscal 1946, receipts were 286.9 million pesos and expenditures 228.1 million. Income included 110.4 million pesos transferred from the Coconut Oil Excise Tax Fund, 58.1 million from the Sugar Processing Tax Fund, 59.7 million from the Exchange Standard Fund, and only 58 million from taxes and other ordinary sources. For the following year, fiscal 1947, expenditures were estimated at 347.2 million pesos and receipts at 183.3 million. The deficit was to be made up by using the balance of the previous year, and by securing budgetary assistance from the U.S. Reconstruction Finance Corporation. Actual receipts, however, especially from income taxes, exceeded expectations.

The budget figures reflected changing emphases on the part of the government. Expenditures for national defense, for example, increased fourfold over prewar figures, and allocations for education doubled. Relatively minor adjustments were made in expenditures for agriculture, commerce, health, and public welfare. An extraordinary appropriation was made in 1946 and 1947 for the Department of Finance, because of a 30 million peso allocation to local and provincial governments and appropriations to cover the Philippine subscription to the Bretton Woods agreement. A significant figure in the fiscal 1946 budget was the 13 million peso appropriation for back pay for legislators and other government employees. This was because Philippine congressmen had voted back pay in full to themselves for the entire period of the Japanese occupation, and to government employees for about six weeks.

There were numerous indications that it was not merely money, but responsible financial administration, that was required in the Philippines. As early as August 1945 a United States Department of Commerce publication stated: "Although national income is very large in terms of currency circulation, no means have as yet been devised of reaching most of this income through taxation."[9] Part of the problem of securing funds was the slowness of some agencies to appropriate moneys already allocated. Other difficulties arose from the legal procedures involved. For example, the rehabilitation allocation of $520 million was a substantial sum, but large payments could not be made until after Philippine ratification of the Trade Act, which could in turn be effective only after constitutional amendment and nation-wide referendum.

Another major component of United States government expenditures in the Philippines after the war was the money used for military purposes and

[8] *Report and Recommendations of the Joint Philippine-American Finance Commission*, H.R. Doc. 390 (Washington, July 8, 1947), pp. 18–24.
[9] *Foreign Commerce Weekly*, August 11, 1945, p. 25.

for the maintenance of American armed forces in the Islands.[10] In the prewar years 1928–40, total American expenditures in the Philippines averaged 78 million pesos a year, of which 40 million was for the Army and Navy. In 1946 United States government expenditures totaled 672 million pesos, of which 579 million went to the Army and Navy.

It is interesting to compare the amount of goods and services used by American armed services with those available to the whole of the Philippine economy. Gross national product for 1946 was 3,228 million pesos; subtracting 106 million of domestic exports, 3,122 million worth of domestic goods and services were retained. To this should be added commercial imports (less re-exports) and other supplies such as UNRRA. This gave a figure of 4,217 million pesos, representing goods and services available in the country in 1946. Over 12 percent of this total, 516 million pesos, was made up of imports into the Philippines for the use of American armed forces, while 3,701 million represented the amount available for Philippine consumption and investment. This may be compared with the figure for goods and services consumed by United States armed forces in 1938, before Philippine independence, which was 3 percent of the total.[11]

It was within this four-sided frame of reference—trade, currency, budgetary needs, and American expenditures—that the question of foreign loans to the Philippines was viewed. In May 1946 Manuel Roxas, the President-elect, invited American investments to his country, saying that if United States capital did not "rush into this economic vacuum," other investors would fill the need.[12] On May 14, 1946, Mr. Roxas told the United States Congress that the Philippine government would need $400 million in reconstruction loans in the next five years and $100 million during the first fiscal year to "support the bare essentials of rehabilitation and social reconstruction." The proposal for a $100 million loan, which would help in balancing the budget, was strongly backed by Mr. McNutt, but the National Advisory Council on International Monetary and Financial Problems, after investigation, reduced the recommended amount to $75 million. In a statement read before the Committee on Banking and Currency, House of Representatives, on July 24, 1946, Secretary of the Treasury John Snyder explained the position. He said:

Although it is the feeling of the National Advisory Council that there are a number of measures which the Philippine Government could itself take to produce income in addition to the amount that is shown in their budget estimates, the National Advisory Council's figure of $75,000,000 is an outside estimate of the amount

[10] Figures taken from various tables presented in Finance Commission Report, op. cit., pp. 93, 104, 105.

[11] This does not mean that the goods imported for the use of United States armed forces would otherwise be available to Filipinos, but it offers a contrast between the needs of American installations and the national income available for the Philippine economy.

[12] New York Times, May 12, 1946.

required even if the Philippine Government took no steps to increase its revenue beyond those outlined in its budget.[13]

Moreover, Secretary Snyder indicated that further study was needed. He continued: "We do not now have sufficient facts upon which to consider the Philippine Government's needs for the next five years. It would be unfortunate if the infant Philippine Republic were to be saddled with an external debt of this size if it were not necessary."[14]

The position taken by Secretary Snyder was supported at the hearings by Mr. Clayton, who spoke for the State Department.[15] He said the $75 million figure was arrived at after checking Philippine expenditures, payable receipts, cash on hand, and the general financial situation. The granting of a $75 million loan was no commitment to grant the Philippine request for $400 million over a five-year period, but was intended only to meet the current deficit of the year with sufficient leeway to provide a $10 million balance at the end of fiscal 1947. With regard to the amounts to be extended and the negotiation of terms, a good deal was left to the discretion of the Secretary of the Treasury. To study further aspects of the Philippine fiscal and budgetary problems, a joint Philippine-American financial mission was dispatched to Manila in January 1947, and submitted its report in July.

In the latter part of 1946 some efforts were made in the Philippines toward conserving and effectively utilizing existing resources. In addressing the Philippine Congress on September 25, 1946, for example, President Roxas proposed a reconstruction plan designed to make the country less dependent on United States capital. He asked for, and later received, authority to create a Rehabilitation Finance Corporation capitalized at about $150 million, patterned after the United States RFC, which would grant loans to private individuals or corporations, government agencies, consumer co-operatives, and agricultural developments, among others. He proposed to finance the agency through sale of United States surplus property worth $100 million allocated to the Philippine government, through withdrawals up to $50 million from the Treasury Certificate Fund, representing excess reserves because of currency lost or destroyed during the war, and by absorption of $10 million of assets of two existing government corporations, the Agricultural and Industrial Board and the Financial Rehabilitation Board.[16]

Disturbed political conditions, however, made effective economic action difficult. Less than three months later a report of a trip made by President Roxas in his campaign for passage of the parity amendment revealed some of the actual conditions. Mr. Roxas and his official party toured the southern Philippines. According to a *New York Times* dispatch:

At every place the party stopped they met reports of excessive unemployment

[13] Hearings before the Committee on Banking and Currency of the House of Representatives on Financial Aid to the Philippines, July 24, 1946, press release, p. 2.
[14] *Ibid.*   [15] *Ibid.*   [16] *New York Times*, September 26, 1946.

and of the spreading influences of graft and corruption among government officials and influential moneyed people alike. . . . At all the stopping places, Bacolod (in Occidental Negros); Iloilo on the Island of Panay; his home town, Capiz, on the same island; Zamboanga and Davao and Cagayan (Misamis) all in Mindanao, Mr. Roxas found graft and corruption prevalent. Maldistribution of crop loans through branches of the Philippine National Bank is one of the worst irregularities.

Through the National Land Resettlement Administration, a prewar semi-government agency, millions of pesos were made available after the liberation for crop loans. Mr. Roxas was informed that rich planters and government officials had obtained the major portion of these loans.

It was found that loans had been made to fictitious tenants, supposedly secured by crops. Later it was found that there were no tenants and no crops and the money could not be recovered. . . .[17]

Political considerations also affected recommended tax legislation. In October the Philippine Congress approved twelve tax bills which, it was hoped, would increase the revenues of the Republic by at least 30 million pesos during the coming fiscal year. War profits and black-market gains were to be taxed, and graduated income taxes were to be levied.[18] On the other hand, in a move to attract new American capital to the Republic, the Congress of the Philippines also passed a law providing for complete tax exemption for new and necessary industries. This act, approved on September 30, 1946, came at a time when there was a desperate need for governmental revenues. The text stated:

Section 1. Any persons, partnership, company, or corporation who or which shall engage in a new and necssary industry shall, for a period of four years from the date of the organization of such industry, be entitled to exemption from the payment of all internal revenue taxes directly payable by such person, partnership, company, or corporation in respect to said industry.

Section 2. The President of the Philippines shall, upon recommendation of the Secretary of Finance, periodically determine the qualifications that the industries should possess to be entitled to the benefits of this Act.[19]

While the Philippines could undoubtedly have utilized both reconstruction loans and private business investment, the general financial situation was not entirely a result of an inadequate amount of dollars poured into the economy, for much depended on how they were used. This was made amply clear in July 1947, in the Report of the Joint Philippine-American Finance Commission. This group, which comprised three Filipino and three American members, had been set up to investigate "the financial and budgetary problems of the Philippine Government and to make recommendations thereon—with refer-

[17] *Ibid.*, December 15, 1946.
[18] *Ibid.*, October 10, 1946.
[19] Congress of the Republic of the Philippines, Republic Act No. 35, September 30, 1946.

ence to taxes, budget, public debt, currency and banking reform, exchange and trade problems, reconstruction and development."[20]

In presenting its recommendations, the Finance Commission warned:

The Commission regards the next few years as a period of national emergency; not in the sense that survival is at stake, but in the sense that emergency measures and an emergency national psychology will be required if the country is to grasp the opportunity for rapid economic development which is presented.[21]

The unique financial position of the Philippines resulted from the flow of imports and dollars both to compensate the Philippine government and people for their war losses, and to achieve American military objectives in the Pacific. It was estimated by the commission that the Philippines, in the next few years, would have received enough foreign exchange to buy about double the amount of goods and services which could be earned by exports alone. How these resources would be used was the key question.

The foreign exchange balance sheet has been particularly important to the Philippines, because of its dependence on foreign trade. There were two major trends discernible to the commission in the future balance-of-payments position. The first was the expansion of United States payments, which would, however, decline sharply by 1949, and almost disappear by 1951. The second was the revival of the export trade, to be followed by a probable decline when trade preferences with the United States were gradually removed after 1954.[22]

Although an important criterion for international comparison, the balance-of-payments position, studied alone, did not give a rounded picture. Internal conditions, such as distribution of income, could not be taken into account, nor could administrative weaknesses, inefficiencies, and inexperience. Foreign exchange assets meant little to a people unable to translate them into the goods and services related to daily living. Where such a large proportion of those assets arose from unearned income, there was no guaranty of future prosperity.

The commission recognized that, to move in the direction of a sound economy, the Philippine government would have to strengthen its control over its fiscal and monetary system. Recommendations of far-reaching significance were made along these lines, particularly concerning taxation, domestic borrowing, the monetary system, a proposed central bank, import controls, credit facilities, and the conservation of foreign exchange.

A review of the revenue sources and collection methods in the Philippines revealed the need for modernization. In 1940 revenues amounted to almost 99 million pesos; 26 percent came from import duties, 28 percent from excise taxes, and 27 percent from license, business, and occupation taxes. Only 12 percent came from income taxes. In 1946, in spite of a fourfold price inflation and large money incomes, tax returns amounted to only 53 million pesos, of

[20] Finance Commission Report, *op. cit.*, p. 1.
[21] *Ibid.*, p. 9.   [22] *Ibid.*, p. 13. See also Appendix Tables VI and VII.

which 29 percent came from taxes on cigarettes. The tax bills passed by the Philippine Congress in September 1946 increased rates and modified administrative procedure, but, particularly in the area of corporate taxes, did not approach the rates payable in most other Asian countries.

The Finance Commission Report criticized the excessive reliance on import duties, excise taxes, amusement taxes, and sales taxes, which together accounted for 72 percent of revenue in 1946. In 1947 income and real property taxes yielded only 16 percent of estimated revenues. It was proposed that the goal of the government should be to make the individual income tax "the backbone of its tax structure. At the same time," the report continued, "there should be a reduction of those consumption taxes which raise the basic cost of living for the great majority of the people."[23]

No matter how admirable a tax schedule the Philippines might put on paper, revenue would not be forthcoming unless there was improved machinery for collection and enforcement. Low revenue directly after the war was to be expected, but inefficiency, evasion, and fraud did not disappear with postwar readjustments. The government itself almost universally understated the possibilities of revenue. The Finance Commission pointed out, for example, that government estimates of income tax collections for fiscal 1948 were under 14 million pesos. This was an increase of only 2 million over fiscal 1940 collections, even though the corporate rate was 50 percent higher than the 1940 rate, individual rates were increased by about 300 percent on brackets up to 100,000 pesos, money incomes were much higher than before the war, and abnormally high profits had been realized in many fields.

The same situation prevailed in the previous year. Although the government had listed in its budget estimate income taxes for fiscal 1947 at only 9 million pesos, actual returns far exceeded expectations. About 19 million pesos were collected, 13 million of which were paid in the last quarter of the fiscal year, during the period of the visit of the Finance Commission.

To strengthen tax collections the Finance Commission recommended that the government raise salaries, improve morale, and increase personnel in collecting agencies, and that it instigate criminal prosecutions in cases of corruption and apply criminal penalties for tax evasion.

Although it was recognized that individual income tax rates in the Philippines were lower than in many other countries, the commission did not recommend immediate increases, but proposed instead more rigid enforcement of existing schedules. A corporate rate of 18 percent for companies with net annual incomes of 25,000 pesos or over was suggested. Sharply increased excise and percentage sales taxes were proposed, particularly on luxury goods. Recommendations on estate, inheritance, and gift taxes aimed to bring them more in line with the ability-to-pay principle, with heavier burdens being

[23] *Ibid.*, p. 29.

placed on the upper brackets. The "pay-as-you-go" system was also suggested, once the collection machinery was improved.

One particularly striking example of the nonco-operation in tax collection cited in the Finance Commission Report concerned returns under the war profits tax. The Philippine Bureau of Internal Revenue estimated that about 30,000 individuals and corporations were liable under this legislation, but on April 30, 1947, three months after the date for filing returns, only 1,920 returns had been received and of these 1,440 showed no tax liability. Only four corporations and 280 individual returns reported taxable increases in net worth.[24]

Receipts from real property taxation were only 10.7 million pesos in 1946, and the real value of the land was considered to be grossly underestimated. The Finance Commission recommended that, with gradual reassessment and rate increases, real property taxation should eventually yield at least 50 million pesos annually. Tightening of collection procedures was again urged, as only 58 percent of assessed taxes was collected in 1946. Other recommendations suggested increases in rates on both forest charges and mining royalties, the imposition of a specific tax on copra production and desiccated coconut, and increased rates on sugar centrals, which would have allowed the government to share in abnormal and windfall profits in the processing of these commodities.

The problems of tax reform and government financing, although important, did not in any sense reflect a situation unique to the Philippines. Other countries with similar semifeudal and agricultural economies and loose economic controls have faced similar problems. The recommendations of the Finance Commission were of particular significance in those areas where they touched the special tie between the United States and the Philippine Republic and sought to reconcile new internal controls with the specifications of the Trade Relations Act.

Perhaps the major recommendation of the commission concerned the monetary system. The authors of the report stated that they regarded the Philippine monetary system "as an unsuitable permanent system for an independent Philippines."[25] The 100 percent dollar reserve with free convertibility into dollars meant that changes in money supply followed changes in the balance of payments. Conceivably, foreign needs and internal domestic needs might not coincide, but the government would have no way of bringing the two into balance. The commission therefore recommended that the Philippine government establish a Central Bank, which would assume responsibility for control of a managed monetary system. This would mean abandonment of the 100 percent reserve, previously criticized as overconservative. It would allow the Central Bank to regulate the reserve requirements, thereby making control of the domestic supply of money more flexible. "Philippine authorities," the report pointed out, "could thus distinguish between their peso and their dollar needs."[26]

[24] *Ibid.*, p. 36.   [25] *Ibid.*, p. 46.   [26] *Ibid.*, p. 47.

When they presented these recommendations, the commission members emphasized that they "contemplate no change in the present par value of the peso" and that they had borne in mind "both the spirit and the letter" of the United States–Philippine agreements on currency and trade.[27] And, so far as international transactions were concerned, it would have been perfectly possible to maintain the currency tie and yet alter the domestic reserve requirements. The background of the Bell Act, however, has shown that a good deal of the pressure for the currency tie came from business groups seeking to safeguard investments in the Philippines, and hoping to make them as secure as domestic American investments. While the recommendations for a managed currency followed sound economic principles and were in the interests of developing the Philippine economy, they represented a definite shift from the previous congressional emphasis on the security of foreign investments. In the long run, however, a stable controlled currency, if used to diversify and industrialize the country, would provide more, rather than less, opportunity for profitable business investment.

Any plan for industrial development in the Philippines would require expansion of financing facilities, particularly for long-term credit. As the report pointed out, of the twelve commercial banks which operated in Manila, five were branches of foreign banks and two were domestically incorporated but owned largely by Chinese capital. The Philippine National Bank was controlled by the government, two other banks were owned partially by the Catholic church, and one largely by local American interests. These banks were concerned primarily with dealings in foreign exchange and the financing of trade, commerce, and agriculture on a short-term self-liquidating basis. According to the commission there was some feeling in the community that "foreign banks were not using their resources, derived in large measure from local deposits, to promote the growth of the national economy."[28] It was recommended that foreign banks be subject to the same supervision by the proposed Central Bank as domestic banks.

Although it had been anticipated that the government Rehabilitation Finance Corporation, inaugurated on January 2, 1947, would facilitate industrialization, that body instead had devoted an excessive proportion of its resources to residential loans and small-scale agricultural credits. The Finance Commission recommended that the Philippine RFC should concentrate on larger programs of industrial and agricultural development, leaving the field of smaller credits to authorized banking firms. A government program of farm credits based on production, which would be followed up with supervision and technical aid, was also proposed.

The Finance Commission recognized the possibility that, despite large dollar balances credited to the Philippine Republic, in the absence of controls resources might be dissipated before lasting benefits were secured for the econ-

[27] *Ibid.*, p. 46.
[28] *Ibid.*, p. 55.

omy. The main danger was that foreign exchange in excessive amounts would be spent for consumption goods, including luxuries. The figures for 1946, for example, showed that about 53 percent of all imports was food and textiles, while only 10 percent was capital goods. While graduated taxation and domestic borrowing would slow down luxury spending, other factors, such as the wide dispersion of U.S. rehabilitation payments to individuals, would create a higher demand for consumption goods by persons who could not have otherwise afforded them. With this in mind, the Finance Commission recommended limiting nonessential imports and inaugurating import licensing procedures. Such a trade control program, the report argued, was "permissible" within the "letter and spirit" of the Trade Act. The act, in fact, did not prevent imposition of import controls, although it did forbid the imposition of duties on United States imports before July 4, 1954. A careful and judicious system of licenses, which would direct foreign exchange resources into commodities needed to serve the economy as a whole, would have an extremely salutary effect in the Philippines. The effect on American exporters could not be measured until the luxury market in the United States became saturated, which would occur in a business recession. At such a time, however, Philippine demand would also be likely to fall off sharply.

It will be recalled that the Finance Commission was originally dispatched to determine the merits of President Roxas' request for a $400 million loan to meet budgetary expenditures for five years. Its terms of reference were broad, however, and its findings covered a wide field. They clearly implied that the mere granting of loans would not solve the economic or budgetary problems of the Philippines, and that the Philippine Republic was not making the most effective use of the resources already at its disposal. The effect of the report on U.S. policy, so far as it can be separated from other factors, was more negative than positive. Subsequently the Philippines received some credits on a project basis, but not, as requested, a large government-to-government loan.

On the whole, the recommendations of the Joint Commission pointed in the direction of greater economic sovereignty for the Philippines. Its proposals on banking, trade, currency, and taxation would, if put into effect, strengthen the economy and cushion it against the shocks of declining preferences in future years. These suggestions, however, indicated what could be done rather than what would be done. The commission's terms of reference did not include a study of the political situation or of major groups and their interest in Philippine development, nor did it have authority to enforce acceptance of its recommendations. An American press analysis called the report "bitter medicine for the Filipino to swallow," and predicted that President Roxas "will have rough political sailing in effecting its full implementation."[29]

[29] *New York Times*, June 9, 1947.

CHAPTER TEN

ECONOMIC CONDITIONS, 1948-50

By .1950, five years after the war ended, per capita production and average levels of living in the Philippines were still in many instances lower than before the war, with little prospect of improvement. In fact, in 1950–51 a severe economic crisis occurred, which engaged the attention of the United States government as well as that of the Philippines. How this came about may be seen from an examination of economic trends in 1948–50.

In 1948 a noticeable slowing down in general business conditions, particularly in merchandising trade, was reported by Dr. Gonzáles, director of the Philippine Bureau of Census and Statistics.[1] Of the three main factors affecting business, both production and distribution declined, and only financial conditions showed an uptrend because of the unabated flow of United States remittances. Payments to beneficiaries by the United States Veterans Administration amounted to over 70 million pesos in 1948, while United States military agencies spent almost 350 million pesos. Including payments of the Philippines War Damage Commission, the total of United States disbursements in the Philippines for the year 1948 was over 670 million pesos.

In spite of this favorable monetary situation, corporate and partnership investments in the Philippines appeared to be on the downgrade. The figures for total investment, for the first nine months of the year, amounted to only 26.3 million pesos in 1948, as compared with 39.9 million in 1947 and 36.4 million in 1946. Investments in stock securities fell 23.6 percent from 1947 to 1948.

In order to increase self-sufficiency, particularly in food and textiles, and expand export markets, the Philippines had to develop productive facilities as rapidly as possible. The production figures for 1948, however, although somewhat improved over the previous year, were still below prewar years for many items. Paddy rice production rose from 2,335,000 tons for the 1947–48 season to 2,401,000 tons for 1948–49, but imports were still required because of population growth. Production of coarse grains also rose slightly, from 466,000 tons in 1947 to 489,000 in 1948. Tobacco production rose to 29,000 tons, still below the prewar average of 32,000 tons. Lumber production reached prewar levels in 1948, advancing by 40 percent over 1947. Electric power generation for Manila was 40 percent higher than in 1947 and more than double prewar. Coal production was estimated at 88,000 tons, exceeding prewar by over 25 per-

[1] Dr. Leon Ma. Gonzáles, "The Philippine Economic Picture," *Philippines Commerce*, December 1948. See also Appendix Tables IX and X.

cent. However, iron ore production was insignificant, gold was only about 20 percent of prewar output, and cement was but 115,000 tons in 1948 as compared with 134,000 tons in 1947.[2]

Sugar production for the 1948–49 season reached approximately 744,000 metric tons, below the prewar figure of 952,000 but a substantial advance over the 1947–48 level. Copra production remained high but abacá production declined, the January–September, 1948, output being 474,160 bales, or 22 percent less than for the same period in 1947. Cigar production in 1948 was 68 million, or 24 percent of prewar, while cigarette production was 67 percent of prewar but less than one percent of actual consumption.

Low production resulted not only in high prices, but also in high unemployment and disturbed labor conditions. There were 212 labor disputes during 1948, as compared with 93 in 1947, with the largest number in lumber and saw-milling and in land transportation. The number of workers involved increased by 26,917, reaching a total of 49,968 in 1948. According to the *Journal of Philippine Statistics*, an official government publication, "In view of the low purchasing power of money brought about by the prevailing high prices of articles of prime necessity, demands of workers for increases in wages predominated. . . ."[3]

Diminished activity in 1948 in such industries as textiles, cigars, shoes, and embroideries, and the fact that the mines had never resumed full operations, were reflected in the high unemployment figures. These can best be judged in relation to the over-all labor supply, which reached 8,984,000 in 1948. This figure included all persons ten years of age or older and able to work. Of these, 1,486,800 were students, leaving 7,497,200 persons actually available for work. Of this number there were 1,229,400 unemployed, representing a heavy drain on the economy.[4]

The cost-of-living index in Manila remained high, declining only slightly from an average of 387.1 in 1947 to 364.1 in 1948. Average daily wages were the same as the previous year, being 7.7 pesos a day for skilled laborers and 4.7 pesos for unskilled. Translated into real wages, based on conditions in 1941, this meant that the skilled laborer was earning at the rate of 2.1 pesos a day, and the unskilled worker at that of 1.3 pesos, as compared with the actual daily rate in 1941 of 2.3 pesos for skilled and 1.2 pesos for unskilled.[5]

In part, the high cost of living reflected the shortage of rice, which was basic to the Philippine diet. But it also resulted from the heavy reliance on imported commodities, particularly food and textiles. The foreign trade balance in 1948 did not change substantially from that of the previous year. Imports rose in about the same proportion as exports, leaving the Philippines with

[2] *Economic Survey of Asia and the Far East, 1948*, United Nations Document E/CN.11/191, June 15, 1949, pp. 50, 52, 59, 76, 90–91.

[3] *Journal of Philippine Statistics*, 1948, p. 84.

[4] *Ibid.*, pp. 84–88.   [5] *Ibid.*, p. 89.

a continuing trade deficit. Total imports for the year were 1,136 million pesos, as against 1,022 million for 1947; total exports were 638 million pesos, as compared with 531 million for the previous year.[6]

A significant fact reflected in the Philippine trade figures is the reliance on a single export crop, copra. In 1948 copra, desiccated coconut, coconut oil, and copra meal or cake together provided over 65 percent of all Philippine exports, in sharp contrast to the prewar figure of less than 8 percent. This was a result of the heavy postwar demand for fats and vegetable oils, which pushed copra prices for April and May, 1948, up to $335 per ton, five and a half times the prewar figure. But as the demand began to be met, prices sagged, and by February 1949 copra was down to $165 per ton. Prices rose again later, particularly in 1950 as a result of the Korean conflict; but this dependence on the fluctuating price of a single crop to provide the bulk of the Philippine earned dollar income was not a sound situation. As the correspondent of the *Wall Street Journal* said in 1949, "Crumbling copra prices are shaking the stilts on which the Philippine Islands have balanced their postwar economy."[7]

Another interesting aspect of the 1948 trade figures was the direction of exports and imports. Unsettled conditions in the rest of Asia and the relative stability of the Philippines increased the importance of the Islands as an outlet for American products. In 1948 the Philippine market accounted for 31.4 percent of the total American merchandise trade with Far Eastern countries, as compared with 16.1 percent in 1937. The Philippines shipped 28 percent of the products which the United States imported from the Far Eastern area in that year, and took 33.3 percent of American exports to the area.[8]

Although imports from the United States continued to overwhelm the Philippine market, exports from the Philippines were being diverted to some extent to different foreign countries. For example, in the first quarter of 1948 imports from the United States amounted to 74.3 percent of the value of total Philippine imports, while exports to the United States were only 58.3 percent of total exports. Other countries taking Philippine products at that time included Japan, 5.2 percent; France, 5.1 percent; Poland, 4.3 percent; Denmark, 3.8 percent; Italy and Canada, each 2.6 percent.[9]

The reappearance of Japan in the foreign trade picture of the Philippines created sharp controversy in the country. It had been revealed in the press in August 1948 that a *modus vivendi* on such trade had been reached with SCAP authorities the previous year, and that actual trade had been under way since August 15, 1947. This news met with a varied reception from the Filipino

---

[6] *Foreign Commerce Weekly*, May 2, 1949, p. 23.

[7] Lawrence E. Hartmus, "Philippine Peril," *Wall Street Journal*, February 15, 1949.

[8] Michael Lee, "Far East Trade Retarded by Civil Strife, Economic Dislocation," *Foreign Commerce Weekly*, June 13, 1949, pp. 39–40.

[9] "Foreign Trade of the Philippines, by Country, First Quarter 1948," *Manila Times*, Mid-Week Review, September 1, 1948, p. 5.

public, and there were even requests on the part of certain newspapers and congressmen for an investigation of so-called "secret agreements." President Quirino, however, maintained that the arrangements with SCAP had not been secret but that little public notice had been given to them at the time when they were made.[10]

The initial proposal on resumption of trade, according to President Quirino, came from the SCAP trade representative in April 1947. An agreement for trade on a government-to-government basis (with SCAP acting on behalf of Japan) was concluded, which provided that credits allocated for Japanese purchases in the Philippines should not exceed the amount of Philippine sales to that country. This was an attempt to reverse the prewar unfavorable balance.[11] The arrival of another mission in the Philippines in 1948, seeking liberalization of the terms of trade with Japan, led to further debate, the character of which reflected Filipino thinking at the time.

In a discussion on the general topic, "Shall We Trade with Japan?" in a Philippine economic journal,[12] Major R. C. O'Hara, SCAP trade representative, described the economic picture in Japan, and stated, "One of the most positive steps that can be taken towards restoring Japan's self-sufficiency is the re-opening of private trade. It is with this purpose that the discussion is vitally concerned." He went on to say that Japan had potentialities for meeting a wide variety of foreign needs, and that the willingness to discuss trade with Japan marked the Philippines as "a country of vision who sees beyond the complexities and confusion of the immediate postwar era."

Filipino opinion was less concerned with the needs of Japan than with the needs of its own country. Amando Dalisay, of the Philippine Department of Foreign Affairs, although supporting some resumption of trade, stated that trade with Japan should be examined from a purely objective business point of view. If the Philippines did not trade at all with Japan, he said, "Our alien friends would of course make purchases in Japan and sell the goods to us by indirect methods." Unchecked dumping of Japanese goods would be destructive to the development of Philippine industry. He therefore proposed limited and selective trading, "based primarily on business common sense and dictated by national economic self-interest."

The Filipino businessman's point of view was expressed in this symposium by Gil J. Puyat and Salvador Araneta, president and vice-president, respectively, of the Philippine Chamber of Commerce. Mr. Puyat proposed limited trading on an item-to-item basis, recalling that in the prewar years raw materials went to Japan, while nonessential consumer goods were dumped in the Philippines. Mr. Araneta emphasized the need for industrialization in his

---

[10] *Manila Times*, August 8, 1948; *Manila Chronicle*, August 7, 1948.

[11] *Manila Times*, August 8, 1948.

[12] R. C. O'Hara, Amando Dalisay, Gil J. Puyat, and Salvador Araneta, "Shall We Trade with Japan?" *Philippines Commerce*, June 1948, pp. 10–15.

country, saying, "We must fight to the utmost the present plans of the SCAP to make of Japan the workshop of Asia. If this should materialize, Japan would have won the war and would have achieved what she fought for, the so-called Co-Prosperity Sphere—an Asia for Japan."

In spite of the public controversy, the trade continued and rose rapidly. In 1948 imports from Japan were valued at 4.2 million pesos, while in 1949 they advanced to 32.1 million pesos. Exports to Japan overshadowed imports in 1948, amounting to 31.0 million pesos, but this figure dropped to 22.6 million pesos in 1949.[13]

The economic realities of the situation meant that few could have stood out against the resumption of some trading relations with the former enemy. But many Filipinos feared the direction in which such trade would develop, and, as predicted, Japan sent consumer goods to the Philippine markets, while Philippine iron ore was exported to Japanese industry. Many factors relating to over-all American policy in the Pacific were involved, however, and the decision to resume trade could hardly have been avoided, considering all the circumstances.

It has been seen that there were numerous production and distribution problems in the Philippines in 1948, while the most favorable aspects of the economy related to financial affairs. One of the soundest administrative efforts also appeared in the latter field, with the establishment of the long awaited Philippine Central Bank. The institution was organized as a government-owned enterprise, with a capital stock of 10 million pesos. The bank was assigned three main jobs: (1) to maintain monetary stability in the Philippines; (2) to preserve the international value of the peso and its convertibility into other freely convertible currencies (primarily dollars); and (3) to promote a rising level of production, employment, and real income in the country.

The decision to establish the bank followed the recommendations of the Joint Philippine-American Finance Commission, but the idea of a central bank in the Philippines was not new. The Central Bank Act of 1948 was in fact the third such law to be considered. The first was passed in 1939, but it did not receive the required approval of the President of the United States. A second bank law was passed during the Japanese occupation, but was never implemented.

The 1948 legislation gave fairly extensive powers to the new institution. The bank could not only manage the currency and credit system of the Philippines, but also grant extraordinary advances to the government within certain periods to finance authorized productive projects. Through its management of the currency issue, the new system would seek to have the amount of money in circulation reflect the needs of Philippine trade and industry, rather than dollar deposits in the United States. The governing board of the Central Bank

[13] U.S. Department of Commerce, *Foreign Commerce Yearbook*, 1950 (Washington, 1952), p. 253.

was also empowered to fix interest and rediscount rates, alter the reserve requirements of banks, operate on the open securities market, provide portfolio ceilings to restrict the nature of bank investments, and buy and sell its own evidences of indebtedness. Furthermore, to maintain international stability and convertibility, the bank could buy and sell gold and impose conditions for dealing in it, buy and sell foreign exchange, restrict and control exchange operations, regulate dealings by banks in futures, and influence the extension of money credit and exchange. As a member of the International Monetary Fund, the Philippines could use these fiscal powers to maintain the required par value of the peso.

The bank's power was dependent to a certain extent on the interpretation of the Philippine Trade Act, which provided that "no restriction shall be imposed on the transfer of funds from the Philippines to the United States, except by agreement with the President of the United States," and tied the peso to the United States dollar, with similar restrictions. As the Philippine financial situation became acute, particularly because of the flight of capital, the bank was given wide latitude in the exercise of its functions. This depended, however, on an interpretation of powers in an emergency rather than on an absolute grant of authority.

The bank faced many administrative difficulties in its early years. There was a need to recruit and train personnel in the field of central banking and to work out procedures of operation. The most important decisions, however, were on matters of policy. While integration with other government agencies was essential, it was also important that the bank retain some independence and not be subject to the rough ups and downs of Philippine politics. To gain and retain the confidence of a country, any central bank must be above party or faction. Furthermore, only limited goals should be established; the best-run central bank could not by itself bring prosperity. As one Filipino economist, Mr. Castillo, commented:

The Central Bank may have only indifferent success as the management lays the groundwork and adapts the new institution to an undeveloped economic environment, yet Filipinos cannot but hope that they have at last acquired an instrument for liquidating financial colonialism in their country and for gaining complete control of their national purse. No financial miracles are expected to result from the establishment of the Central Bank, but with it the people can face the future more confidently, heavily overcast though the economic skies may be.[14]

The time has passed when the raising or lowering of an interest rate could be regarded as a basic change in financial policy, with easily predicted results. Economists have shown how many manipulative devices can, under certain conditions, have an effect opposite to what was intended. Thus a devaluation

[14] Andres V. Castillo, "Central Banking in the Philippines," *Pacific Affairs*, December 1948, p. 371.

of currency might under certain circumstances worsen instead of improve an unfavorable balance-of-payments position because of loss of confidence and a resulting flight of capital. What happens to dollar income is important only in relation to prices, and this in turn is largely dependent on what happens to production. The Central Bank could be an important machine for easing credit and facilitating business activity, but it could not act on its own as a development agency. It was a useful economic tool for government programs, but not a substitute for them.

It was in 1949 that the Philippine economic situation took a serious downward trend, as a result of both agricultural and industrial difficulties. Not only did copra prices and production fall, but there was also a drop in production of abacá, the next most important crop in postwar years. This contributed to the unfavorable trade balance. Industrial production did not revive, unemployment continued, dollar resources were being used up, and the fiscal position worsened. General political instability and unrest around the election period all added to the problems of the young Republic.

The output of various products in 1949, in comparison with prewar production, was as follows: abacá, 69 percent; copra, 110 percent; sugar, 63 percent; cigars, 26 percent; cigarettes, 60 percent. Other data pointed up low production in many fields. During the fiscal year 1948-49 the Cebu Portland Cement Company produced 3,688,196 bags of cement, while the total requirements were about 6 million. The only textile mill operating in the Philippines, owned and run by the National Development Company, produced about 9 million square yards of cloth and 3.6 million pounds of yarn during 1949. Before the war the Philippine requirements for textiles amounted to about 130 million square yards, of which 20 million were made locally and 110 million imported. The population increase raised the estimated needs to about 170 million square yards.

The revival of production was particularly poor in the field of mining, where heavy wartime losses had been sustained. The value of gold production in 1949 was approximately 20 million pesos; the production of copper, lead, manganese, chromite, and iron ore amounted to 16.9 million pesos; and of cement, gypsum, coal, and rock asphalt to just under 10 million pesos. For gold this was 23 percent, and for base metals, 24 percent, of prewar production.[15]

Of major importance was the fact that declining prices in the world market had affected the production and shipment of the two main postwar export crops. Abacá production fell from 110,000 short tons in 1948 to 82,000 in 1949. At the same time prices fell from 68 pesos per picul (139 pounds) in January 1949 to 51.5 pesos in July. There was an even sharper decline in copra. Copra

[15] Data on production in 1949 taken from United Nations Document E/CN.11/I&T.15, Economic Commission for Asia and the Far East, Committee on Industry and Trade, "Industrial Development and Planning Programmes and Priorities," Annex K, Republic of the Philippines, April 4, 1950.

exports, which amounted to 2.2 million pounds in 1947, were only 1.3 million pounds in 1948, and dropped again to 1.2 million pounds in 1949. The value of these shipments fell from $177.2 million in 1947 to $154.7 million in 1948 and then to the low figure of $89.6 million in 1949.

The seriously adverse balance of trade, which had eased somewhat in 1948, became even more acute in 1949. Exports for the calendar year 1949 were 507.6 million pesos, and imports were 1,172.8 million. This imbalance prevailed in spite of the inauguration, at the beginning of 1949, of import controls designed to limit luxury imports.

The passage of the initial Import Control Law (Republic Act No. 330) occurred after six months of discussion and haggling between business and government over matters of jurisdiction, quotas, and percentage allocations. There were sharp differences of opinion between Filipino and American business in the Republic on the value of the legislation. For example, the Philippine Chamber of Commerce stated editorially: "The import control regulations . . . are most reasonable in character. Far from disrupting an already established trade, it seeks to regulate importations which will enable the Philippines precisely to place that trade on a national basis."[16] The *Journal of the American Chamber of Commerce* in the Philippines, however, declared: "Business will now have to adjust itself to the situation thus created, but it need not make a noise as if it likes it, and the American Chamber of Commerce does not like it. . . . Wise spending is always desirable, but a sound general assumption in the adult world is that those who have money know best how to spend it."[17]

The control law listed various commodities in two categories, luxury goods and nonessential imports (items which could be produced locally or for which substitutes could be found). These products were under license, and imports were limited to a percentage of either the quantity or the money value imported during the base year July 1, 1947, to June 30, 1948. Some of the cuts specified were as follows; automobiles, 40 percent; perfume, 50 percent; wines and liquors, 50 percent; cigarettes, 30 percent; and cotton textile apparel, 40 percent. Twenty percent of the imports subject to control was set aside for new firms.[18]

As can be seen from the trade figures, this attempt at regulation failed on two counts. In the first place, the cuts were not so drastic or the enforcement so rigid as to reduce imports by any sizable amount. In the second place, the controls were not accompanied by a program of domestic production to meet actual needs, as the rise in imports and the actual figures on agricultural and industrial activity indicated.

[16] *Philippines Commerce*, December 1948, p. 7.

[17] *Journal of the American Chamber of Commerce*, January 1949, pp. 3–6.

[18] Executive Order No. 193, by the President of the Philippines, prescribing rules and regulations to carry into effect the control and regulation of imports of nonessential and luxury articles into the Philippines as provided for in Republic Act No. 330, December 28, 1948.

Although some progress had been made toward such restoration of Philippine production, by 1949 it remained below that of prewar years. The combined index of volume of production in agriculture, manufacturing, and mining for 1949 was 91.3, based on the year 1937. Mining alone amounted to only 49.1 percent of the prewar figure. Agricultural recovery was impeded by the disturbed political conditions, and by the fact that the total area under cultivation in 1949 was only some 4.902 million hectares, less than the area in use before the war.

Recovery in production of commodities for export was extremely uneven in 1949, in part because facilities in the Islands had not been fully reconstructed and in part because world-wide demand was uncertain. The over-all index of volume of exports for that year, based on 1937 figures, was 81.0. For individual commodities the following degree of recovery was seen: desiccated coconut, 142.0; copra, 222.0; abacá, 27.0; sugar, 47.5; coconut oil, 38.1; canned pineapple, 373.0; chromite, 305.3; iron ore, 61.3; all others, 37.0. These index figures referred to volume, rather than to value, and therefore threw more light on actual levels of reconstruction than on the amounts of foreign exchange income procured.

In any comparison of prewar with postwar production, however, an essential fact was that the Philippine population had increased by some 25 percent, which of course meant that needs were similarly higher. This population rise, coupled with the decline in production, meant that increasing amounts of consumer goods had to be imported to maintain even the low prewar levels of living. Thus in 1949 about 8 percent of the total imports of the Philippines consisted of canned and other processed foodstuffs, and about 20 percent was textiles and textile manufactures. Furthermore, for the period 1946–49 the Philippines took about 85 percent of its imports from the United States. This meant that Philippine domestic prices automatically reflected high postwar American prices. This price level affected not only luxury items such as automobiles and radios, but also food, medicines, and clothing, the essentials of living.

Filipino wages, however, remained low, bearing no resemblance to the level of American wages or profits which helped to determine the prices of American exports. According to official government figures, the Philippine index of real wages in 1949, as compared with 1941 levels, was 96.5 for skilled industrial workers in Manila, 114.8 for unskilled workers, and 89.9 for agricultural workers. The daily wage rate for agricultural laborers in 1949 was 1.7 pesos, in addition to two free meals, according to the Bureau of the Census and Statistics. Wage rates in the sugar mills in Luzon ranged from 2 to 4 pesos a day, while in Manila the average daily rate for a skilled worker in 1949 was 7.6 pesos and for an unskilled laborer 4.9 pesos, with substantially lower rates for other cities.

Regardless of political persuasion, there appeared to be general agreement among Filipinos that wage levels were inadequate. According to Amado V. Hernández, president of the Philippine Congress of Labor Organizations, the average daily expenses of a working man with a family of four in Manila were 6 pesos, while his average daily earnings were only 4 pesos.[19] The differential had to be met with supplementary earnings from others in the family, through use of savings or war claims payments, borrowing, selling of possessions, or mortgaging of future earnings, which meant constant debt. Even this estimate seemed conservative, however, when compared with a study made by the Catholic church in the Philippines, which concluded that a minimum budget for a city family of five working in industry required an income of about 4,000 pesos a year.[20]

A further index of the level of living was the way income was apportioned among various items. In May 1949, for example, a wage earner's family in Manila spent approximately 55.9 percent of its monthly income on food, 14.7 percent on shelter, 2.6 percent on clothing, 7.0 percent on light and fuel, and 19.8 percent on miscellaneous items, such as health, transportation, cigarettes, recreation, household and other expenses.[21] With over 77 percent of income going for food, shelter, light, and fuel, many necessities had to be neglected. The low incomes, lack of margin for savings, and prevailing unemployment all indicated that the economy had not, by 1949, begun to meet the basic needs of the people.

The uncertainties of the economic situation were bound to result in political tensions, while at the same time political conflicts lessened the prospects for peaceful economic solutions. As 1949 progressed, feeling mounted over the forthcoming presidential elections, the first since formal independence was granted. The bitterly fought electoral battle not only reflected, but also contributed to, existing unrest and instability.

The presidential election of November 7, 1949, was marked by widespread violence and reported fraud, and among the repercussions were a challenge in the Supreme Court and an armed rebellion in certain provinces against the legitimacy of the administration. The contesting candidates included the incumbent, Elpidio Quirino of the Liberal party, who was re-elected; José P. Laurel, candidate of the Nacionalista party; and José Avelino, who represented an opposition faction of the Liberals. The open split between Avelino and Quirino had occurred early in 1949 when Avelino, then Senate president, was ousted from his post on charges of graft and corruption, particularly involving disposal of surplus property. This action was later upheld by the Philippine Supreme Court, and Avelino entered the presidential elections as an independent candidate.

---

[19] Amado V. Hernández, *Progressive Philippines* (Manila, July 1949), p. 16.

[20] *Report to the President of the United States by the Economic Survey Mission to the Philippines* (Washington, October 9, 1950), p. 91.

[21] *Journal of Philippine Statistics*, 1948, p. 130.

Not all of the issues of the campaign were sharply defined. Although Laurel was the former puppet President under the Japanese, the collaboration question was not of vital importance as all three candidates had been accused of co-operating with the enemy at one time or another. Quirino was well known for his support of the Philippine Trade Act, while Laurel had criticized American policy in the past on nationalistic grounds. As the election date approached, all candidates hastened to support continuing close relations with the United States, and to voice their opposition to communism.

President Quirino was returned to office following a heated campaign. Neutral observers who reported on the course of the election spoke freely of widespread violence and intimidation. One correspondent stated:

Election Day violence killed scores and injured hundreds. The official results, at best, are a dubious expression of public opinion. Armed men seized ballot boxes and kidnapped election officials. Tens of thousands of votes were falsified; the returns from whole districts simply vanished. Election officials drawing as much as $7.50 per day for their work delayed the count as long as possible and, in some cases, handed over all the ballots to the highest bidders. Many Filipinos feel that the elections settled nothing.[22]

There were protests against the election procedures and results from many quarters. Former President Sergio Osmeña resigned from the Philippine Council of State. The most serious postelection occurrence was the armed rebellion which took place in Batangas province, which was apparently led by Nacionalista supporters. This revolt was of such magnitude that it required units of the air, sea, and land forces of the Philippine Army to restore order. In a separate move the Hukbalahap, Communist-led opposition, called for the overthrow of the Quirino administration.

By the turn of the year events in the Philippines had quieted down. But although surface tranquillity may have been restored, widespread disillusionment remained about the effectiveness of the ballot box as a true measure of public opinion. Increasing numbers of Filipinos had participated in antigovernment activity, and the legality of the administration had been strongly challenged.

The political issues of the election period were not without their economic repercussions. As often happens when confidence in any administration declines, there was a general movement of capital out of the country. This was accelerated by the fear of imminent devaluation of the peso. The clearest indication of this was the drop in net foreign exchange reserves of the Philippine government and of Philippine banks, which fell from $410 million on January 1, 1949, to $290 million on October 31, 1949. During the first eight days of December alone, Philippine reserves declined by some $14.5 million. According to the recommendations of a mission of the International Monetary

[22] *U.S. News and World Report*, November 18, 1949.

Fund, which was studying Philippine finances at the time, the imposition of exchange controls was "unavoidable."

The government finally took action to check further depletion of resources, and placed all transactions in gold and foreign exchange under licensing control on December 9, 1949. The consent of the President of the United States, required under the terms of the Philippine Trade Act, was secured on the basis that this was an emergency measure. The controls imposed by the Central Bank were sweeping and affected all bank assets, securities of all kinds, and debts payable in foreign countries. No foreign payment could be made without the bank's permission, and the incurring of future debts abroad was also prohibited.

In commenting on the exchange situation, one American newspaper reported:

The newest Government control order caused fresh consternation in business circles, following as it did the drastic import control measures and credit curtailment for purchases abroad of more than eighty luxury and semi-luxury commodities. The exchange control pointed up the seriousness of the Philippine financial situation with shocking impact.[23]

Not only was the international fiscal position of the Philippines in a serious state at the end of 1949, but domestic finances had also been adversely affected by the tempestuous election. President Quirino admitted the gravity of the situation on November 14, 1949, when, at his first press conference after re-election, he said that the government's most urgent problems were the reorganization of public finances and the execution of a total economic mobilization program. Two days later, on November 16, the Secretary of Public Works announced the suspension of all public works programs, in order to channel all available government funds to essential services.

This emergency retrenchment on public expenditures was necessary because of the uncertain state of public finances. The regular session of the Philippine Congress had adjourned without passing a budget for the fiscal year ending June 30, 1950. As a result, all government expenditures from July through November, 1949, were authorized by the President under an executive order, based on his emergency wartime powers. A Supreme Court decision of September 1949, however, invalidated this order on the ground that the wartime emergency had passed, and as a result further presidential allocations would be unconstitutional. The disturbed political atmosphere meant that, instead of an immediate convocation of Congress to handle this matter, the legislators were not called into special session until the end of December 1949, after the critical election was over. In the interim the public purse was in effect unavailable for public services.

[23] *New York Times*, December 10, 1949.

By the beginning of 1950 it was apparent that drastic measures would have to be taken to check the deterioration of the economy. The state of public finances was more than a legal problem; mounting expenditures and inadequate tax returns meant that the Philippine government was facing a serious deficit.

The budgetary outlays of the government had risen steeply over the years. For 1946 expenditures were 213 million pesos; for 1947, 381 million; for 1948, 358 million; for 1949, 425 million; and estimated outlays for 1950 exceeded 502 million. A few major items absorbed most of these funds. Proposed expenditures for 1950, for example, included 134.6 million pesos for education; 58.4 million for national defense; 51.4 million for maintenance of law and order; 79.6 million for economic development, primarily for roads and other construction; and 69.8 million for investments. Furthermore, after the adoption of the regular 1950 budget, the Defense Secretary asked Congress for an additional 30 million pesos for defense. At the same time the Quirino administration sought to raise another 10 million pesos by private contribution to a "Peace Fund" to finance police operations against the Huks.[24]

In spite of these large expenditures, revenue did not rise in a proportionate degree. For 1950 anticipated income from taxation was only 273.5 million pesos, while estimated total revenue was only 331.3 million, which was far below the proposed expenses.

The low level of government income was not due to poverty of resources, to lack of money in circulation, or to a decline in national income, for all of these remained at high levels. For the most part, it resulted from poor collection of scheduled taxes, and from an inadequate and retrogressive tax system. Direct taxes in the Philippines accounted for only about 18 percent of actual tax collections, and customs duties made up another 10 percent, while items such as excise taxes were some 72 percent of the total. Necessary new corporations were exempt from taxation for four years, while old established business was lightly charged. The corporate tax rate in the Philippines was only 12 percent, whereas it averaged some 35 percent in Japan, 44 percent in Pakistan, 50 percent in Burma, over 50 percent in India, and 40 percent in Indonesia.[25] Such levels of taxation were obviously insufficient to finance the demands of a modern government, to meet the high military budget, or to begin to underwrite the projected industrial development program.

International as well as domestic finance problems continued to plague the Philippines in 1950. The exchange controls instituted the previous year had halted the more obvious shifts of capital abroad, but had placed limitations on foreign investors. In August 1950 the Central Bank relaxed restrictions on the remittance overseas of earnings and profits, and allowed firms to transfer

[24] *New York Times*, January 3, 1951.
[25] *Economic Survey of Asia and the Far East, 1949, op. cit.*, pp. 440–41.

abroad earnings or capital representing up to 30 percent of their investment in the Islands through the end of 1949.[26]

The steady drain on foreign exchange resources continued, and the initial moderate import controls were extended for 1950, with quotas assigned as percentages of the 1948 allotments. Drastic cuts were made for passenger automobiles, soap, textiles, silk, cigarettes, chewing gum, and refrigerators.[27] Even these reductions did not have much effect, however, since importers were able to shift from controlled to noncontrolled items.

As in many other phases of the Philippine economy, an over-all, rather than a piecemeal, effort was needed to conserve exchange. Such an attempt was finally made in the new Import Control Law of May 1950, which placed all imports under licensing. Goods were classified into various types, with percentage cuts made for the different categories, rather than for individual items. "Prime goods," such as meat, jute, and medicines, were cut from 20 to 40 percent; "essential" goods, including coffee, cheese, and inexpensive radios and phonographs, from 40 to 60 percent; "nonessential" goods, such as paper, tobacco, shoes, rayon, and linen, from 60 to 80 percent; and "luxury" imports, including certain fresh and canned vegetables, silk, and liquors, from 80 to 95 percent. Certain nonquota goods could not be imported in excess of 1948 levels, except for dollar-producing and saving materials such as agricultural machinery.

A highly controversial section of the new Import Control Law set aside 30 percent of import quotas for new Filipino importers, the figure to rise to 50 percent by 1952. Because of the parity provision in the Trade Act, United States nationals were accorded the same privileges as Filipinos. However, there were strong American protests against this special consideration for new importers, since it was likely that new firms would be Filipino rather than American. In that sense the provision was considered discriminatory against established firms in the Islands, many of which were owned by United States nationals.

Shortly after the imposition of controls, a noticeable reduction in Philippine imports could be seen. For the period from January to June, 1950, total imports dropped 40.6 percent below those for the same period in 1949. In addition, the composition of imports changed somewhat. Capital goods imports in the first six months of 1950 were some 213 percent above those of the previous year, while raw material and consumption goods imports dropped by 49.9 and 68.0 percent, respectively, from the 1949 figures.

Although designed for the primary purpose of limiting luxury imports, the controls also had other, less favorable repercussions. For one thing, the loss of excise duties resulted in some reduction in government revenue. In the

[26] *Far East Trader*, "Review of 1950," January 1, 1951, p. 10.

[27] *Foreign Commerce Weekly*, January 23, 1950, p. 24.

second place, domestic products were not available to substitute for many of the formerly imported goods, and shortages in consumer commodities exerted a strong inflationary pressure on the Philippine market. Price controls were not as effective as they might have been, and circumvention of the regulations was widespread. Some resentment was expressed against the carrying out of the controls by the administration. On September 9, 1950, the *Manila Bulletin* stated: "It should be plain by now, that the institution of Import Control is an almost hopeless mess, inadequately provided for by the Government in the first place, and allowed to degenerate from a poor beginning into a nest of corruption, favoritism and active coercion of the public into paying money for 'lost' documents."[28]

The inadequacies of the regulations, however, did not mean that controls were not needed. Instead they showed that the restrictions were essentially negative in character, and could not by themselves reverse the trend of the economy. Without a positive program for increased domestic production, the limitations placed on imports accentuated the need for consumer goods for the growing Filipino population.

In the all-important area of production, the year 1950 did not bring substantial improvement. Agricultural output remained fairly steady, with some increases, but these were not sufficient even to supply the domestic needs. Abacá production was estimated at 790,000 bales for 1950; the sugar crop, suffering from drought and typhoons, was estimated at about 680,000 short tons; tobacco production was about 26,000 tons; and the rice crop approximated 58.9 million cabanes, an increase of 4 percent over the previous year. On the industrial scene production did not approach prewar levels, and consumer goods continued to be in great demand.

The shortage of commodities was reflected in the business situation and in the cost of living. By the end of 1950 retail sales were 40 percent less than for the previous year, and inventories some 40 to 50 percent less. Prices rose because of shortages, and the trend toward increased inflation continued, reflecting the economic problems attendant on the Korean conflict.

In addition, the financial position of the government seriously affected the levels of living. The failure of Congress to provide for continuation of public works projects resulted in large-scale unemployment in the summer of 1950. During the acute financial crisis at the end of September, the Philippine National Bank branches stopped accepting Treasury warrants, including those for salaries of schoolteachers, which were some 56 million pesos in arrears. This situation was temporarily relieved by a loan in October of 22 million pesos from the International Monetary Fund.

The rural unrest in the Philippines persisted during 1950, in spite of the continuing anti-Huk campaign of the Philippine Army, which conducted a

[28] *Far East Trader*, January 1, 1951, p. 11.

full-dress military offensive, equipped with field artillery, bombing planes, and mobile armed units. According to a report in the *New York Times*, the plans for reorganization of the Defense Department had been worked out "in close consultation with the Joint United States Military Advisory Group."[29]

This renewed campaign of Huk suppression seemed to have dispersed, rather than annihilated, the opposition. Brigadier General Calixto Duque, Philippine deputy chief of the armed forces, said in an interview that, despite progress against the dissidents, "If we kill 800 Huks, then 800 people take their place."[30] Huk activity was demonstrated in a series of raids by about 5,000 reportedly Communist-led peasants on eleven towns in central Luzon on August 26, 1950, a national holiday marking the first uprising against Spain. The raids were apparently not intended to be the beginning of a sustained revolt against the government, but rather were designed to replenish Huk supplies, particularly medicines, to secure the release of Huk prisoners, and to spread leaflets critical of Philippine support for the Korean campaign.

While continuing their guerrilla tactics, the Huks at the same time put forth a long-range program for economic and social changes in the Islands. A Huk estimate of their own position was outlined in an interview in the Sierra Madre foothills with Luis Taruc on July 2, 1950, obtained by Manuel P. Manahan, Philippine publisher. Mr. Manahan secured the following information from the Huk leader:

Q. What is the extent of the Huk movement throughout the Islands?

A. Almost all strategic points in the major Islands have been penetrated and the masses are rallying to support the movement.

Q. What is the possibility of another amnesty? Have you received any feelers?

A. The word amnesty itself has become like poison to us. We consider amnesty and peace negotiations with the present government out of the question. Regarding peace feelers we have received inquiries from two sources, Avelino and Quirino. Avelino before and after the election, from Quirino recently now that he is desperate.

Q. Is there such a thing as a Huk time-table?

A. There is no such thing as a time-table. . . . However we expect this [a revolution] to happen within the next two years, from our own analysis and the movements of the American imperialists.[31]

In dealing with the Huk problem President Quirino stressed military methods and sought American aid. For example, it was reported that the possibility of United States financial assistance for an all-out campaign against the Huks was apparently the subject of a conference between President Quirino, John F. Melby, head of the United States Military Aid Mission, and United

---

[29] *New York Times*, March 5, 1950.
[30] *New York Times*, August 25, 1950.
[31] *Manila Times*, July 5, 1950.

States Ambassador Myron Cowen in Manila on September 21, 1950.[32] The following day, September 22, President Quirino, in spite of strong objections from the Nacionalista party, issued an executive order directing the organization of barangays in every barrio, in an attempt to secure civilian participation in the anti-Huk campaign. Each barangay was to establish a patrol service to supervise the barrio, to keep registers of residents and transients, and to ensure civic co-operation with the administration.

The following month, on October 20, the President asserted that an "actual state of rebellion" existed in many localities, and two days later he suspended the writ of habeas corpus for any persons detained then or thereafter on charges of sedition, insurrection, or rebellion. This last act brought forth criticism from Senator Tanada, Filipino legislator, who said that "No greater abuse of democracy can be found in Philippine history, outside of the Japanese regime, than that of President Quirino's suspension of the writ of *habeas corpus*."[33]

The problem of the Huks, as it existed and was being dealt with at the end of 1950, illustrated the danger that the long-range economic needs and development programs of the Philippines might be handicapped or even defeated by more immediate political considerations. Philippine energies and wealth were diverted to the negative task of controlling opposition, instead of being concentrated on removing the underlying causes of dissatisfaction. Economic backwardness and poverty could result only in recurrent crises and dissension, unless the existing pattern was broken by constructive measures to build a strong and prosperous nation.

Some salutary measures had been enacted, it is true, but too often a legislative step forward was accompanied by administrative steps backward. Thus the law providing for a 70–30 crop distribution between tenant and landlord was poorly enforced. Exchange, import, and price controls were in practice often evaded or ignored. The basic need, however, was vigorous action by government to stimulate development of the natural resources and productive potential of the Islands. We must now consider the Philippine government's efforts in this direction.

[32] *Far East Trader*, October 4, 1950.
[33] *Manila Chronicle*, February 18, 1951.

CHAPTER ELEVEN

THE YOUNG ECONOMY: SURVEYS AND PLANS

THE Philippine government has long been aware of the need for national economic development, and the history of the country has shown numerous efforts in this direction. Although concrete progress was limited, a review of earlier plans provides a frame of reference for viewing recent trends in Philippine economic thinking.

It is important to note that official encouragement of necessary enterprises was evident from the time of the administration of President Woodrow Wilson, when the Philippine authorities established the Philippine National Bank, acquired the Manila Railroad, and set up various other projects. All of these enterprises relied heavily on government participation, especially in the initial stages. This orientation has been criticized in some quarters as being contrary to the American free enterprise system, but in fact it followed the pattern for Philippine development laid down while the Islands were still in the possssion of the United States. At that time a mixed economy of public and private enterprise was considered to be appropriate for an independent Philippines. To allow for this type of activity the Philippine Constitution provided (Article XIII, Section 6):

The State may, in the interest of national welfare and defense, establish and operate industries and means of transportation and communication, and upon payment of just compensation, transfer to public ownership utilities and other private enterprises to be operated by the Government.

The main agency to implement this policy in the Commonwealth period was the National Development Company, a public corporation set up to serve as an agency of the government in the furtherance of its economic policies. Several subsidiaries were also established over the years to carry out various phases of activity. Among these were the National Food Products Corporation, the National Rice and Corn Corporation, the National Warehousing Corporation, the National Footwear Corporation, the Cebu Portland Cement Company, the Insular Sugar Refining Company, and the Rural Progress Administration, and People's Homesite and Housing Corporation. In addition, the National Development Company engaged in textile manufacture and experimental farming, and invested in the Philippine Air Lines.

Other government agencies were established to cope with various problems not handled by private enterprise. Among these were the National Abacá and

Other Fibers Corporation, set up to aid in stabilizing prices; the National Coconut Corporation, to help in research as well as in price stabilization; the National Tobacco Corporation, to rehabilitate that industry; the National Power Corporation, to develop water power; the Manila Railroad; the National Land Settlement Administration; the National Cooperatives Administration; and the Manila Hotel, intended to promote tourist trade.

Although elaborate plans had been made, real economic development had barely begun when the Japanese attack occurred. After the war such development became a further link in the chain of postwar needs that began with relief, rehabilitation, and reconstruction. In dealing with the over-all national problems the role of government assumed increasing importance.

Shortly after the war attention was directed to the urgent agricultural problems. A Philippine–United States Agricultural Mission, reporting in 1947, recommended a number of steps to strengthen production for both consumption and export.[1] The appointment of a Technical Planning Board was strongly advised, and priority for production, processing, and marketing of agricultural products, both on the farm and in the factory, was suggested. Resettlement, mechanization, and diversification of farming were also considered important. Specific recommendations were presented on production of the four major export crops—sugar, abacá, copra, and tobacco—as well as for the major food crops—rice and corn—in addition to other proposals for education and extension work.

The major attention in investigation and reporting, however, was soon to be directed to the general problem of industrialization. A number of proposals were put forth. The three major ones were the Hibben Memorandum, an outgrowth of the Joint Philippine-American Finance Commission; the Beyster Plan, a private study prepared for the Philippine government; and the Cuaderno Program, drawn up by the Philippine Secretary of Finance.

Recognizing the need for long-term development, the Joint Finance Commission accompanied its short-term recommendations with an evaluation of Philippine resources and economic perspectives.[2] This was prepared in 1947 by Thomas Hibben of the United States Department of Commerce for the use of the commission, and published by it for the information of the general public. To achieve some degree of self-sufficiency, and to improve production of export products, Mr. Hibben suggested expenditures of 2.18 billion pesos during the following five years. This sum would be solely for economic development, and would not include residential housing or public services. Transportation would require 1.1 billion pesos, including 545 million for

[1] *Report of the Philippine–United States Agricultural Mission* (Washington, June 1947), pp. 41–44.

[2] Thomas Hibben, "Philippine Economic Development, A Technical Memorandum" (Manila, June 7, 1947), included in *Report and Recommendations of the Joint Philippine-American Finance Commission*, H.R. Doc. 390 (Washington, July 8, 1947).

roads, 123 million for railways, and the rest for air, shipping, and other facilities. Of the total amount for services, including transport, power, and communications facilities, less than one-third would be spent for labor and locally
produced materials.

The memorandum stressed the need to increase the production of foodstuffs, since self-sufficiency would conserve foreign exchange. An investment
of 175.4 million pesos was proposed for food production, including land
settlement, irrigation and drainage projects, and expansion of fishing facilities.
Industrial development would require an investment of 283 million pesos
over the five-year period, according to Mr. Hibben. Suggested expenditures
included iron and steel, 95 million pesos; chemicals and related products, 41.3
million; and light industries, such as textiles, shoes, paper, and glass, 146.7
million. To rehabilitate and revive the export industries, an investment of
167 million pesos was proposed, including allotments to sugar of 50 million
pesos, abacá and ramie 25 million, gold and silver mining 35 million, and coconut oil and vegetable lard 20 million.

The program envisaged by the Hibben Memorandum was put on a five-
year basis, since this was approximately the period during which rehabilitation
payments would be highest and preferential trade would be conducted on the
most favorable terms. Completion of the above proposals, according to Mr.
Hibben, would have provided:

. . . at least 75,000 homesteads, 80,000 hectares of irrigated land, self-sufficiency
even with increased population and higher living standard demand in rice, corn
and vegetables; self-sufficiency and possible export of fruits, nuts, fish and meats;
greatly reduced import requirements in shoes and leather, chemicals, textiles,
paper, glass, clay products, iron and steel; maintenance of prewar levels and possible
increase in export of sugar cane products, coconut products, abacá and other fiber
products, lumber, tobacco products and mine products; increase in the output of
power; and transportation and communications facilities to meet the demand of
a growing industrial and prosperous agricultural economy.[3]

The memorandum gave no detailed estimate of proposed sources for investment capital. Since it was essentially for the use of the Joint Commission, it
was never considered for legislative action. As a result, its chief value was its
balanced emphasis on both agriculture and industry and its use as a yardstick
against which to measure other plans.

In attempting to arrive at a comprehensive program for development, the
Philippine government sought the advice of a firm of American consulting
engineers, the H. E. Beyster Corporation of Detroit, Michigan. Under the
supervision of this organization, the technical staff of the Philippine National
Development Company prepared a "Proposed Program for Industrial Re-

[3] *Ibid.*, p. 66.

habilitation and Development," which was published in Manila on June 24, 1947.[4]

The Beyster Plan stressed rehabilitation of the prewar economy, and was less ambitious for industrialization than the Hibben Memorandum. Beyster proposed expenditures of 3.2 billion pesos for a fifteen-year period, with one-half assigned to development purposes, exclusive of shipping and power transmission facilities, and the other half devoted to housing, hospitals, schools, and other public works. In the field of development, major items proposed were 118.7 million pesos for a steel industry, and other sums for a chemical industry, fisheries, marketing facilities, textiles, and pulp and paper manufacture. A total of 134.3 million pesos was allotted for roads.

Generous treatment was accorded to the sugar industry, for which Beyster proposed 270 million pesos for rehabilitation, including 120 million for the sugar mills. This may be compared with the Hibben estimate that 50 million pesos would be adequate, even at prevailing inflated costs, although the estimate of war damage in the industry was 55.6 million pesos at 1940 prices. The approach of the Hibben Memorandum was that every single operating unit should not be restored, but rather that consolidation, modernization, and elimination of marginal producers were necessary if the Philippines expected to compete in the world sugar market after the loss of American preferences.

There was similar disparity in the recommendations on mining. The Hibben Memorandum stated that reconstruction of old mines and development of new ones should absorb an investment of about 40 million pesos. The Beyster Plan, however, estimated losses as equivalent to 78 percent of the total invested value of the industry in 1940. Allowing for replacement at current market prices, Beyster figured that new investment would "require an actual expenditure of approximately four times the amount of assessed damages" or some 484.8 million pesos.[5]

The Beyster Plan also was never put into effect, and was of interest more for the kind of thinking it represented than for its specific recommendations. In the first place, this report proposed that over half of the total development expenditures go to rehabilitate prewar industries and facilities, especially sugar and mining. This would have re-established many marginal producers and tended to restore the former overspecialized economy. In the second place, although the proposals did point up areas in need of rehabilitation, they did not offer any over-all plan for development. Furthermore there was no indication of how investment would be directed. Private capital flows to areas of greatest return, and not necessarily to areas most in need of development. In economies such as the postwar Philippines there was more money to be made

[4] "Proposed Program for Industrial Rehabilitation and Development," prepared by the Technical Staff, National Development Company, under the supervision of the H. E. Beyster Corporation (Manila, June 24, 1947).

[5] Ibid., p. 81.

from "buy and sell" trade with a rapid turnover than from long-term investment. Because total resources of materials and of foreign exchange were limited, this was a serious problem. The Beyster Plan neither set up desirable goals nor proposed how the objectives it did outline could actually be achieved.

The plan finally approved by the Philippine government was a more modest five-year proposal evolved in 1948 by Philippine Secretary of Finance Miguel Cuaderno. It emphasized agricultural development, in the hope of making the country self-sufficient in food products by 1952 and also of increasing the dollar value of export crops. Although Secretary Cuaderno anticipated that private foreign capital would be an important source of funds, capital was also to come from taxation, domestic borrowing, borrowing from commercial banks, and from the Philippine Central Bank.

Dr. Amando M. Dalisay, Executive Secretary of the Philippine National Economic Council, held out high hopes for the success of a short-term program of economic development along these lines. He stated that the threefold objective for the government plan was as follows:

First, to adjust the Philippine economy to the decline in the United States Government payments and provide the necessary adjustments to the progressive application of American tariffs after 1953. Second, to effect the initial stages in the process of structural adjustments necessary in the change of the national economy from sole dependence on export crops to an economy better fortified against the severe fluctuations in the demand and prices of export crops in foreign markets. And third, to provide for the reconstruction, extension, and augmentation of transportation and communication services so as to enlarge the scope and possibilities of the domestic market and promote greater regional specialization in production.[6]

These were all desirable goals, but somewhat ambitious, considering the scope of the program which was recommended by the National Economic Council and approved by the President. Of total capital investment of 1.7 billion pesos proposed for the five-year period from 1949 to 1953, 419 million was to be allocated among agricultural projects and 1,311 million among industrial enterprises. The total represented dollar-exchange needs of approximately $441 million for the importation of machinery, and requirements of about 967 million pesos for locally produced materials. Top priority was assigned to production of rice, corn, fruits, sugar, abacá, maguey, ramie, tobacco, peanuts, and coconuts, to improvement of fisheries, livestock, and forest products, to development of the mines, of water power, and of land, air, and sea transportation, and to small industries such as a nail plant, a paper and pulp plant, fertilizer plants, and handicrafts. Second priority was given to projects in the fields of water supply, port improvement, schools, hospitals,

[6] Amando M. Dalisay, "P.I. Short Term Program of Economic Development," *Bataan*, January 1950, p. 9.

markets, housing, highways, flood control, airports, jute production, and improvement of dry-dock facilities.

By April 1950 the Philippine government had allocated over 52 million pesos to finance its development program. Among the projects approved were the following:

	Pesos
Ocean-going vessels	4,692,000
Textile project	700,000
Rice and corn project	7,925,000
National shipyard and graving dock	515,230
Steel mill	40,000
Paper- and bag-making	891,000
Lumot diversion project	880,000
Irrigation project	11,000,000
Davao project	1,615,000
	28,258,230

In addition, 1,875,000 pesos were subscribed for shares of stock of the National Development Company, 2.5 million for reimbursements of advances made by that company, and 20 million to finance projects of the Rehabilitation Finance Corporation.[7]

The Philippine government faced serious obstacles in implementing this program, particularly inadequate public finances, foreign exchange, and technical personnel. As a result, the 1948 five-year plan was revised in August 1950. The new program, which extended to 1954, proposed expenditures of some 429 million pesos with 234 million representing the cost of imported equipment and materials, and the remainder allotted for peso requirements. In the choice of industries to receive high priority, six criteria were emphasized: preference was to be given to industries which would either save or earn foreign exchange, which could be brought into production quickly, which would act as stimulants to other industries, which would require relatively lower capital investments, in which the ratio of local to imported raw materials would be high, and in which an economic operating capacity could be based on domestic requirements.[8]

In the approved program a good deal of emphasis was placed on hydroelectric and power development, but these projects went slowly, owing to lack of adequate financing. The application of the Philippine government to the

[7] United Nations Document E/CN.11/I&T.15, Economic Commission for Asia and the Far East, Committee on Industry and Trade, "Industrial Development and Planning Programmes and Priorities," Annex K, Republic of the Philippines, p. 8.

[8] *Philippine Agricultural and Industrial Development Program, Revised, 1950*, Report of the Philippine Economic Survey Mission, Hon. José Yulo, chairman (Manila, August 11, 1950), p. 146.

International Bank for Reconstruction and Development for a power development loan has been under discussion since 1948, but to date no material aid has been given. The Maria Cristina project in Mindanao was under consideration, and development of power resources was proposed to give an initial capacity of 80,000 kilowatts, of which 60,000 kilowatts would be used by a complementary ammonium sulphate fertilizer plant, yet to be constructed. The reluctance of the International Bank to make the loan was due in part to the financial risks involved in establishing a large project primarily dependent on a single consumer, a plant which was still only in the planning stage.

In certain fields not involving such large sums, the government went ahead on its own. Completed projects under the National Development Company included the Cebu Portland Cement Company; the Insular Sugar Refining Company, which was producing in 1949 at 22 percent of capacity; a single textile mill with 30,000 spindles and 50 looms; a nail factory with a yearly output of some 150,000 kegs; and the Batangas Finishing Mills and Agusan Sawmills, with a capacity of one million board feet per month.[9] Not only was the total program far from adequate to meet the need, however, but there was confusion and uncertainty over the proper role of government in furthering business activity.

At the same time that plans were made for public financing of development and industrialization schemes, Philippine officials repeatedly stated that the government would act only in areas where private capital would not venture. Several times the government sought to unload public ventures, including lumber and textile mills, on to private enterprise, but with little success. Occasionally, Philippine business objected to undue interference in its operations, as in 1948 when a manufacturer of hollow concrete blocks protested the public sale of blocks by the Peoples' Homesite and Housing Corporation at a price below that in the market. The government agreed at the time that the blocks should be withdrawn from sale as long as private producers could offer a similar product at a reasonable price, and that the government corporation would not enter the market until prices rose above a certain limit.[10]

Business complaints against government in industry, however, and repeated government assurances of its willingness to lease, sell, or place under private management almost all of its projects did not mean that private enterprise was ready to take over. In actual fact there were few projects which were considered to be good business risks. In the fiscal year ending June 30, 1948, for example, the Manila Railroad incurred a loss of 3.3 million pesos; the daily operating loss of the National Development Company's textile mill amounted to 6.5 thousand pesos; and the lumber finishing mill in Batangas was shut down. Business might make verbal assaults on public enterprise, but it was

[9] United Nations Document E/CN.11/I&T.15, *op. cit.*, pp. 11–14.
[10] Emilio Abello, "Philippine Resources Immense, but American Capital Is Needed, Welcomed," *Bataan*, April 1949, pp. 23–32.

unwilling to take over losing propositions. The Philippine government, therefore, remained in policy a supporter of private enterprise, but in fact an entrepreneur in public projects primarily by default.

This does not imply that private enterprise and foreign firms were not interested in doing business in the Philippines. Actually very substantial sums were invested in the Islands after the war, but a disproportionately high amount went into nonproductive enterprises. This indicated the need for the Philippine government to encourage the types of activities which would be more productive and thereby serve the widest national interest. But there were grave differences of opinion on what direction such development should follow. Varying emphasis had been placed on the need to promote industrial as against agricultural resources. Other differences arose over whether the Philippines should follow a policy of protection or of free trade, on the relative roles to be played by private and by public enterprise, and on the importance of domestic as against foreign capital.

The shift in terms of trade in favor of agricultural commodities, for example, raised the question whether development should not rely on increased export of the same prewar products in order to build up needed foreign exchange. There are two objections to this method. In the first place, a country as small and dependent on trade as the Philippines can hardly hope to cushion the effects of the notorious ups and downs of agricultural commodity prices. The experience of the depression years, and even the postwar fluctuations in the price of copra, indicate that agricultural prices set in the world market are unsteady bases for any economy. In the second place, there has been half a century of experience in relying on the ever growing export of such products to the American market, and yet it has not been shown that the position of the average Filipino peasant has improved in the period. Tenancy is more prevalent, rural debts are still large, and living conditions have changed little in fifty years despite the potentialities of modern technology.

A decision to emphasize industrial development, however, does not mean that it is possible to ignore the land problem. Any plan for overambitious industrialization is bound to fail, not only because of the lack of sufficient investment capital, but also because of the limited domestic market. To encourage the home market the living levels of the entire people must be raised, and this is possible only through a thoroughgoing program of rural reform, reduction of peasant debt, adjustment of tenure laws, handling of absentee landlordism, and other measures to alleviate peasant poverty. Thus while rehabilitation of large-scale agriculture will not in itself solve the long-run economic problems, neither will grandiose industrial schemes. A balanced program of rural improvement, coupled with support of badly needed industry, would meet a basic need in the Philippines.

To build up such domestic industry some Filipino economists have advocated a system of protection through tariffs and economic controls. For example, in supporting such a proposal, Salvador Araneta has quoted from the American economist Paul Samuelson, who stated:

Probably, the infant-industry argument had more validity for America a century ago than it does today, and has more validity for present-day backward nations than for those which have already experienced the transition from an agricultural to an industrial way of life. In a sense such nations are still asleep; they cannot be said to be truly in equilibrium. All over the world, farmers seem to earn less than industrial workers. Consequently, there is everywhere a relative growth of industry and a decline of agriculture. Populations migrate cityward, but the movement is not rapid enough to achieve an equilibrium of earnings and productivity. A strong case can be made for using moderate protection to accelerate these economically desirable long-run trends. Such a defense of protection might more appropriately be called a "young-economy" argument rather than an infant-industry one.[11]

In order to prosper, however, the young economy must do more than protect its products. It must develop resources and become increasingly self-reliant. This is no Robinson Crusoe doctrine—the underdeveloped country must also buy and sell abroad. But it must have sufficient strength so that such trade can be conducted from the best possible bargaining position.

This bargaining position is closely affected by the foreign economic relationships of the country and its legislative and financial obligations. In the case of the Philippines, the relationship with the United States has been of paramount importance. Despite the large flow of American money to the Islands and the preferential arrangements, there have been repeated criticisms of restrictive economic ties between the two countries, in particular of certain parts of the Philippine Trade Act of 1946. For example, a Survey Mission of the International Monetary Fund, which studied the Philippine situation, reported in January 1950:

The Bell Trade Act, under which the Philippines and the United States admit each other's goods duty-free, has had the effect of discouraging the establishment of local Philippine industries and has thereby contributed to the tendency to over-import. . . .[12]

Filipino economists have also been ready to attribute some of their difficulties to their foreign economic ties. One postwar study entitled "The U.S. Recession and Its Effects on the Philippines," prepared for the Philippine National Policy Association, stated:

One of the most sordid manifestations of our inheritance is our dependence on the United States for our economic well-being. Handicapped by the joint action of

[11] Paul Samuelson, "Economics, an Inventory Analysis," p. 568, quoted in Salvador Araneta, "Pro and Con of Protectionism, A Filipino View," *Philippines Commerce*, December 1948, p. 10.

[12] "Report of the Philippine Mission of the International Monetary Fund," submitted to the fund's executive board (Washington, January 17, 1950).

free trade and the bases, our economy could not expand beyond production for the foreign market, which in our particular conditions, is largely the United States.[13]

This report stressed the importance of industrial projects. "If there are no projects to absorb agricultural production," it declared, "we have to continue our dependence on foreign markets, which does not insure stability and prosperity for our agricultural population. On the other hand, no industrial project is likely to prosper unless purchasing power is developed among the agricultural population. And said purchasing power cannot develop without basic adjustments in our present farm and rural economy."[14] The report went on to state:

Obviously, the primary requisite for the implementation of these programs, should we meet the financial and technical requirements, is the abrogation of the Bell Trade Relations Act and the consequent repeal of Parity, together with all their onerous effects on our new proposed industries.

Impliedly also, as an unwritten requirement of an industrialization program, we will have to revamp our rural relationships and re-establish them on the basis of semi-industrial economy.

Whether the government will pursue a policy in accordance with the requirements stated above, it is not certain. If its performance in the past, and up to the present is an index, we may almost be sure that it will not, and by this reluctance to embark upon decisive changes, it will frustrate its own aims of industrialization.[15]

During the immediate postwar period, in 1945 and 1946, such matters as quotas, tariffs, and preferences were uppermost in discussion of American economic policy in the Philippines. Since that time the focus has shifted to global programs of American aid to other countries, such as the Marshall Plan, and particularly to Point Four and other forms of economic aid to underdeveloped areas like the Philippines. For the United States such programs raise difficult questions as to how far such expenditures must be under American supervision in order to achieve the desired results; for the receiving countries they raise equally difficult questions as to how far they can accept American aid without incurring unwelcome obligations.

In discussions of help for underdeveloped countries, there has been an unfortunate tendency to assume that century-old difficulties could be easily resolved through relatively small amounts of dollar aid. Furthermore, when such programs have failed, this has often been ascribed to the weakness and inefficiency of the recipient country, rather than to the fact that too much was

[13] José L. Llanes, with the assistance of Cornelio V. Crucillo and Bonifacio Quiaoit, *The U.S. Recession and Its Effects on the Philippines*, National Policy Association, Technical Bulletin No. 4, Manila, November 17, 1949, p. 22.

[14] *Ibid.*, p. 33.

[15] *Ibid.*, p. 37.

expected in the way of results. For example, Secretary of State Dean Acheson, speaking on January 12, 1950, said of the expenditure of some $2 billion by the United States in the Philippines:

Much of that money has not been used as wisely as we wish it had been used, but here again we come up against the matter of responsibility. It is the Philippine Government which is responsible. It is the Philippine Government which must make its own mistakes. What we can do is advise and urge and if help continues to be misused to stop giving the help.[16]

While the moneys received have not always been used to the best advantage, the matter of responsibility cannot be dismissed so easily. Fifty years of American rule, following the long Spanish regime, have given the Filipinos only limited experience in self-government. Furthermore, the absence of a clear-cut postwar American policy on collaboration gave free rein to the Roxas administration, which was itself too deeply involved in charges of wartime guilt to take a firm stand on postwar corruption.

[16] Dean Acheson, "Crisis in Asia—An Examination of U.S. Policy," speech before the National Press Club, January 12, 1950, in *Department of State Bulletin*, January 23, 1950, p. 117.

CHAPTER TWELVE

THE BELL MISSION AND AFTER

By 1950, as a result of events in China, Korea, and elsewhere, the United States faced a situation in which its influence in Asia was seriously threatened, not only by the Communist countries but also, in a different way, by strong nationalist and neutralist currents in non-Communist countries. Thus the Philippines assumed a new importance both in American strategic planning and in American diplomacy. For, unlike most other Asian countries, the Philippines had as a rule, though with some exceptions, given full support to United States policies, and its representative in the United Nations, Brigadier General Carlos P. Romulo, had been an active spokesman of the American viewpoint in world affairs.

This support was demonstrated in 1950, when, after an initial period of hesitation, Filipino troops were dispatched to Korea to join American forces there. Furthermore, the Philippines did not go along fully with the twelve-nation Asian-Arab bloc in the United Nations which sought mediation of the Korean conflict.

Perhaps the major issue of foreign policy on which the Philippine administration's position differed from that of the United States was the question of reparations payments from Japan. While there was some doubt about the extent to which Japanese machines slated for reparations could actually have been absorbed by the Philippine economy, it was hoped that such equipment might be of some use in industrialization of the Islands. The decision of the United States in 1949 that Japanese reparations deliveries be halted, therefore, met with strong protest from the Philippine delegate to the Far Eastern Commission, General Romulo. In describing Filipino reactions to the American decision at the time, General Romulo declared:

I can recall only one instance in recent years of a report which created jubilation in Tokyo and consternation in Manila, and that was the news of the Japanese sneak attack on Pearl Harbor.

Times must indeed have changed very much since then to produce this curious duplication of events in reverse. Or perhaps we should say that this is a sneak attack, only an infinitely more insidious one—a delayed action attack that will some day explode in the very faces of those who now deplore the cost of the Japanese occupation. . . .[1]

The matter of reparations again assumed importance in public discussion

[1] *New York Times,* May 20, 1949.

in March 1951, during the visit to Manila of John Foster Dulles to talk over the terms of the proposed peace treaty with Japan. The Manila press at the time gave major attention to the reparations question and to the Philippine demand for an $8 billion claim against Japan. General Romulo again commented on the importance of placing the needs of the Philippine economy above those of Japan. The fact that no further reparations were specified in the peace treaty, although it left room for future negotiations on the subject and suggested that Japan might process raw materials for nations having war damage claims, drew sharp criticism from Filipino sources. The Philippines signed the treaty in San Francisco in September 1951, but it did not abandon its efforts to secure compensation for the wartime destruction.

Aside from the reparations question and the broader problem of the postwar treatment of the former enemy, however, the Philippine government has been ready to support numerous other aspects of American foreign policy. But from the point of view of the United States, while verbal agreement and United Nations votes were important, the internal difficulties of the Islands made them a weak link in the American security chain in the Pacific. The Philippines could be a useful ally in the Far East only to the extent to which its government was strong and stable and provided effective management of the national economy. By 1950 Philippine economic difficulties had reached a point where re-examination of American policy seemed to be called for. Accordingly, in July 1950, President Truman dispatched an Economic Survey Mission to the Islands.

The mission was headed by Daniel W. Bell, former Undersecretary of the Treasury and private banker, and included five members and a staff of twenty-four assistants. The group made an extensive survey of economic conditions in the Philippines, getting behind the much-talked-of "showcase" and into the shop. Its report, released in October 1950, included a searching analysis of current economic and social problems, backed up by valuable and formerly unpublished data on the economy, and accompanied by specific recommendations.[2]

The Filipinos had sought assistance from the United States, but had hoped for a joint mission composed of nationals from both countries to investigate the needs. They were therefore sensitive to the activities of the all-American survey group, and feared particularly that a severe indictment of the administration on the grounds of graft and corruption would be forthcoming. In anticipation of such a reprimand, a sensational press statement was released in Manila shortly before the Bell Report was made public. This comment, attributed to one of President Quirino's private secretaries, included the following as a typical paragraph:

The Filipinos, there is no question, are inefficient all right—even in their graft-

---

[2] Cf. Shirley Jenkins, "Philippine White Paper," *Far Eastern Survey*, January 10, 1951, pp. 1–6.

ing—due, no doubt to simple lack of sufficient experience. With more time and greater chances, they may yet show they can equal, or even surpass, the stink familiar, and now taken for granted, in Washington and such very proper exemplary centers of power, prosperity and culture.[3]

This release met with severe criticism, and was followed by an official apology and the reprimand and later dismissal of the author. But it is worth noting on the record as an unusually frank statement of a point of view not uncommon in underdeveloped areas.

Although the Bell Report frankly stated that problems of graft and corruption existed in the Islands, it wisely did not give excessive emphasis to this aspect of Philippine affairs. Such difficulties, as events have shown, have not in themselves distinguished developed from underdeveloped areas. Furthermore, they have frequently been only symptoms of the underlying basic problems which required solution. Instead the Bell Report gave major attention to the pressing economic needs of the people and to suggestions for alleviating some of the worst problems. Just over a hundred pages in length, the report was accompanied by nine technical memoranda on the following subjects: agriculture, Bureau of Customs, Bureau of Internal Revenue, fiscal and administrative operations, foreign trade, industrial development, internal distribution, mining, and taxation.

In its review of the current situation in the Philippines, the Bell Report declared:

The basic economic problem in the Philippines is inefficient production and very low incomes. While a substantial recovery was made in production after liberation, agricultural and industrial output is still below the prewar level. In the past ten years, however, the population has increased by 25 percent. Although home production has been supplemented by large imports, the standard of living of most people is lower than before the war.[4]

Among the major causes of the economic difficulties, according to the report, were the following:

While production in general has been restored to almost the prewar level, little of fundamental importance was done to increase productive efficiency and to diversify the economy. . . .

The failure to expand production and to increase productive efficiency is particularly disappointing because investment was exceptionally high and foreign exchange receipts were exceptionally large during most of the post-liberation period. . . . The opportunity to increase productive efficiency and to raise the standard of living in the Philippines in the postwar period has . . . been wasted because of misdirected investment and excessive imports for consumption. . . .

[3] *Far East Trader*, "Review of 1950," January 1, 1951, p. 13.
[4] *Report to the President of the United States by the Economic Survey Mission to the Philippines* (Washington, October 9, 1950), p. 1.

The inequalities in income in the Philippines, always large, have become even greater during the past few years. While the standard of living of the mass of people has not reached the prewar level, the profits of businessmen and the incomes of large landowners have risen very considerably. . . .[5]

The Bell Report supported its generalizations with a detailed statistical analysis of various aspects of the economy, including problems of production, the character of postwar investment, the behavior of prices, wages, and national income, government finance, monetary and credit policy, the international-payments position, and import, exchange, and price controls. This was followed by various recommendations for reconstruction and development in the fields of agriculture, industry, finance, commerce, social welfare, public administration, and technical assistance, and by proposals for American aid.

Unlike previous plans for the expenditure of large sums on elaborate new projects, the Bell Report laid particular emphasis on the need to make better use of existing facilities. The mission was critical of the lack of such activity in recent years. Regarding agriculture, for example, the report declared that the Philippine–United States Agricultural Mission of December 1946 had made excellent recommendations but that, "unfortunately, after four years, no important part of the report has been adopted."[6] The Bell Mission's own recommendations on agriculture included proposals to combat plant disease affecting abacá production; extension of research to improve both sugar and tobacco production; expansion of food-grain production; study of problems of land use, clearance, irrigation, and settlement; and furthering of fishing and forestry activities.

The report gave careful consideration to the problems of land tenure in the Philippines, and asserted that:

The strained relationship between the landlords and their tenants and the low economic condition generally of the tillers of the soil compose one of the main factors retarding the recovery of agricultural production. . . . The land problem remains the same or worse than four years ago and the dissident trouble has spread to wider areas.[7]

In its analysis of the nature of rural discontent, the report declared:

The Philippine farmer is between two grindstones. On top is the landlord, who often exacts an unjust share of the crop in spite of ineffective legal restrictions to the contrary. Beneath is the deplorably low productivity of the land he works. The farmer cannot see any avenue of escape.[8]

The Bell Mission went on to propose that the law on the books providing for a 70–30 division of crop between the tenant and the landlord be enforced,

[5] Ibid., p. 2.
[6] Ibid., p. 50.
[7] Ibid., p. 55.
[8] Ibid.

that a program of resettlement and resale be carried through, and that rural credit be made available at moderate interest rates.

With regard to industrial development the report took a cautious approach. It warned that:

Industrial development cannot come from the establishment of a few large projects which somehow generate an industrial economy. It comes from the establishment of many enterprises, each particularly suited to the economic capacity of its managers, its workers and its market. The benefits of more efficient production can be fully realized only through more efficient distribution within the economy.[9]

The mission saw need for expansion in manufacturing, power, fuel and mineral production, transportation, and public works. On the controversial question of the role of government in industry, the report said: "It is clear that the Government will have to take an active part in stimulating economic development in the Philippines." But it added that "By the most generous evaluation, the larger number of the Government corporations are inefficient, wastefully operated, and in some instances they have been misused."[10] The mission proposed a reorganization of such public enterprises under a new Philippine Development Corporation, as well as various measures to improve distribution of products to both consumers and producers.

In the discussion of various aspects of fiscal, investment, and credit policy the main recommendation of the Bell Report concerned ways of increasing tax revenue. According to its findings, the Philippine budget could be balanced and tax receipts increased by some 60 percent, under existing conditions of national income. The report also proposed revision of the tax system along more progressive lines, instead of continuing the heavily retrogressive pattern.

Increases were suggested in cigarette, liquor, and gasoline excise taxes, in sales taxes on nonessential items, in corporation and individual income taxes, and in estate and gift taxes. For local governments, an increase in property assessments to levels reflecting true values was proposed. Furthermore, the Bell Report recommended for a two-year period two emergency measures to improve the Philippine international balance-of-payments position. These were a special levy of 25 percent on all imports except rice, corn, flour, canned milk, canned fish, and fertilizers, and a tax of 25 percent on all exchange remittances.

In seeking to explain some of the more apparent causes of Philippine economic difficulties, the report could not avoid discussing various aspects of the Philippine Trade Act. For example, it stated:

The principal Philippine objections to the Trade Agreement have been to the provisions which limit the Government's power to allocate exports of "quota" products, and to the so-called "parity provision" guaranteeing national treatment

9 *Ibid.*, p. 61.
10 *Ibid.*, p. 67.

for United States citizens and business enterprises in the development of natural resources. The absolute quotas on Philippine exports are regarded as limiting opportunities for expanding Philippine trade with the United States as Philippine production grows and the United States market expands. There has also been some feeling that the exchange provisions are a limitation on Philippine sovereign rights.

Some provisions of the Trade Agreement, such as the absolute quotas (except in the case of sugar) and the internal tax preference given Philippine coconut oil, are prejudicial to the attainment of the objectives of United States commercial policy on a multilateral basis. These provisions of the Act which limit Philippine sovereign prerogatives, i.e. the "parity provision," the "non-discrimination" provision, and the limitations on the Philippine Government in allocating quotas established for certain products, do not in practice provide the proper type and degree of protection for American interests.[11]

The report criticized provisions of the Trade Act which limited Philippine authority to change the par value of the peso, saying: "The President of the United States has no responsibility for the fiscal, credit and investment policies that may necessitate such action. For this reason, he ought not to be burdened with the responsibility of giving formal approval for exchange controls or changes in exchange rates if they should be needed."[12] The mission suggested modification of the existing Philippine Trade Act to accord more fully with new conditions, and conclusion of a Treaty of Friendship, Commerce, and Navigation between the United States and the Philippines, which would also "provide equitable conditions for investment."

In addition to discussing agriculture, industry, and finance, the Bell Report ventured into the fields of labor, health, education, public administration, and technical assistance, in a somewhat cursory survey. Recommendations included extension of public health and educational facilities; establishment of minimum wages for agricultural and nonagricultural workers; encouragement of trade unions that would be "free from Communist influence, domination by the Government, interference by management, and racketeering by labor laders"; reorganization of the civil service; and extension of technical aid.

While the Bell Report's analysis of the economic problems of the Philippines was of general interest, the major assignment of the mission was to make recommendations regarding American aid. The report proposed both technical and financial help, under specified criteria. The first recommendation on aid, actually part of the discussion of development plans, was the suggestion that a United States Technical Mission be made available to the Philippine government for a period of some five years. "The members of the Technical Mission," according to the report, "must be competent not merely to give general advice, but also to assist Philippine officials in the actual day-to-day opera-

[11] *Ibid.*, p. 85.
[12] *Ibid.*, p. 88.

tions and in the formulation and implementation of changes in policy which must be brought about."[13]

With regard to direct financial aid to the Philippines, it was proposed that the United States grant over the following five years some $250 million, primarily on a project basis. The report laid special emphasis on the importance of supervision of the suggested assistance, and declared:

The aid from the United States will be more effective if the United States retains control of the funds and their use for development purposes in the Philippines. . . .

The head of the United States Technical Mission to the Philippines would be authorized to release funds for grants for approved purposes. Expenditures would be made directly by the United States Government where construction is required. . . .

In order to avoid the dissipation of American aid, the Philippine Government would be required to maintain sound financial policies as a condition for continued aid. The Philippine Development Corporation would not be authorized to make any loans directly to the Philippine Government. The Philippine Development Corporation would consult with the United States Technical Mission on the most effective manner in which the resources at the disposal of the Corporation can be used for development. Furthermore, the Philippine Development Corporation would offer full facilities to the United States Technical Mission to determine for itself how funds made available for development, whether supplied by the United States or out of its own resources, are in fact being used.[14]

The Bell Report has been reviewed in some detail because of the sharpness and clarity of its presentation of the postwar Philippine economy, as well as the political significance of its proposals. Such astuteness on matters of finance, trade, and industry, however, has not been unusual in reports on the Philippines, as evidenced by the "Report of the Joint Preparatory Committee on Philippine Affairs," in 1948; the recommendations of the Technical Committee to the President of the Philippines, "American Philippine Trade Relations," in 1944; and the "Report and Recommendations of the Joint Philippine-American Finance Commission," in 1947, among others. It might, in fact, be said that the way to crisis in the Philippines has been paved with good reports.

Such surveys, however, valuable as they may have been, suffered from some of the same weaknesses as the Bell Report. Essentially the study of Philippine affairs was subordinated to the major problem of the various missions, that of determining effective areas for American policy. Thus official United States reports necessarily lacked historical perspective on the background of the problem, in terms of the needs of the country being viewed. For example, the Bell Report analyzed the Philippine Trade Act, not primarily in terms of

[13] *Ibid.*, p. 100.
[14] *Ibid.*, pp. 105–6.

its effect on the Philippine economy, but rather from the point of view of whether or not it served American commercial policy in the Pacific. Further-more, the Bell Report did not attempt to discuss either the political realities in the Philippines or the degree of change necessary to reach full implementation of its own recommendations. In fact, the data presented on the national economy served only to emphasize the difficulties of securing such implemen-tation.

In the Philippines the Bell proposals faced opposition because of the pro-vision for American supervision of the aid program, confronted hurdles be-cause of the tax and wage criteria, and met further obstacles to implementation on account of prevailing instability and nation-wide unrest. These reactions, although outside the scope of the survey mission, nonetheless formed the frame of reference within which the Philippine picture had to be viewed.

Some of the difficulties with regard to historical perspective and point of view were illustrated in comments on the Bell Report by the Filipino econo-mist Salvador Araneta, secretary of the Philippine Department of Economic Coordination. In a series of memoranda analyzing the Bell findings, prepared for President Quirino, Secretary Araneta stated:

> One of the great merits of the Report is the strong emphasis which it places on the need to bring about what may be called the social and economic reformation of the Philippines. We fully concur in the need and in the justice of achieving the major goals in this direction that are recommended in the Report.

> It is to be regretted, however, that the Bell Mission fails to emphasize that our social and economic ills are age-old problems and that some of them were the cause of the Philippine Revolution at the end of the last century. To an impartial student, it should be apparent that there is a regrettable over-emphasis in considering these as mostly post-war problems, left unsolved by the inaction of the present Philippine leadership in the Government. . . .

> Perhaps what the Bell Mission has failed to realize or appreciate fully are the fundamental difficulties of a new independent government. Largely shaped and conditioned by the demands and responsibilities of a colonial system, the new gov-ernment has to face the pressing challenge of reorganization and re-orientation to the problems and difficulties of an independent, sovereign country. . . .[15]

In discussing aspects of economic policy which have delayed Philippine recovery, Mr. Araneta referred to the role of American capital, which, he stated, came to the Philippines to rehabilitate the prewar industries and con-tinued as before to dominate the import and export business. American capital, he maintained, did not seek to establish new industries, not because of nation-alistic Philippine economic policy, but because free trade did not make such

[15] "Memorandum for His Excellency, Elpidio Quirino," comments on the Report of the Bell Mission (Manila, November 1, 1950).

enterprises profitable. Mr. Araneta proposed a system of selective free trade to replace the existing provisions of the Philippine Trade Act, and declared:

The war broke our trade relations with America and destroyed most of the industries depending on free trade. Consequently, after liberation, before the pre-war industries dependent on free trade had been rehabilitated, I was in favor of abandoning entirely our free trade arrangement with the United States to start a new economy for the Philippines. We lost in the fight against the Bell Act, and now our Philippine economy is in the process of rehabilitation, as it had existed before the war, with sugar, coconut oil, cordage and cigars again depending on their free entry into the American market. . . .

Our experience for the past three years, I believe, has shown that free trade means the preservation of the status quo, inimical to the creation of new industries, that are necessary to replace the ones that are to be destroyed with the gradual cessation of free trade. And under the Bell Act free trade is followed by another period of diminishing preferences, i.e. of slow strangulation, which evidently enough cannot provide the necessary atmosphere of economic welfare to create new industries that could replace those that are being strangulated.[16]

While the points made by Mr. Araneta did not negate the findings of the Bell Mission, they illustrated an important Filipino attitude on some of the economic difficulties of the Islands.

Aside from the matter of allocating responsibility, the mission's report met with severe criticism from many Filipinos for the emphasis which was placed on the need for supervision of projected aid. It was even reported that government advisory groups had turned down the plan, feeling that "the Bell proposals would constitute an infringement of sovereignty."[17] The visit to Manila of William C. Foster, United States ECA administrator, apparently served to placate some official protests. In speaking to members of the Philippine Congress Mr. Foster stressed the "partnership concept," but he added frankly: "It must be clear that a partnership implies rights, as well as obligations on both partners. As partners we, of course, have a normal interest in the proper conduct of affairs. Like any partner, we reserve the right not to invest when we feel such investment would not yield proper returns."[18]

Negotiations in Manila between President Quirino and Mr. Foster resulted in an agreement, on November 14, 1950, for implementation of the Bell program.[19] The Philippine government agreed to give the main proposals of the report its "serious and immediate consideration," and to formulate a legislative program to deal with some of its recommendations. These included tax legislation designed to produce not less than 565 million pesos in revenue, a mini-

[16] *Ibid.*

[17] *Far East Trader*, November 22, 1950, p. 261.

[18] *New York Times*, November 9, 1950.

[19] "Philippine Self-Help Steps Outlined in Agreement," *Bataan and Asian Review*, December 1950, pp. 7–8.

mum wage law for agricultural workers, and a "joint resolution expressing the general policy of Congress to accelerate the carrying out by congressional enactment of the social reforms and economic development measures recommended. . . ." The United States, for its part, agreed to furnish technical assistance to the Philippines, to resume negotiations for a Treaty of Friendship, Commerce, and Navigation, to re-examine the provisions of the present trade agreement, and, "In consideration of the determination of the Philippine Government to act boldly and promptly on the major program . . . the President of the United States intends to recommend to the United States Congress the appropriation of the necessary funds . . . envisioned . . . at $250 million."

This agreement cleared the way for legislative action, both in the Philippines and in the United States. While awaiting approval, however, both reform and aid remained in a state of suspense for at least six more months.

This delay resulted from a number of political difficulties which the Philippine legislators faced when dealing with the proposed reforms, difficulties which underlined some of the realities of Philippine life. The Philippine Congress sat in continual debate for five months before coming to a decision on the proposed legislation. This delay was due in part to the unpopularity of the measures on wages and taxes, and in part to internal political disagreements which led to a stalemate on all action. Thus one correspondent, in reporting on the Philippine congressional discussion of the proposed minimum wage law for agricultural workers, stated:

Organized opposition to it, originating with entrenched landowners and sugar interests, was even more stubborn than that of the business interests against the required tax legislation. . . .

Rivalry between the two houses of Congress and bickering over personal leadership has consumed more time than the actual deliberation on the necessary legislation.[20]

This political dissension within Congress was an outgrowth of the splits which occurred at the time of the 1949 elections, and reflected the inability of the administration to retain its former adherents. Although Avelino had been badly defeated in his try for the presidency, his followers retained their senatorial positions, and continued as an opposition group in the Liberal party. As a result, the Avelino Liberals, the old Nacionalistas, and the Independents came together to form a new Democratic bloc, which held a majority in the Senate. Thus the so-called "Little Senate," the once-powerful group of Quirino Liberals, was reduced to impotency. On the other hand, when there was some defection from the Democratic bloc, as in February 1951, when Senator Tanada voted with the "Little Senate," the result was a ten-to-ten tie and an utter stalemate in action.

The Democratic bloc, although it had certain potentialities, continued in the

20 *New York Times*, March 19, 1951.

spring of 1951 to be a negative association of minority members, with the power to stop proposals of its opponents but without a positive platform of its own. The political impasse in the Philippines continued because none of the groups in Congress came forth with a real program to meet the needs of the Philippine economy, a platform which could effectively rally popular support. This impasse had a bearing on the recommendations of the Bell Report, since the proposed reforms could be enforced only by a determined and widely supported administration. The 1951 elections, which were the cleanest in Philippine history and resulted in a setback for the party in power, represented progress from the point of view of developing a genuine two-party system; but neither party offered to the electorate a comprehensive and constructive economic program for the nation.[21]

Agreement on the legislative criteria for the Bell Report was finally reached by the Philippine Congress in the spring of 1951, but on terms below those proposed in the mission recommendations. On March 28, 1951, President Quirino signed Republic Acts 600 and 601, which increased corporate income taxes and established a special excise tax on sales of foreign exchange. Instead of the flat 16 percent corporate tax, rates were raised to a general tax of 20 percent on the first 100,000 pesos of net income, and 28 percent on net income in excess of that amount. The tax on net incomes of building and loan associations was raised from 9 to 12 percent, and a levy of 10 percent was imposed on net incomes of "private educational institutions." A special excise tax of 17 percent was to be applied to the peso value of transactions in foreign exchange, for a two-year period.[22]

This action was followed by the signing on April 6 of the minimum wage law, which established a base wage for agricultural workers of 87.5 cents a day, to increase in the following three years to a minimum of $1.25. Outside of Manila base pay for industrial workers was set at $1.50 a day, to increase the following year to $2.00, while minimum wages for industrial workers in Manila were established at $2.00 a day.[23]

In a message to President Quirino, made public on April 14, President Truman stated the American intention "to proceed rapidly and actively carry out its commitments in the programs upon which we have agreed,"[24] and some $15 million was authorized for interim aid for the Philippines. By the end of June the money had been fully appropriated for approved projects, including the purchase of fertilizer, irrigation pumps, pesticides, and equipment to complete a textile mill. Support was extended for a public health program, for the establishment of cottage industries, and for surveys of coal reserves and railroad needs. Another indication of American interest was the fact that on June 16

21 Cf. James J. Dalton, "Ins and Outs in the Philippines," *Far Eastern Survey*, July 30, 1952.
22 "Philippine Economic Conditions Analyzed," *Bataan*, June 1951, p. 9.
23 *New York Times*, August 5, 1951.
24 *Far East Trader*, May 2, 1951.

the Export-Import Bank notified the Philippine government that it was prepared to discuss extension of credits for productive projects.

While project aid such as the ECA was prepared to advance could be extremely important in injecting vigor into certain sectors of the economy, it could not provide the over-all development necessary for the Philippines to utilize most effectively its agricultural and industrial resources, its materials and man power. Furthermore, the success of a program of project aid cannot be predicted, as it depends to a large extent on the general political and social environment of the country at the time.

One factor which could not be overlooked in estimating the success of project aid in revitalizing the economy was the ever-present threat of Hukbalahap resistance. Although any reliable estimate of Huk forces has been difficult to obtain, a brigadier general in the Philippine Army stated in February 1951 that, on the basis of captured documents, the Huk organization claimed an active membership of some 30,000, and about 5 million sympathizers.[25] At the same time, the Philippine government continued vigorous suppression campaigns, including the sentencing to death after trial, in the spring of 1951, of six members of the Philippine Communist party, while nine were committed to life imprisonment and others to varying jail terms. In July 1951 the acting president of the Philippine Senate, Quintin Paredes, stated that the Philippine Army was holding some 2,000 persons suspected as subversives.

The problems of implementing an economic program for the Philippines are illustrated in the ups and downs of the fiscal position in 1951. By the spring of that year the Philippines was in a somewhat improved financial situation as compared with the previous year. Although the national deficit remained a matter of concern, the budget was on its way to being balanced for the first time since independence. Foreign exchange reserves had improved steadily, rising from just under $351 million in January 1951 to $393 million at the end of May, an increase of about $143 million over the end of 1949. For the first five months of the year exports were valued at about 410 million pesos, and imports at 300 million, resulting in an excess of exports of some 110 million pesos. This may be compared with the same period in 1950, when the excess of imports over exports was 81 million pesos.[26]

Unfortunately, this promising picture did not last for long. The administration in the Philippines soon succumbed to the pressure to get rid of onerous controls. At the end of May 1951, as soon as a favorable balance and safe dollar reserve were obtained, President Quirino decontrolled a sizable list of essential commodities including food, medicines, textiles, and some building materials. This resulted in a rush for import licenses. The Central Bank of the Philippines estimated that the dollar value of licenses issued in the first half of 1951, some $485 million, exceeded the total for the whole year of 1950. Procurement

25 *Sunday Herald* (Manila), February 11, 1951.
26 *Foreign Commerce Weekly*, July 23, 1951, p. 14.

difficulties delayed delivery on many items, so the effect on trade and balances was not immediate. Fulfillment of outstanding orders, however, would in certain ways have put the country back to the critical situation it faced in 1949. The situation caused widespread concern and indicated how precarious was the newly found Philippine prosperity.[27]

By June 1951, after ten months of export balances, the scale tipped the other way. Imports, valued at 89 million pesos, were the highest since 1949, while exports of 69 million pesos were the lowest since November 1950. The cost of living continued to rise, reaching an index of 412.3 in June as compared with 398.2 in January 1951, while exchange reserves again declined, to $383.3 million in June and $337.7 million in September 1951.

It is interesting to note that twelve government-owned corporations reported an over-all profit of 7.9 million pesos for the fiscal year ending in June 1951, as against a loss in the previous year of 1.3 million pesos. Eight of these firms registered profits, with the Government Service Insurance System earning 6.6 million pesos, the Metropolitan Water District of Manila 2.0 million, and the Cebu Portland Cement Company and the National Development Company 1.5 million each.[28]

During the latter months of 1951 there was a downward trend in export prices for some commodities. Significantly enough, a major reason for this trend was considered to be the prospect of an end to the Korean conflict. Thus the *Foreign Commerce Weekly* reported in January 1952: "As a consequence of heavy output and a more favorable outlook for a negotiated peace in Korea, abacá prices continued to decline."[29] Later in the month the same publication stated: "Copra prices moved downward in early December as a result of improved prospects of a Korean peace."[30]

The recession in the Philippines continued over the first six months of 1952. Retail trade was slow, cash and credit were tight, and the international reserve position continued to decline. Foreign exchange receipts suffered from the drop in United States expenditures, which fell from $207.6 million in 1949 to $99.8 million in 1951. From the beginning of its operation in the Philippines in April to the end of December 1951, the ECA, now the Mutual Security Agency, had issued procurement authorizations of $27 million.

The economic difficulties of 1952 were accentuated by a series of labor strikes in April for higher wages, and by a number of strike actions in June. These included a strike of over 2,000 workers in a lumber mill in Negros, and other labor activity in the sugar refineries, lumber mills, and banks. At the same time a bill exempting home needleworkers in the embroidery industry from the legal minimum wage became law without the President's signature.

27 *New York Times*, August 5, 1951.
28 *Foreign Commerce Weekly*, November 26, 1951, pp. 14–15.
29 *Ibid.*, January 14, 1952, p. 17.
30 *Ibid.*, January 28, 1952, p. 16.

This deflationary trend which characterized the Philippine economy was apparent in a number of critical economic indexes. The Filipinos were aware that their economic situation was not one of prosperity or stability, and they turned again to re-examine their relationship with the United States.

Shortly after the beginning of the downward trend, in July 1951, an outstanding Filipino jurist, Justice Claro M. Recto, criticized the undue reliance of the Philippines on the United States, and declared:

> More than two years ago I suggested that we should promote closer relations with our neighbors in Asia on the basis of an independent nationalism. . . .

> The Philippines can never hope to exercise any real influence in Asia so long as it is identified, rightly or wrongly, in Asian eyes, as an American puppet, having no policies but the policies of the United States. . . .

> Even laying aside such realistic considerations as the geographical isolation of the Philippines, and the military and industrial weakness of our country, it should be clear to any disinterested observer that Asian nationalism will never accept the "leadership" of any puppet or protectorate, whether western or soviet, no matter what attractive gilding is provided for it. . . .[31]

While Justice Recto sought a political move in the direction of an "independent nationalism," other Philippine leaders were concerned with the dollars-and-pesos effects of the Philippine-American tie. In his State of the Nation address at the convening of the Philippine Congress on January 28, 1952, President Quirino called for a review of the provisions of the Philippine Trade Act of 1946, and said that some readjustment of the trade arrangements was essential to suit changing conditions and achieve a more stable and balanced economy for the Philippines. The newly reactivated National Economic Council was designated to draft proposed changes. In addition, a resolution favoring revision of the act was passed early in March by the House Committee on Foreign Affairs. In hearings before the congressional committee opposition to the Bell Act as it stood was registered by the governor of the Central Bank, the Secretary of Commerce, and the president of the Philippine Chamber of Commerce, on the ground that complete free trade results in the dependence of the Philippine economy on the United States market and stifles local industrial growth.[32]

Late in April 1952 a preliminary report with proposals for revising the Trade Act was submitted to the President by the National Economic Council. These proposals included recommendations for the institution of selective free trade for a limited period between the Philippines and the United States, in lieu of graduated duties and declining duty-free quotas; elimination of restrictions on the Philippine government in the control and administration

[31] *Manila Bulletin*, July 23, 1951.
[32] *Foreign Commerce Weekly*, April 21, 1952, p. 17.

APPENDIX TABLES
AND INDEX

TABLE VIII

PHILIPPINES: AREA UNDER CULTIVATION FOR PRINCIPAL CROPS

(In thousand hectares)

	1940	1946	1949	1950*
All crops	5,073	3,891	4,902	5,075
Food crops	3,442	2,603	3,486	3,623
Palay (rough rice)	2,080	1,650	2,164	2,214
Corn	913	571	866	909
Fruits and nuts	201	186	203	215
Root crops	178	148	172	187
Beans and vegetables	49	30	49	64
Other foods	21	18	32	34
Export crops	1,631	1,288	1,416	1,452
Coconuts	1,051	960	965	985
Sugar cane	230	29	129	130
Abacá	292	272	283	291
Tobacco	58	27	39	46

* Preliminary.
Source: National Economic Council, cited in *Central Bank Statistical Bulletin*, Manila, December 1950, p. 132.

TABLE IX

PHILIPPINES: PRODUCTION OF SELECTED COMMODITIES

(In thousand metric tons)

	1937	1949	1950
Palay (rough rice)	2,420.7	2,491.3	2,606.1
Corn	437.7	534.1	573.7
Root crops	333.9	528.2	646.5
Fish and fish products*	—	238.0	215.7
Meat and poultry products†	—	165.1	216.1
Sugar	1,076.1	692.9	654.0
Copra	521.9	698.1	780.1
Abacá	200.6	74.5	82.2
Leaf tobacco	36.3	21.9	26.4
Coconut oil	213.0	102.3	135.0‡

* Commercial fisheries.
† Production for food only.
‡ Preliminary.
Source: Bureau of the Census and Statistics and National Economic Council, cited in *Central Bank Statistical Bulletin*, Manila, December 1950, p. 133.

TABLE X

PHILIPPINES: INDEX OF PHYSICAL VOLUME OF PRODUCTION
(1937 = 100)

	1949	1950*
Combined index	91.3	95.9
Agricultural	92.2	98.3
Manufacturing	94.7	97.3
Mining	49.1	58.6

* Preliminary.
Source: Bureau of the Census and Statistics, Bureau of Commerce, Bureau of Forestry, Bureau of Mines, Sugar Quota Office, cited in *Central Bank Statistical Bulletin*, Manila, December 1950, p. 150.

TABLE XI

PHILIPPINES: NUMBER OF NEWLY REGISTERED CORPORATIONS
BY KIND OF BUSINESS, 1945–50

	1945	1946	1947	1948	1949	1950
Agriculture	7	58	72	18	21	49
Cinema	5	27	23	24	10	10
Construction	20	30	20	8	5	13
Educational	8	44	53	79	51	67
General merchandising ...	189	288	118	73	70	114
Insurance	5	3	6	4	6	9
Lumber	20	71	44	20	16	17
Manufacturing	7	29	22	29	26	103*
Mining	—	9	11	12	17	13
Printing	11	19	12	3	16	19
Real estate	2	9	13	13	20	17
Transportation	13	69	48	22	16	16
Other	58	154	167	164	123	86
Total	345	810	609	469	397	533

* Of this number 15 were manufacturers of cigars and cigarettes, 13 of clothing and other wearing apparel, 11 of food, and 13 of drugs, chemicals, and allied products.
Source: Securities and Exchange Commission, cited in *Central Bank Statistical Bulletin*, Manila, December 1950, pp. 58–59, 64.

TABLE XII

Cost-of-Living Index of a Wage Earner's Family in Manila
(1937 = 100)

	1949	1950
All items	385.3	378.0
Foodstuffs	405.3	378.0
House rent	470.9	470.9
Clothing	224.9	307.0
Fuel, light, water	320.3	295.7
Miscellaneous	280.6	350.2

Source: Bureau of the Census and Statistics, cited in *Central Bank Statistical Bulletin*, Manila, December 1950, p. 180.

TABLE XIII

Philippines: Employment in Reporting Nonagricultural Establishments

	1949	1950
Total	109,621	109,299
Mining and quarrying	10,764	12,937
Manufacturing	55,850	54,693
Transportation and communication	26,116	25,888
Commerce	16,891	15,781

Source: Compiled directly from questionnaires returned to the Department of Economic Research by 556 co-operating establishments in the Philippines; cited in *Central Bank Statistical Bulletin*, Manila, December 1950, p. 188.

TABLE XIV

Wage Rates, Wage Indexes, and Real Wages in Industrial Establishments in Manila

	Wage rates in pesos		Index (1941 = 100)		Real wages in 1941 pesos	
	Skilled laborers	Unskilled laborers	Skilled laborers	Unskilled laborers	Skilled laborers	Unskilled laborers
1941	2.29	1.24	100.0	100.0	2.29	1.24
1945	5.83	3.27	254.6	263.7	0.85	0.66
1946	6.73	4.53	293.9	365.3	1.29	0.87
1947	7.54	4.66	329.2	375.8	1.94	1.20
1948	7.47	4.69	326.2	378.2	2.05	1.28
1949	7.61	4.90	332.3	395.2	2.19	1.41
1950	7.60	4.29	331.9	346.0	2.25	1.27

Source: Bureau of the Census and Statistics, cited in *Central Bank Statistical Bulletin*, Manila, December 1950, pp. 206–7.

INDEX

Abacá, 5, 16, 40, 73, 98–102, 106, 124, 129, 131, 137, 140–42, 144

Agriculture, 5, 18, 40–41, 68, 75, 98, 102, 104, 131, 137, 139, 141, 144, 147, 154, 173

Air transport, 101–2, 107–8, 140, 142

American Chamber of Commerce (Philippines), 80, 130

American Economic Survey Mission (Bell Report), 9, 11–12, 17, 25, 51, 152–59, 161

American Producers of Oils and Fats (U.S.), 35

American Sugar Cane League, 72

Army of the Philippines, 9, 13–14, 18, 103, 133, 137, 151, 162

Asia, relations with Philippines, 15, 19–20, 26–27, 29, 81, 152, 164, 167

Avelino, José, 12–13, 52, 93, 132, 138

Bell Bill, *see* Trade Act, Philippine

Bell, C. Jasper, 21, 49, 54, 56–57

Bell, Daniel W., 152

Bell Report, *see* American Economic Survey Mission

Beyster Plan, 141–44

Black markets, 52–53, 99, 116

Budget, 5, 110, 113–14, 122, 134–35, 155

Buttons, pearl and shell, 37, 65, 67, 85

Cabili, Tomas L., 48

Central Bank of the Philippines, 17, 120, 127–29, 134, 144, 162, 164

Chinese in the Philippines, 9, 15, 26, 39, 44, 52, 104

Cigars, 37, 65, 71, 107, 124, 129, 159

Cigar Manufacturers Association (U.S.), 71

Clayton, William, 56, 61–63, 116

Coconut oil, 34, 36–37, 55, 62, 65, 67, 73, 100–101, 113–14, 125, 131, 141–42, 156, 159

Collaboration, 43, 82, 84, 86, 98, 133

Commonwealth government, 26, 36, 44, 49, 95, 112–13, 140, 167

Communist party (Philippines), 5, 6–9, 82, 162

Congress (Philippines), 13, 18, 23, 25, 35, 86,

88–89, 91, 95, 114, 116–17, 119, 134, 137, 160–61, 164

Constabulary, 7, 9, 98

Constitution (Philippines), 30, 56, 62, 67–68, 87, 89, 91, 93–94, 140

Construction, building, 102–4, 107

Copra, 5, 16, 28, 34, 40, 73, 97–102, 106, 108, 120, 124–25, 129, 131, 141, 163

Cordage, 34–37, 55, 65–66, 70–71, 73, 75, 85

Cordage Institute, 70–71, 73

Cost of living, 99–100, 102, 104, 108, 124, 132, 137, 175

Cuaderno Program, 141, 144

Cuba, 35, 55, 60, 72–74

Currency, 57, 59, 68, 76, 88, 102, 110–12, 116, 120–22, 127, 129, 156, 165

Democratic Alliance, 82–83, 86–87

Democratic party (Philippines), 14–15, 160

Democratic party (U.S.), 32, 34

Dewey, Admiral George, 2, 31

Dulles, John Foster, 16, 152

Elections: of 1946, 11, 82–84; of 1949, 11, 132–33, 160–61; of 1951, 12–13; of 1953, 14

Embroideries, 54, 103, 107, 124

"Equal rights" for American nationals, 26, 30, 36, 56, 59–62, 65–68, 75–76, 80, 82, 85–86, 88–95, 116, 136, 149, 155, 165

Exchange Standard Fund, 113–14

Finances, 5, 45, 57, 110–22, 127–29, 133–36, 145, 154–55, 162–63, 172

Finance Commission, Joint Philippine-American, 104, 110, 116–22, 127, 141

Gold, 103, 107, 124, 129, 142

Gold Standard Act, 111–12

Gonzáles, Leon Ma., 103–4, 123

Hare-Hawes-Cutting Act, 35

Hausserman, John W., 76–77

Hawes, Harry B., 61, 71–72